Cultural DNA

Cultural DNA

Gender at the Root of Everyday Life in Rural Jamaica

Diana J. Fox

UWI PRESS

University of the West Indies Press

Jamaica • Barbados • Trinidad and Tobago

University of the West Indies Press
7A Gibraltar Hall Road   Mona
Kingston 7   Jamaica
www.uwipress.com

ISBN 978-976-640-219-8

A catalogue record of this book is available from the National Library of Jamaica.

Cover illustration: Rex Dixon, *Interrupted Helix* (acrylic on paper,
15 × 11 inches, 2009).

Book and cover design by Robert Harris.

Set in Stone Serif 9/14 x 24

Printed in the United States of America.

Contents

Illustrations

Preface

THIS ETHNOGRAPHY IS SHAPED by the turbulent decades that the discipline of anthropology, cultural anthropology in particular, underwent in the 1980s and 1990s. During these decades anthropologists challenged the ethnographic enterprise that had emerged originally in the late nineteenth century as part of European colonial expansion into the non-Western world. Anthropologists in the 1980s sought to refigure their discipline as a collaborative field, rather than one which sought knowledge of colonized peoples to further the imperialist enterprise. Practitioners re-imagined themselves as seekers of an interpretive knowledge through an interactive process with research subjects who helped to define research agendas, rather than producers of authoritative accounts of cultural "others". As a result, new forms of ethnographic writing emerged, giving voice to the serendipitous process of uncovering anthropological knowledge, the deep involvement of the researcher with her subjects of research and all of the various moral and personal challenges and insights this endeavour produced. Feminist ethnographers played a central role in this process by highlighting the value of subjectivity on the part of both ethnographer and research community and encouraging open reflection about doing ethnographic fieldwork.

This text is an experimental ethnography that engages many of the writing strategies born from this period, detailing my own personal process of excavating anthropological knowledge about the gender systems of rural Afro-Jamaicans. As such, the book has two interlocking objectives: one is to document the process of doing feminist ethnographic fieldwork in order to reflect on the production of anthropological knowledge about gender and its links to authorial subjectivity. The second is to offer an analytical description of the nature of gender in rural Jamaica. Feminist anthropologists generally adopt a cultural constructionist view of gender, one that was formulated in the

1970s by theorists across many disciplines, including anthropology. This theory – with historical precursors as far back as ancient Greek thought[1] – asserts that gender is the social and cultural construction of biological sex. According to philosopher Judith Butler, gender is an artifice that is derived from customs that embed power relationships. Largely concurring with this understanding, my intent in part is to elucidate the nature of gender as a sociocultural creation, that is, the social and cultural meanings attributed to biological sex, through an ethnographic case study of the rural community of Frankfield, Jamaica. In so doing, I draw on and critique existing studies of gender, with particular attention to indigenous Caribbean theorizing. Briefly, this includes Trinidadian feminist Patricia Mohammed's and Barbadian feminist Eudine Barriteau's notions of gender systems, as well as Mohammed's conceptualization of gender negotiations. It also includes Jamaican anthropologist Barry Chevannes's understanding of the socialization and enculturation of males in a number of Caribbean communities. Non-Caribbean theorists are similarly important in my analysis. I find valuable, although also problematic in its limited capacity to address substantive social change, Butler's concept of gender performativity. Butler argues that through gestures, dress, action and speech we perform socially inscribed gendered ideologies, in essence becoming our gender through its practice. Butler also claims that gender expectations can be resisted through subversive performances that in essence mock dominant expectations, and while examples of these kinds of transformative performances have been documented, recently, for instance, in Jamaica by Gina Ulysse (2007), they are not systemically transformative. This means that, while affecting individuals and perhaps groups, transformative performances do not effect legal or policy change. In exploring my own assumptions and knowledge acquisition process, feminist standpoint theory comes into play. Proffered by feminist scientist Sandra Harding (1991), this body of thought explores how knowledge is socially situated; that is, standpoint theory examines how the questions and approaches adopted by researchers as well as interpretation of results are informed by the power-imbued social structures within which individuals are located.

Another set of ideas, intersectionality theory, has also influenced my appreciation of how the gendered identities of different segments of the Jamaican population are informed by social and cultural categories such as race, colour, gender, class and sexuality. How these intertwine and are punctuated by power differentials, and how Jamaicans perceived me as socially situated, are also important theoretical strands. In the process of engaging with the above conceptual paradigms, I began to piece together what I consider to be an integrative analysis, developing a metaphor that has allowed me to grasp simultaneously the multiple and contradictory features of gender – its systemic features, its fluidity and malleability, and its historical continuities.

WHY THE TITLE? ANTHROPOLOGICAL ANALOGIES AND THEORETICAL INSIGHTS

In my effort to conceptualize the characteristics of gender, I follow a longstanding anthropological tradition: I designed a metaphor as a heuristic device to analyse the relationship between gender and culture. Yet anthropological metaphors have pitfalls which are worth identifying early on, as I seek to avoid them in my own application. In particular, anthropologists have favoured analogies of culture and society based on descriptions of the natural world. Perhaps these have been existential attempts to explain how human beings and human social life both mirror and diverge from other forms of life. Among the most persistent of these analogies emerged in the earliest days of anthropological theory, when nineteenth-century cultural evolutionists employed an "organic analogy" to generate a model of society as an organism undergoing unilineal evolutionary transformations. In later decades, the analogy was differently employed by British structural-functionalists, who, while rejecting cultural evolutionary models as spurious and unscientific, nonetheless viewed society as a stable set of interacting relationships, like an organism seeking homeostasis. In the 1950s in the United States, the organic analogy again re-emerged in neo-evolutionary, materialist paradigms examining societal adaptations to local environments as the driving force behind cultural development.

All of these applications, found both in the tradition of social anthropology of the British and French schools and the cultural anthropological tradition of the North American variety, regarded anthropology as a science in pursuit of societal and cultural laws. Yet in the process of invoking a potentially useful analogy, the model is perceived as the reality – societies are regarded as actual organisms. Anthropologist Jerry D. Moore (2004, 248), commenting on the use of anthropological analogies and metaphors, states, "It is curious how frequently anthropological theorists have turned to key metaphors to explain their insights (for example the organic analogy) and then have treated those metaphors as if they had a social rather than only a heuristic existence. The unexamined metamorphosis from metaphor to scientific law occurs frequently among anthropological theorists."

While I am mindful of the problems of anthropological analogizing, the value of the metaphor is compelling both in its descriptive and interpretive capacities. Like my anthropological predecessors, I have developed a metaphor drawn from the world of nature to help me tell this *cultural* story of gender in rural Jamaica, steering clear of a literal application.

The metaphor is this: gender is to culture as deoxyribonucleic acid (DNA) is to biological life. The title of this book, *Cultural DNA: Gender at the Root of Everyday Life in Rural Jamaica,* builds on my use of this strictly *figurative* analogy between gender and DNA.[2] I argue that this analogy is helpful in understanding the complex qualities of gender as a product of culture, as well as the ways it is systemic, reproduced and simultaneously transformed by each generation. I wish to be quite clear: I am not reducing gender to genes. I am in no way arguing that the culturally ascribed roles or idea systems associated with biological males and females are the result of genetic distinctions between men and women or reducible to the outcome of evolutionary processes of natural selection. While the acts of giving birth and nursing infants are biologically based, sex-linked behaviours, social historians and anthropologists have demonstrated that human societies ascribe various social roles and meanings to them, structured by class, race and other factors. Thus, even behaviours tied to nature have social meaning and are influenced by human social and cultural categories, just as nature itself is conceptualized through these lenses. Hence, feminist scholars have unequivocally condemned the essentialist idea that "biology is destiny" and that biological males and females always occupy roles that are sharply differentiated (Wylie 1991, 34). Another example strengthens the point: there have been times and places where household work has been men's work, and men have been regarded as naturally better able to do this type of work. This was the case in Zambia, beginning in the colonial era when African men served white colonizers in the domestic sphere as servants. Here, the masculine household space was shaped by race, gender and sexuality – white colonial fear of black female sexuality led to the hiring of men. Today, this colonial history has become folklore in the form of stories told about the unhinged sexuality of young Zambian women or middle-aged Zambian women beyond childbearing years who seek domestic service. They are often rejected by other Zambian women who might hire them, worried that as servants, these women will move into the bedroom and take over the house. Thus men perform domestic work, their association with domesticity an artifice born from ideologies of sexualized racism in the context of white colonial power later perpetuated by elite black Zambian women (Hansen 1986, 18). The behaviour patterns, beliefs, values, norms and ideologies about masculinity and femininity that have grown up in human societies are shaped by cultural, social and economic circumstances, as well as power dynamics, race relations, class, and a host of other factors. In short, a complex intersectional weave of relationships debunks any facile and fraught association between gender and genes. Gender, by definition, is human-made.

Thus, by invoking DNA metaphorically, I am offering neither a sociobiological assertion nor one of biological essentialism. Rather, I employ the metaphor of DNA to generate an elucidatory, analytical image of gender as a part of human culture that embodies many of the descriptive qualities that scientists assign to DNA. In so doing, I link together fundamental insights into the nature of gender that have been noted previously by feminist scholars across a range of disciplines as stated above, and I contribute a new perspective through the DNA metaphor. The specific nature of this challenge emerges throughout the chapters and is ultimately clarified in the conclusion. I begin this process now by elaborating on the analogy between gender's relationship to culture and DNA's relationship to biological life.

GENDER IS TO CULTURE AS DNA IS TO BIOLOGICAL LIFE

I offer readers a lay description of DNA since it is from this description that my metaphor emerges. The visual of DNA in figure one provides a loose model onto which I impute my analysis of gender. DNA is a nucleic acid carrying genetic directives for the biological development of all cellular forms of life as well as many viruses. It has been called the molecule of heredity as it encodes a set of plans, much like a blueprint, that makes each species unique. DNA, along with all the instructions it contains for organisms to develop, survive and reproduce, is passed along from adults to their offspring, replicated and used to transmit traits. DNA resides in the nucleus of cells as well as in cell structures called mitochondria, which generate the energy the cell needs for life. Visually, the molecule is organized as two winding, chemical strands resembling a twisting ladder that scientists call the "double helix". The double helix makes up the backbone of the molecule. The rungs of this ladder are made up of pairs of four interchangeable chemical building blocks or nucleotides (adenine, thymine, guanine and cytosine) called "bases", which pair according to rules and which are held together by weak hydrogen bonds that can be "unzipped", separating the strands (Genetic Science Learning Centre 2010; National Human Genome Research Institute 2009).

Throughout the book, I underscore four characteristics of gender that I liken to DNA – four rungs or building blocks – directing my thoughts about the concept of gender and its relationship to culture. The two metaphorical strands that constitute the backbone of gender are masculinity and femininity, separate yet intertwining and connected by the four building blocks. Metaphorically, just as DNA resides in the nucleus and mitochondria of cells, gender can be imagined as the nucleus of culture, culture as the metaphorical "cell", providing key instructions for its organization as well as the energy or work needed to reproduce itself.

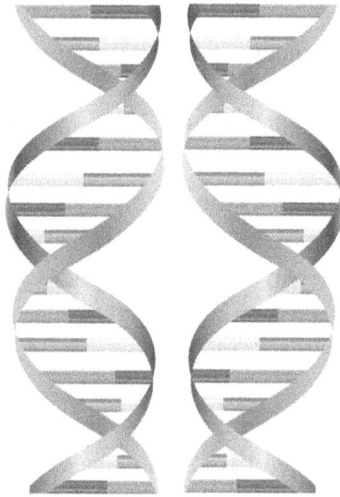

Figure 1: Two DNA strands. This diagram is taken from the National Human Genome Research Institute (http://www.genome.gov.)

Before identifying the bases that constitute the gender "molecule", we must first note that DNA is systemic in nature. It renders the whole organism and exists fully in each cell. Changes or mutations generate organismic/systemic change, thus creating new species. Similarly, gender exists as a system. In my conception of it, the gender molecule consists of two strands, masculinity and femininity, which are both separate and intertwining. One can imagine that the intersection of intertwining strands marks the creation of a new gender category or may reflect specific moments of relative egalitarianism, parity or cultural value attributed to the roles of women and men. At the same time, the unwinding of the strands can metaphorically imply dissonance and emerging inequality between men and women, as scholars have noted occurred in the aftermath of the agricultural revolution when women's productive roles were reduced, childbirth rates increased dramatically and laws emerged to regulate women's reproductive behaviour.[3]

The notion of a gender system has been elucidated by two leading Caribbean feminist scholars noted above. Mohammed (1998) defines gender systems as constitutive of the rules governing social, sexual and reproductive behaviour of men and women in any given society; these systems include the social roles assigned to men and to women, the cultural definition of masculinity and femininity, the sexual division of labour, the rules surrounding marriage and kinship behaviour, and women's position relative to men in political and economic life. Barriteau regards gender systems as relations of power constituent of both material and ideological dimensions. The ideological features include gender identities: masculinities, femininities and alternative gender identities; gender-role identities and culturally specific constructions of masculinity and femininity. Material relations of gender consist of access to material and non-material resources of status, power and privilege as well as socio-economic allocation of resources (Barriteau 1998, 198). Barriteau argues that historically, two persistent features of Caribbean gender systems are their ongoing "ruptures and contestations, and an absence of gender justice" (p. 197).

I draw from features both of Mohammed's and Barriteau's notions of gender systems – indeed they overlap – as well as Mohammed's path-breaking insight that societies encompass multiple and contradictory gender systems. I will demonstrate that everyday life in rural Jamaica is informed by more than one gender system, one dominant and others subversive, although my focus will be on the black Jamaican rural gender system that shapes daily life in Frankfield. I also draw from Barriteau's emphasis on the materiality of gender, and her characterization of gender systems undergoing ruptures and contestations. It is these ruptures and contestations that contribute to the production of new gender systems, along with political and legal changes, economic transformation, and other factors that I will point to throughout the book.

The strands of the gender molecule are held together by bases or rungs constituted by building blocks, of which there are four. As described above, in the actual DNA molecule these refer to nucleotides. In my metaphor, the rungs represent qualities of DNA rather than nucleotides that are central to biological life, and which I liken to qualities of gender and its role in culture. The first rung represents the longevity of DNA maintained through its reproduction in biological life. DNA is replicated and reformulated in each new life in a unique new combination but one which is constituted from all previous generations. In the same way, elements of gender systems, including definitions of masculinity and femininity or the division of labour, for example, are reproduced through socialization and enculturation. Children are taught how to behave and think about themselves and others through the lens of gender ideals. As Simone de Beauvoir famously stated at the beginning of *The Second Sex*, "one is not born but rather becomes a woman" (1989, 265) and the same is true with men. Yet in each generation the rules for gendered behaviour, the ideals and ideologies can be altered from the previous generation. Mohammed has noted that "like most *culture*, [gender norms] are also passed on from one period to the next, and the terms and conditions are changed by the struggles between masculinity and femininity" (1998, 23; emphasis added).

Hence, the second building block in the metaphor: DNA is not fixed or immutable, and nor is gender. Mutability, malleability, plasticity, flexibility and fluidity are all terms I will use to describe the second characteristic of gender and its role in culture, likened to DNA and its role in biological life. Today and in the future, natural and chemically induced mutations, biological engineering, micromanipulation technology, nucleic acid engineering and other technologies are altering DNA to bring about selected characteristics. Gender, like DNA, in this figurative way, is not fixed but transformed accidentally and contingently through cultural processes, as well as consciously. As Ulysse points out in her ethnography of Jamaican informal commercial importers (ICIs – women involved in international trade), these women are involved in "self-making" practices through which they fashion their gender identities asserting notions of self through various processes including beautification. Scholars of gender history have demonstrated gender's plasticity as concepts surrounding masculinity and femininity acquire new characteristics over time and may even develop completely new associations. The ICIs of Ulysse's study "socially assert the femininity they have been historically denied" as working-class black females (2007, 54–56), literally engendering themselves as feminine. Like DNA mutations producing new characteristics that are either helpful to a species' survival or lead to its demise, new gender identities and patterns may improve dynamics between men and women, and hence survivability, or they may not, instead generating increasingly entrenched inequalities. The former can be seen in Ulysse's assertion that the beautification practices of the ICIs amount to a performance of femininity involving "a clever manipulation of the interlocking gender, class, and color codes that have historically constrained them" (p. 56). The latter (entrenched inequalities) can be seen in the plantation society that emerged in Jamaica in the eighteenth century, creating a syncretic gender system born out of English and African forms of patriarchy, as well as patrilineal and matrilineal modes of descent. While the repressive economic and ideological system of slavery further deepened and rendered more violent the preceding systems, it also produced multiple forms of gendered resistance against the Slave Codes that aimed to restrict the behaviour of men and women differently based on false, racist assumptions of an over-generalized "African" masculinity and femininity. DNA reminds us of the mutability of gender categories emerging as potentially liberating, enhancing survival, or restrictive, violent and reminiscent of a species' demise. Thus both longevity and mutability are two building blocks that are paired together to form a rung in the gender molecule's ladder. At any given time, gender systems embody both elements of the past as well as new features that are the result of gender's flexibility.

The third and fourth building blocks are two sides of a coin and therefore also paired: DNA is often described as a signature, a unique snapshot of biological identity. This is the third building block: individuality and uniqueness, terms I will use interchangeably. This individuality, however, emphasizes the ways in which the collectivity of human biological history, the fourth building block, is ultimately distilled in individual human lives. From this local distillation, portions of the larger story of humanity's biological evolution can be recounted. Similarly, gender is also a cultural signature writ small on the individual, such that the collectivity that is culture is uniquely patterned within and imprinted upon individuals. Just as elements of the broader culture are reflected in individuals, so are the wider patterns of gender embodied as personal gender identities. The stories people tell about their lives as men and women are reflections of both their unique circumstances and the context within which their circumstances have unfolded.

The analogy that gender is to culture as DNA is to biological life can therefore be visualized through the depiction of DNA as a metaphorical "gender molecule" situated within the nucleus of culture. The four building blocks – longevity, mutability, uniqueness and collectivity – are paired into longevity-mutability and uniqueness-collectivity, holding together the intertwining strands of masculinity and femininity as a gender system.

It is important to underscore that this model does not represent a "totalizing" or a "meta-theory" that is deterministic about the impact of gender systems to the exclusion of other ideologies and cultural constructions of human life. In fact, it is completely contrary to feminist theory to do so since feminism recognizes the interlocking interaction of a multiplicity of cultural formulations in understanding gender. In other words, feminism has resolutely established, through intersectionality theory, that there is in fact no notion of gender that is somehow suspended out of these interconnected constituents. There are also other features of society that are themselves foundational to culture that interact with gender. Historical context, political economy, environmental and ecological conditions, along with spiritual beliefs and broader cultural themes such as personality or temperament, as Margaret Mead pointed out in the 1930s, are entwined with gender as constitutive of culture. Understanding of these many factors shaping gender now pervades feminist scholarship, and I draw on some of them.

There are a number of assumptions that permeate the ethnography. First, ideas about gender are deeply interwoven into the fabric of cultural life: they are not mere embellishments, accessories or extensions of more important foundational societal features such as economic, political or religious systems of thought and practice as mentioned above. Gender ideals, symbolisms and power relationships permeate all of these, playing a pivotal part in their own configurations. A second assumption is that male dominance is a near-universal attribute of gender systems even though it is quite clear that patriarchies consist of variations in gendered power, such that race, ethnicity, class, religion and other factors position some women with greater power than others, and some women with greater power than some men. At the same time, I acknowledge that there have been and continue to be societies with greater or lesser gender equality; there is great variation in gender patterns globally. Nonetheless, simultaneously, gender inequality is persistent and pervades the majority of contemporary human social arrangements. Third, such near-universal dominance is the result of ideologies that sustain power and privilege, and which are upheld as cosmic and eternal (Keesing, cited in Moore and Sanders 2006, 265). Last, the problem of the body – that is, the attempt to understand and explain biological differences between men and women – has become part of the problem of gender identities and meanings. The ways in which biology and culture interact with respect to male and female behaviour are still not fully understood. Yet theorists tend to congregate along ideological lines stressing either biosocial reasons that explain human behaviour through the principle of natural selection or cultural constructionist perspectives that emphasize socialization and enculturation as the driving forces behind male and female behaviour. I recognize that this is an ongoing problem in feminist analysis. Following Martha Nussbaum's incisive critique of Butler's work in which she points out that Butler (and I would add the cultural constructionist approach to gender in general) does not address the ways in which biological realities of the body impact on our understandings of gender. Nussbaum states: "Even where sex difference is concerned, it is surely too simple to write it all off as culture; nor should feminists be eager to make such a sweeping gesture . . . In short: what feminism needs, and sometimes gets, is a subtle study of the interplay of bodily difference and cultural construction" (1999, 8). While acknowledging that this kind of analysis is crucial, I will address bodily differences through a cultural constructionist lens, as the fundamental symbolic axis around which ideologies are perpetuated in the everyday and through the cosmic. In rural Jamaica, these bodily differences are understood by many as foundational to gender-role differentiation, applying the kind of divinely ordained, culturally produced biological essentialism that feminist scholars reject, but which is nonetheless found in many parts of the world. At the same time, as we will see, gendered bodily differences are also raced and classed, produced and moulded through the historical hegemony of Jamaica's plantation society. As anthropologist Sherry Ortner (1996, 441) has put it, the human body is the vessel through which gendered meanings and power relationships are "read" and performed.

ORGANIZATION OF THE BOOK

Envisioning the chapters in the book itself as a series of building blocks, I begin with my first journey into the Jamaican countryside in 1991, when I was still a graduate student. The chapter introduces the community of Frankfield, located in the centre of the island of Jamaica in the parish of Clarendon. It is an arrival story that seeks to bring readers into this cultural terrain and familiarize them with the methodological approach and the contributions of this ethnography to the literature on gender in the Caribbean region. Chapter 2 adds another building block to the strand of metaphorical DNA that symbolizes the centrality of gender in Jamaican culture. Its aim is to locate stories about the origins of Frankfield within a broader national narrative, drawing from the intersection of archival research and local lore. The chapter tacks back and forth from stories and reports about the parish of Clarendon, to the community of Frankfield, to island-wide accounts of gendered life, in an effort to elucidate the feminist anthropological knowledge production process.

The third chapter pursues the same analytical framework outlined in chapter 2, focusing on building a gendered history of Frankfield by stitching a patchwork narrative drawn from archive, folklore and cultural memory. Chapter 4 outlines the specifics of the community's rural black Jamaican gender system. Chapter 5 invites readers to move in more closely to particular individuals' lives, further highlighting the idea of the simultaneously unique and shared signature of gender by urging readers to think about how the personal narratives of a group of men and women from Frankfield embed assumptions about the gender ideals discussed in chapter 3. Their narratives are personal threads in a cultural spiral. They are gendered narratives, stories of "ordinary" people that I argue are crucial in appreciating the wider systems of which they are a part and the new gender systems that they are in the process of producing. Chapter 6 builds on themes presented in chapter 4. I discuss the application of feminist ethnographic research methodologies on collaborative projects with community members, in service learning projects and HIV/AIDS workshops. Here I am concerned with the American college student experience in Jamaica as a self-reflexive lens that produces personal portraits of their own gendered, racialized and class identities set against insights into the Jamaican gender system, garnered through these projects. Finally, chapter 7 offers concluding remarks, reaffirming what has been said about gender in rural Jamaica and exploring the potential application of the DNA metaphor to other cultural settings historically, in the present and also perhaps in tentative projections for gender in the future.

Acknowledgements

I AM INDEBTED TO numerous individuals and organizations, without whom the completion of this book would have been impossible. Since the research for the book has been in process since 1991, I secured funding to travel to Jamaica and other parts of the Caribbean from many sources, for which I am most grateful. These include two Third World Studies research grants and two faculty development grants from the Massachusetts College of Liberal Arts in North Adams, MA; one summer research grant; three faculty/librarian research grants; the Fiore Prize in World Justice grant; and a Faculty ATP Mentor grant, from Bridgewater State College, Bridgewater, MA. I also pursued research under a Fulbright fellowship in 2005–2006 and a Fulbright senior specialist grant in 2007, when I had the opportunities to work with colleagues at the Centre for Gender and Development Studies at both the Mona and St Augustine campuses of the University of the West Indies (UWI).

Colleagues at both campuses provided me the opportunity to present an overview of my research, and I received valuable insights and support from the staff. At the Mona Unit, I received insight and commentary from Barbara Bailey, June-Ann Castello and Althea Perkins, in particular, for reading portions of the text and offering comments. I was also given warm and friendly support by the entire staff, particularly Lourraine, whose recent passing marks a significant loss, and Florence, both my first contacts there, who encouraged me to apply for a Fulbright. Thanks also to Margaret, Georgia and Rodderick for their humour and open arms, and, from the wider Mona campus, to Barry Chevannes for his comments during a presentation I gave. Thanks also to Pablo, friend and reliable driver/chaperone, for stimulating political conversation and safe driving over many years, from Kingston to Frankfield, and all over "de rock".

At the St Augustine Unit, I am indebted to Patricia Mohammed for reading an early draft and later revealing herself to me as one of the peer reviewers for UWI Press, for which she offered invaluable insights as well as her ongoing critique and emotional support: I would not have pursued the theoretical component without her assistance. Thanks also to Rhoda Reddock for encouragement and theoretical insights on the role of the feminist ethnographer, and to the staff of the unit for their friendly assistance, particularly Glenda, Donna and Michelle. Thanks to the peer reviewers at the UWI Press for detailed and constructive criticism.

I could not have completed this work without the many years of patience and understanding of my family. Throughout, Al held down the fort when I travelled to Jamaica and Trinidad. His belief in me, and enthusiasm for my work, pushed me along during rocky times. In the 1990s my stepsons, Ishmael, Michael and Donte, waited patiently at home for my return. Since she was born in 2002, our daughter Sophia has travelled with me to Jamaica on numerous occasions, unwittingly providing insight into mothering and child-rearing practices and helping to cement family ties in Frankfield. Her sweetness, humour and curiosity connected me to children in Frankfield as well. Over the years my mother, Vivian, has provided scholarly and emotional counsel; she is always with me. Thanks to my brothers, Michael, for always urging and encouraging me to "write something significant", and Greg, who has also always offered support, enthusiasm and advice.

Thanks to so many students over the years, including Eric, Andy, Danielle, Carrie, Geraldine and others, and, in particular, my former student Heidi Savery: friend, research assistant, nanny and, ultimately, godmother to Sophia. Heidi travelled with me to Jamaica four times as a research assistant and nanny for our daughter. Ron Dalton – friend, colleague, godfather – has provided the same. Thanks also to Jessica Clothieaux, longtime friend, who provided rich commentary on various drafts. Lifelong family friend and anthropologist-mentor, Eleanor Chasdi, read the entire manuscript and offered welcome critique and valuable comments. And thanks also to my other "bestest" friends, Pammy and Robin – *always* supportive.

I would like to express my appreciation for the guidance, support and friendly assistance of the folks at the UWI Press. I first met Linda Speth while a Fulbright scholar at UWI Mona. She came out of her office to warn me about crossing the lawn with my small daughter because tarantulas had been spotted! This lead to a tour of the Press, a discussion about the book still in progress, and her support and suggestions throughout the process. Shivaun Hearne and others at the Press have also been instructive and helpful. I am deeply thankful for the careful, insightful comments of Erin MacLeod, who has cheerfully urged me on and worked with me to complete final copy-editing issues. Her attention to detail is unmatched. Thank you, Erin!

Finally, *but by no means least*, thanks to the kind and generous people of Frankfield, so many of whom appear in this text: Lynette Dunkley and Baldina Heron, who have become two such special people in my life, and their kin Colette and Kippling, whose love, affection and many, many kindnesses turned anthropology into a family for me. To Moses, Danny, Janine, Joan and her children, Sam, Balti, Priest, Elfie, and the many other residents of the community, who have welcomed me year after year into their town – schools, churches, homes – as one of their own and without whom this book would not exist. For those whom I have neglected to mention – my apologies, you are here in spirit.

Chapter 1

Arriving, Departing and
Arriving Again

The aim of anthropology is the enlargement of the universe of human discourse
– Clifford Geertz (1973, 14)

ANTHROPOLOGY BECOMES REAL

In May 1991 I boarded a plane in Hartford, Connecticut, and travelled to
Kingston, Jamaica, for the first time. I was a graduate student at the University
of Massachusetts at Amherst. Hoping to enlarge my own universe of cross-cultural knowledge, I had recently been hired by a medical anthropologist to learn
about the values, beliefs and attitudes surrounding the growing use of crack
cocaine on the island. I was part of a team of student research assistants studying to become professional anthropologists. As part of our preparations, we
received an overview of the illegal drug situation, learning that cocaine was
infiltrating Jamaica through shipments from Columbia. These original infil-
trations were oddly accidental: boats leaving Columbia and traversing international waters with the illegal cargo would dump their loads into the sea
when spotted by the coast guard. The bags, equipped with a time/weight
device, would immediately sink and later wash up on the southern shore of
Jamaica, where they were discovered by struggling fishermen (who rapidly
became wealthy dealers) and women "mules" would transport the substance
around the island. I remember being shocked to learn that crack cocaine had

1

penetrated rural Jamaica; that fact contradicted my assumptions that the drug was an urban phenomenon. By the time I left the island, this and most of my other unschooled preconceptions had been shattered: that first trip was transformational. It was my first fieldwork, and the learning curve I experienced was steep. But my rocky climb had ended abruptly after I was held up at machete-point while I was wandering, rather naively, through a shantytown neighbourhood in Papine, a community bordering the north end of the University of the West Indies campus. Walking with another graduate student on the team, we were clearly out of place with our white skin and shopping packages. Two young men ran up behind us, grabbed our wrists, and pointed machetes menacingly at our stomachs and throats: we handed over our packages and bags containing our travel documents. Shaken, with the last bits of my already thin confidence dissolved, I left before completion of the study. Yet I departed a different person than when I had arrived as a result of my exposure to a new cultural reality, an experience I would see repeated years later in my own students. On many occasions since, I have travelled with small groups of four to five students who have lived with Jamaican families, pursued independent research and assisted me with my own. We studied gender roles, economic development and local understandings of HIV/AIDS; yet that first journey set the stage for all others, opening up relationships and a field site that would become a second home to me.

But in 1991, what would be real for me today was far from my consciousness. Except for our debriefing on the cocaine trade, I knew very little about Jamaica other than that it was home to my favourite reggae artists and had been frequented by many of my college friends during spring breaks. Jamaica is the third largest island in the Caribbean, located south of Cuba in the cluster of islands known as the Greater Antilles. The island itself is divided into fourteen parishes. All of the participants in the study were assigned a community in which to evaluate the crack issue. Mine was Frankfield, a small, rural agricultural town in the north-west of the parish of Clarendon, approximately sixty-four miles from Kingston in the central, southern part of the country. On the morning of my departure to Jamaica, I left behind my future husband and stepsons, little boys who cried wrenching tears and clung to me from the back of our pick-up truck. As I pulled away and waved goodbye, I felt horrible leaving them. Yet once on the plane, I did what so many anthropologists-in-the-making have had to do: I anticipated the unknown.

Arriving later that afternoon in the crowded, bustling Norman Manley

International Airport in Kingston, the capital city on the south coast of the island, I tossed my backpack over my shoulder and wandered outside into a wall of hot humidity. I soon saw my "guide", a professor from the United States whom I had never met before, named Kathy.[1] She was friendly, cheerful and brave, I thought, as we climbed in her rented car with the steering on the right, British style, and she whisked me off to the home of a US Drug Enforcement Agency official in the hills above the city. At a gate stationed by guards, we were buzzed into a grand estate, graced with a gorgeous swimming pool over-looking the city. After a refreshing swim, we headed off for my first meal of spicy jerk chicken and Red Stripe beer at a local restaurant/bar, hopping with reggae and open to the night air under a thatched roof. Returning relaxed and too tired to imagine the next day's journey into the interior, I soon fell asleep to my one and only night of air-conditioning.

The next morning, refreshed, we set out for Frankfield. Leaving Kingston, we passed through the sprawl of a shantytown. At a traffic light, children appeared from the tin-roofed board shacks and approached the car windows to sell bottled water, bags of cashews or boxes of doughnuts. I sat upright, sud-denly feeling ill at ease about the luxury I had experienced the night before. I had read extensively in graduate school about "Third World" economies and the unequal distribution of wealth to a small minority, while the impoverished majority eked out a living on less than a dollar a day. Jamaica had a growing middle class, and by 1999 the World Bank would no longer classify Jamaica's economy as Third World status. Between 1989 and 1999, the poverty rate fell from 30.5 per cent to 17 per cent (World Bank 2007). After many years of trav-elling around the island away from the touristy north coast, it is obvious even to newcomers to the island that there is a growing middle class; yet there is also persistent poverty that is apparent in the rural interior and parts of any city, and throughout the country, infrastructure is deteriorating. Many children in rural areas apprentice on farms and throughout the island they work for shopkeepers to earn petty wages. Increasing numbers must forgo school to assist their families in small informal businesses, or because their families are unable to afford fees required for school entry and the cost of school uniforms and shoes. Moreover, throughout the island's cities, children work in the infor-mal sector selling foodstuffs and working in tourist markets. After only one day on the island, however, I had not yet seen these emerging and established communities of the middle class, though I had briefly witnessed polar ends of the economic spectrum.

We stopped at a red light, and a young boy, maybe five or six years old, hopped off a brick wall and ran up to my window, rapped on it and held up a small plastic bag of cashews. I stared at him for a moment, and then, too late, reached for my purse just as the light changed to green. We were off, and he was gone; I turned to look behind me, perusing the image of his eager face. As we drove, the scene of what just happened played over in my mind; to me at this early stage in my development as an anthropologist, this little boy was the quintessential "other": an assumed image so distant from "self" that the identity becomes fixed and reified as a set of characteristics, rather than being recognized as a fluid and complex being. I had grown up in an upper-middle-class home outside of Boston, Massachusetts, and knew no want as a child; I had never seen a shantytown. That morning, as we wound through traffic on our way out of "Town" (the Jamaican term for Kingston, as no other urban centre in the country compares to this sprawling metropolis), I searched for something in my experience that could bring me closer to that momentary interaction with the little boy. As I tried to make sense of my embarrassment at my first glimpse of so-called Third World poverty, a wave of anthropological insight washed over me: I recalled the notion of empathetic understanding, a term I had learned in graduate school. Anthropological notions emerge slowly; the formal definitions of conceptual frameworks that are implemented in the fieldwork process underscore the value of this ethnographic "rite of passage". Empathetic understanding posits the possibilities of overlapping realities, despite widely differing worldviews. It is a way of thinking about oneself as an anthropologist in relation to the researched subject-other that challenges researchers to draw from one's own lived experience to help identify with the lives one is immersed in. The objective of empathetic understanding is to close the gap between a familiar self and an assumed, distant other by keeping in the forefront of one's mind the shared humanity of one's research subjects. The goal here is not to gloss over important differences to say that we are the same, but to open doorways for critical reflection on the conditions and cir-cumstances that shape our lives. I was charged, as an anthropologist-in-train-ing, to think about ways I might identify with the little boy, rather than to assume total distance.

I recount this fleeting yet deeply valuable experience in order to indicate something about the anthropological process of understanding as I acquired it. In so doing, I am positioning myself in this text within what anthropologists have called the "new ethnography" – disciplinary-wide responses to more than two decades of critique of the genre of ethnography emerging from both inside and outside of anthropology. Ethnography in its most basic sense is both a process of implementing a research methodology and an outcome – the story of fieldwork and a cultural portrait. How I came to understand and think about the little boy from the shantytown and my fieldwork process is deeply informed by currents of thought emerging from these critiques.

Many anthropologists today are explicit about the process through which fieldwork is transformed into anthropological knowledge, challenging long-held assumptions about the ethnographer, whose experience of simply "being there" was believed to confer authority over the subject of inquiry. The concept of empathetic understanding became a valuable heuristic device for me, and I began to employ it regularly, prodding myself to think about how other anthropological concepts could assist my understanding of Jamaican culture. Even today those abstract ideas and anthropological theories, which seek to explain and interpret cultural life, become vivid and alive to me while I am in the field. On that particular day, while driving through the Kingston shanty-town, a central tenet of an increasingly vocal feminist anthropology was put into practice for me.

Since the late 1980s, feminists have argued that it is overly simplistic to think about the anthropologist/subject relationship in terms of a pair of binary opposites constituted by the familiar cultural self and the exotic cultural other. This questioning arose from the feminist challenge to pure objectivity in scientific and social scientific research.[2] Scholars have pointed out that the researcher's location in society, or our "positionality", shapes our interests and the questions we ask. This positionality is constructed by one's location in society: gender, race, ethnicity, class and other interlocking features of identity. Cross-culturally, women researchers grow up socialized to appeal and be sensitive to the emotions of others. Many are taught empathy as a "feminized" social tool. Empathetic understanding as a feminist methodology stems from women's socialization experiences and requires a conflation of self with other in order for cross-cultural identification to occur. It serves as a corrective to ethnographic objectivity as the primary ideal of fieldwork. While feminist ethnographers also maintain that important differences certainly exist across cultures, even when the anthropologist is a native of the research community, if we focus solely on differences, we exclude the appreciation of shared values, beliefs and norms that emerge either independently or through multiple transnational channels such as media exposure, migration and other forms of travel. If researchers think about our own cultural identities in relation to those under study as potential points of intersection as well as divergence, then the line between subject and object, self and other, blurs (Behar 1993, 301–2).

Empathetic understanding is only possible if those of us who travel and do research in places that are new to us carry with us the assumption that shared points of view, however differently arrived at, will indeed exist. As students of culture, we cannot afford to overlook points of shared meaning in life and how they intersect with our differences. Many of the undergraduates I have travelled with over the years struggled, as I had, to understand the relative poverty of working-class Jamaicans, in relation to their own self-identified working-class or lower-middle-class identities. They were often confronted with requests for money while wandering about Frankfield, generating embarrassment and confusion about how to respond, when they had little money for themselves, travelling on a shoestring budget and working full time at home to put themselves through college. At the same time, they were comparatively wealthy in terms of the material abundance they lived with at home, their opportunities to acquire wealth and status, and their freedom to travel. According to one student named Eric, who came with me three times to Frankfield,

> We would often have to explain to folks that back home we were "poor college students"; hence, we were unable to provide much money for handouts, and would explain that back home we have very little money ourselves for anything but the "basics". Sure, the levels of poverty do not compare, but this explanation often produced a sense of understanding on the part of people asking for money, as well as enabling us to be viewed through a slightly different lens in some cases. (Eric Molleur, personal communication, 11 March 2004)

This kind of analysis harnesses relational thinking, one of the centrepieces of a feminist ethnographic methodology that refuses to reduce the complexities of the world's peoples and their cultures to a stark "us" and "them" or "self" and "other". As anthropologist Sally Cole has stated concerning the impact of employing this fundamental insight of feminist research: "The creation of a self through opposition to an other is blocked, and therefore both the multiplicity of the self and the multiple overlapping and interacting qualities of the other cannot be ignored . . . offer[ing] the promise of finally undermining the assumption of anthropology that we stand outside" (cited in Behar 1993, 359). I introduce these concepts early on in the book both as part of my own ethnographic encounter with a new cultural reality and to underscore one of the main conceptual building blocks that I will employ to construct this book: empathetic understanding as a heuristic device to problematize dichotomies such as "us/them" and "self/other".

On day two in Jamaica, then, driving through a shantytown, "empathetic understanding" became my key phrase. I held onto the notion as something tangible amid the unknowns I was entering into, and it proved to be important for the remainder of the day, as well as in many days yet to come.

As we wound up the narrow, potholed roads into the mountains, we saw people adorned in their Sunday best. By now it was hot and humid, and I was amazed to see men and boys in suits, women in stockings and heels with flowered hats and girls in frilly dresses, all on their way to church. This was an image that would become familiar, but in all the years I attended church as a participant observer, I myself never became accustomed to wearing pantyhose in ninety-degree temperatures, and from the beginning risked disapproval with open-toed sandals and simple T-shirts.

The sights, sounds and smells of that initial journey to Frankfield, now so well-known, immersed me in my new world. I took mental notes as we drove along, already composing my first journal entries: "towns lie along the main road in a straight line; children are hauling water in buckets from roadside standpipes; and boys are tending goats; the hillsides are dotted with banana trees, coconut palms, yam crops twisting around poles" (field notes, May 1991). On some hairpin turns, when two cars could barely pass, I looked at the valley plunging below, gasping both at its magnificent beauty and how closely we teetered towards the edge. Not only were the roads deeply rutted, in some instances with great, gaping crevices and no guardrails, but one wrong little turn . . . what was that statistic I learned in graduate school? More anthropologists die from car crashes on poor-quality remote roads than from any other cause.

Finally, about three hours after we had left Kingston (today the journey is much shorter due to a new toll road) we pulled into Frankfield, a fading green sign welcoming visitors to town. Today, a new, bright yellow Western Union sign stands alongside it. People finally have a way to receive remittances in their hometown from relatives working overseas. We cruised slowly down the main road, full of schoolchildren: girls in their bright blue dresses and starched white shirts, boys in their tan pants and tops, apparently on break for their lunch hour. Girls held hands and giggled as I rolled down the window and asked directions to the high school. Along the way, Kathy had informed me that the first task of the day on arriving in Frankfield was to find me a place to live. The high school, she said, would be the place to begin our search. Gulping down my astonishment that this had not been previously arranged I smiled wanly, as the reality of my situation sank in. I would be on my own: I would have to rely on those proverbial inner resources. Whatever those resources were, I was soon to find out. Reflecting now on this experience, I am well aware that first fieldwork is quite a different reality for newbie anthropologists. The prevalence of cellular telephones and email dramatically transforms the experience of isolation. In 1991, Frankfield had one public telephone booth, where I would wait in line to call home once per week to reassure my anxious parents. Telephone service was first introduced in the area in 1965 with ten lines, and was extended in 1996 so that now most of the homes in Frankfield have telephone service.

We pulled through the gate of the Edwin Allen Regional High School, all eyes upon us. Although Jamaica has an active tourist trade bringing "foreign"[3] to the island daily, rarely do they leave the north coast where most of the resorts are located. Some more adventurous travellers go to the south coast, but it is rare to see a white face in the island's interior. Just over 90 per cent of the population is black, 7.5 per cent is mixed and 0.2 per cent is white. Other minority groups including East Indian (1.3 per cent), Chinese (0.2 per cent) and Lebanese (0.1 per cent) comprise the remaining population (Wedenoja and Fox 2004, 551). We clearly stood out. In the 2000 version of the *Lonely Planet* guide to Jamaica, there is just one paragraph devoted to Frankfield, which describes the community as a "dishevelled town [that] has a 'lost in the hinterland' feel . . . all eyes will follow you warily as you move through town" (Baker 2000, 528). If you are just passing through, that might be an initial impression, but like all human communities, what makes them "tick" is not revealed in a quick drive through. The *Lonely Planet* author, however, seemed to think so little of Frankfield as a destination for travellers that in subsequent editions it is not even mentioned. Frankfield has a residential population of around 3,544 with an additional daily population of about two thousand, which is mainly the result of the Edwin Allen Regional High School which draws both children and teachers from communities throughout the area. According to the Statistical Institute of Jamaica, the official population of the town was 3,373 in 1991.[4] The town extends for about a mile from its entrance by the Church of God, arriving from Chapelton, to Angel Bridge going towards Spalding. As we drove along, arriving at the high school, crowds of students lined the road up to the school; a soccer game was underway in the large field at its base, and cheers and jeers resounded for the teams. We soon found our way to the office of the principal. Here was a man, I would come to learn, who was a highly respected member of the Jamaican middle class, admired through-out the community and often invited to preside over the many formal cere-monial events that mark Jamaican public life, although he lived an hour away in the city of Mandeville, where many middle-class and well-off Jamaicans reside. Kathy told him why we were here and what we needed, while I smiled politely, trying to look like someone whom a family would want to have live with them. He decided that the school reverend might have some ideas about where I could stay.

Kathy accompanied the principal to find the reverend while I waited in the hallway and surveyed my surroundings. In a moment, a small, round woman, grandmotherly, with a sweet and pretty face, wearing a white nurse's uniform, poked her head out of a doorway. She gave me a warm, generous smile that immediately relaxed me, and began to ask me questions: "And who are you, my dear?" As I began to tell her about myself she volunteered that she had recently been to Arizona, where her great-niece was a basketball star at the Uni-versity of Arizona. Surprised, I informed her that I had attended the University of Arizona for two years, where I had received my master's in anthropology. I remember being bewildered that here in this small, mountain town in the cen-tre of this island, lived a woman who knew the city I had lived in for three years. Our crash course on Jamaica had not said much about travel and migra-tion. I wondered where else she had been. And I thought, "Once upon a time, she left this place for the first time and arrived somewhere totally different. She knows how I feel." Again, the notion of empathetic understanding washed over me as I imagined this nurse, travelling for the first time to Tucson from her familiar home here in Frankfield. I thought of her feeling anxious in a new environment and thus extending herself to me as she did now to ease my own anxiety. Later on, when I learned that welcoming visitors and relatives to her home was a standard part of her daily life, I asked her about her ability to be so generous and gracious to others. "I've travelled in my life and *know* what it's like to be alone somewhere far from home", she had said, confirming my assumptions. "I just want people to feel *relaxed*, at home. Make a cup of tea. Lie down, *anything you want!* You know?" I was to hear these types of phrases repeated many times as I returned with new groups of students; this was a wel-come mantra that worked, putting me and others at ease.

So it ended up that when the reverend, the principal and Kathy returned and saw the nurse and me engaged in conversation, the reverend's eyes brightened: "Nurse Dunkley," he said, "won't you take in this American student for the summer? I see that you've already made friends." For a moment she hesitated, "Well, I have boarders already, you know, my granddaughter, and a student attending Edwin Allen . . . but," she gave a sidelong glance at me, and perhaps saw my hopeful expression, "I think we can make room . . ." I sighed with relief. And thus began my friendship and kinship with "Nurse", a title of respect bestowed on all nurses, so highly regarded are they in Jamaican society.

Kathy said goodbye and took her leave; I got in Nurse's little orange car, and we headed to her home, a one-storey structure, just outside the centre of town, a place where I would come to have "people", an adopted family, and I would be told one day that "this is your home too". But I did not understand "fictive kin"[5] on that day or for many years later, for it took perhaps a half a decade for those bonds to grow and for life in Frankfield to become recognizable and beloved. Still, even as we drove to Nurse's home, stopping numerous times along the way to greet people who called out, "Good afternoon, Nurse!", I felt her maternal, protective wing. The next day, though, when I ventured out into town on my own to calls of "whitey" and "white lady" I felt myself to be isolated, alone and, yes, "other". Yet while I assumed that I was being perceived as an alien, white female face, I did not know that my initial association with Nurse by townsfolk would immediately cloak me in her reputation, or that my behaviour would reflect on her. I had performed one of many anthropological gaffes by forgetting that I, too, was under scrutiny, imputing on Frankfielders an overly simplistic view of what they thought of me, when in actuality, I was already being assigned a place of class, race and gender in the community and, indeed, the society.

Frankfielders were familiar with Nurse as a travelling woman who housed many friends and relatives from foreign. As a guest of Nurse, a highly regarded, church-going Methodist, middle-class member of the town, I later understood that I was expected to behave like a respectable "lady": to dress modestly, to ignore the calls of men in the street, to stay in after darkness settled on the town, to comport myself as a member of the elite classes, historically associated with whiteness. Already I was more than "other". My female identity was at once raced and classed through ideas about white womanhood inherited and passed down from the British colonial slave era. As Ulysse observes of this period, "all white females (whether born in the mother country or the colony) were considered to be 'ladies', while black females were women and girls" (2007, 26). Although I was unaware of it at the time, I was immediately embedded within a feature of one Jamaican gender system: the longevity of a particular colonial configuration of race, colour, class and gender. At the same time, it would also become clear that another gender systemic coexisted with the persistence of this one, as the once clearly articulated relationships among class, race, colour and gender have become reconfigured. Portia Simpson's brief tenure in 2006–2007 as Jamaica's first black female prime minister and the vilification she received that contributed to her being ousted are indicative of the ongoing struggle among coexisting gender systems marked by tensions between features of a gender system that signify longevity and emergent features indicative of mutability. As Garnett and Danielle Roper point out in their article, "Christianity and gender in the Caribbean: Is Portia Hagar redivivus?", printed following her electoral defeat:

> If we understand the historical figure of the black maid working in the master's house, it reveals that the involvement of the black working-class in government threatens the social, racial and class hierarchy in Jamaican society. Hence the construction of Portia Simpson Miller as a maid, or as a virago, calls upon the underlying social prejudices of our society that inform the voters' decision and ultimately maintain patriarchal and elitist power in Jamaica. (*Jamaica Gleaner*, 21 October 2007)

Yet it took some time for me to realize not only how I was being positioned but the enormous complexities of competing gender systems and their compositional race/class/colour make-up. In the beginning I focused on my discomfort in spite of my feminist anthropological leanings that exhorted me to think more complexly.

The discomfort I felt for many years in Jamaica as a racial and religious minority would provide an opportunity to embrace empathetic understanding, in order to reflect on the dynamics of race and otherness in my own environments in the United States. Indeed, when, a few weeks later, the calls turned from "white lady" to "brownin' " as I tanned, I realized that the fluidity of racial categorization and the ideas of colour that comprise it were only one component of my malleable gender identity. In Jamaica, and the Caribbean more broadly, "colour", based on visibility, is an axis of gender identity linked to "race". "Browning" in Jamaica is a term of colour that has come to replace "mulatto" and is associated with the middle class; as one Frankfielder put it to me, justifying why he was asking me for money, "yuh rich!", reflecting the transition from the colonial white power structure to the contemporary brown elite (Austin-Broos 1984, cited in Ulysse 2007, 13). Current anthropological thinking about race as a sociocultural construction was becoming a reality for me, and my experience of being labelled with Jamaican racial and colour identifiers permitted me to reflect on race and racism at home, which in turn permitted me to put into practice another anthropological heuristic that all fieldworkers experience: self-reflexivity.

In addition to immediate responses to my raced and classed gender identity, people were also forming opinions about me as one who, though privileged in resources, was lacking in cultural knowledge. I was a curious child, seeking socialization and wishing to be embraced, tutored and well liked. I hoped I would not offend, although I did at times; and like any child, I was reprimanded that my reaction to something was improper, or later I was instructed in private on a more appropriate response to a situation. These ranged from breaches of norms, such as being improperly dressed for an occasion (I was too informal and did not wear stockings, thus violating codes of "ladyness"), or not accepting money from my host family to run an errand in town and insisting that I pay for everything myself (an act I initially thought was generous, but later realized was demeaning to my hosts, unintentionally asserting white status over brown), to more egregious errors, such as not returning home early enough in the evening or speaking out and offering my opinion when it was not asked for, warranted or appropriate. Reflecting now on those early trips, it is clear that I was being taught to behave appropriately as a white lady in the context of Jamaican society. As I got older and more familiar with the community, these sanctions eased. People evaluated me less rigorously along gender/class/colour/race codes of behaviour and included knowledge of who I was as a human being in their interactions with me. Yet other markers of status emerged and were integrated into the relationships I developed with Frank-fielders. These included my status as a professional, acquiring my PhD so that people began to call out to me "Doctor" or "Professor" as I walked through town. In addition, when I began to bring my young daughter to Frankfield, new instructions emerged about mothering, limiting my mobility even further after fall of darkness, or even regulating when I could walk out into town during the day in order to protect my child from the heat of the sun. My professional status did not mitigate these restraints; in fact, my continued casual dress and informality lead people to comment that I did not behave in a removed and elite fashion as they expected a professor, and particularly a white lady professor "from foreign", to behave. Nonetheless, at all stages, in my visits to Frankfield I have been coached in the norms of behaviours appropriate to the gender decorum of the specific role I occupied at the time. These insights, produced through the anthropologist's toolkit, are a central goal of the methodology of participant observation, established generations ago by one of the discipline's founders, Bronislaw Malinowski, in his "effort to understand the subjective experience of another culture through the immersive strategy of ethnographic research" (Moore 2004, 145).

I grew over the years in cultural knowledge and in tactful ways to learn about the community I was immersed in. I was indeed embraced, so that eventually I found my voice: I was able to express my opinion and even argue, and to reveal that I was Jewish to a largely Christian fundamentalist community, and, no, I had not been saved. Yes, I was and remain a sinner in the eyes of many. Did I worry about that? I certainly did, although now I believe unnecessarily so. It was not until 2001, ten years later, that my fears were put to rest when my friend Richard, a hat maker, told me, "People respect you around here; you know that no harm will come to you; people look out for you." But even now I still receive warnings and reprimands when I overstep boundaries or behave in culturally ignorant ways. Socialization and enculturation are lifelong processes for members of a society; for anthropologists becoming culturally fluent is also an ongoing process.

ARRIVING IN TIME FOR A WEDDING: DEFINING THE RESEARCH AGENDA

I have travelled to Frankfield at least twelve times, including that first visit, and again in 1995, 1997, and at least annually through 2007. Each time is a rich story in itself, and in the pages that follow I will share anecdotes, descriptions and analyses from many of these visits that illuminate the central idea of this text. That idea is this: Jamaican ideas about femininity and masculinity are constitutional of everyday life. Yet gender, as feminist scholars have argued cogently in recent decades, does not stand alone, isolated from other intersecting influences of race, class, ethnicity, religion, and other attributes of identity, meaning and stratification. All of these attributes are pivotal in Jamaican life, along with numerous other factors such as environment, political climate and the articulation of the Jamaican economy with global capitalism, which impacts job availability, unemployment and other economic indicators. My aim here is to demonstrate that all of these crucial features of Jamaican society are simultaneously intersectional with gender meanings and practices, so that, for example, women are the predominant workers in the free-zone areas while men are the managers, light skin is regarded as a signifier of female beauty, older women are the predominant churchgoers, men still retain dominant political leadership, and so forth. On my first visit I did not think much about the centrality of gender in Jamaican culture, much less its articulation with race, colour and class, although I gathered pieces of information, including bits about the sexual division of labour and the norms of respectable female modesty in dress and sexuality, where I did note distinctions in colour and class especially emergent in black female rejection of ladylike modesty exhibited through tight, revealing clothing and flashy jewellery. These pieces have become part of my cumulative knowledge once I did decide to focus on the topic. This decision occurred during my second trip, four years later, when I heard Nurse Dunkley give a speech at her nephew's wedding. The speech inspired me to take a close look at Jamaican views of men and women and to dig beneath the surface to try to interpret how gender moulds rural Jamaican life, establishing opportunities and imposing limitations on people.

Why did I return to Jamaica? When I left the first time I was miserable, and I questioned my skills as a fieldworker. Soon after I had been mugged at machete-point in Papine, I returned to Frankfield from Kingston. I had decided to go back to the United States, and I informed Nurse and her family that I was going home early. At my announcement, they all burst into tears, weeping and imploring me to stay, telling me, "Frankfield isn't like Town." I was stunned at their disappointment, at the feelings they had generated for me, and at their heartfelt conviction that I should not leave the island with negative feelings. Over the years following my departure, that memory stayed with me more poignantly than the fear associated with the mugging, and I did come to realize that no, Frankfield was not "Town". When I left, I took this moment with me, so that my decision to return was a confirmation of the warmth that had flowed between us and the hope that there was something more to build.

Now I had my doctorate, I was a first year professor at a small state college in western Massachusetts, and I was ready. Gaining the doctorate is, in effect, a rite of passage into professional anthropology. For me, it conferred a certain confidence at least in my ability to think anthropologically, gaining the approval of my professors. I hoped this time when I returned I could combine the thinking and doing.

Nurse met me at the airport with her adopted son. Over the years, as is common in rural Jamaica, Nurse had informally adopted many children, somewhere in the neighbourhood of twenty when we last sat down to count, and she is still at it at the age of eighty-two, with an additional young man and woman housed under her roof attending Edwin Allen Regional High School. Some of these children were nieces and nephews, others neighbours' children, all of whom she loved, fed, clothed, disciplined and schooled. Nurse has only one legally adopted child. He survived his twin brother who died soon after birth. Nurse took him home as hers after she helped deliver him when he was abandoned by his mother in the hospital.

Seeing her waving at me outside the airport gate, I hurried to her and we hugged warmly. "Girl, I knew you'd return," she said. "I told you I would," I replied, smiling. This time, I do not remember looking out the window at all, until we reached the mountains. We chattered away, catching up on each other's lives although I had written regularly over the years, keeping in contact. Pulling up to the driveway of Nurse's home, her niece and grandniece met me with great big hugs and laughter. The dining room table was set with lace and china, and Nurse's niece, who ran a "cook shop" (restaurant), had prepared a feast: whole fish (snapper) sautéed in onions and hot peppers with her special sauce, rice and peas cooked in coconut milk, candied yams, and a lettuce salad commonly known as "vegetable salad". We sat down, and Nurse gave a moving and lengthy grace, a regular ritual for which she is known and even teased, thanking her saviour for my safe arrival and for the meal we would share.

That night, settled into "my room" (I did not even realize until years later that this was Nurse's grandniece's room, and my arrival required her to share a room and bed with her mother) in the spacious, queen-sized bed, smelling the mosquito coil, I listened to the sounds of Frankfield waft in through the wooden shutters. Country homes do not have glass on the windows but wooden shutters instead, often encased in elaborately artistic iron grills (known as burglar bars). I settled into the cacophony of the crickets and cicadas, the boom boxes blasting reggae, the rhythm of dancehall emanating from the nightclub in town, and the sound of cars going up and down the hill. It was, after all, Saturday night, and Frankfield was alive with weekend noises of partying and the delicious smell of "jerk" clinging to the air. As some of my students would learn a few years later, it is hard to be a vegetarian in Jamaica unless you are a Rastafarian – since certain sects of the Rastafari faith encourage vegetarianism. Your meals are in the form of the ubiquitous goats and cows that roam the roads and yards; chickens and pigs are common as well although confined to pens. Once a vegetarian myself, I became accustomed to seeing cows' heads being cut up on chopping blocks.

I put my earplugs in, the only way I would get a sound sleep and avoid being woken up early by a rooster or a bellowing cow, eagerly anticipating our trip to the town of Santa Cruz in southern Clarendon where we would attend the wedding of Nurse's nephew early the next day.

The elaborate Baptist wedding ceremony was videotaped, including the bride's veil, which was the longest I had ever seen. It seemed to stretch the entire length of the church hall. After the exchange of vows, we all piled into cars and headed to the home of the bride's parents for the reception in the hills above the town. We sat in folding chairs lined up in rows, while women passed out cups of "mannish water", a thick, pungent, grayish soup made of goat parts, including the testicles (a regular treat at major Jamaican gatherings), and then box lunches of fried chicken, rice and peas, and salad made from locally grown vegetables. The bride and groom then stood under a canopy beside a towering cake while the best man introduced speaker after speaker to give a toast. This, too, was being videotaped. The bride, a black woman, was a maid for a white expatriate couple (who were doing the filming), the husband working for the Inter-American Development Bank. At one point during the ceremony they had approached me, much to my discomfort, assuming a connection via our shared whiteness. Upon learning that I was a mere graduate student – a different class of whiteness – they resumed their filming, and I soon learned that at the end of the ceremony, people could stay to watch the whole event they had just participated in all over again. There was also a sound system involved: each time someone said something important or funny, the volume was cranked up for about ten seconds for effect and people clapped and cheered. Then, Nurse was invited up to speak. She seemed surprised but pleased. Making her way through the crowd, she smiled and clasped hands with people sitting along the narrow aisle. Reaching the canopy, she turned momentarily to the audience. Then looking directly at her nephew she spoke, in English, not patois,[6] in recognition of the formality of the event and of her own education and authority:

> Having lived some years, I have a few words of advice for you. You must consider
> your wife's opinion and consult with her in everything you do, because women

are equal with men today. Just because you are the man doesn't mean you can just go off and do what you want. Otherwise your marriage won't work. You must be home for your wife's needs and your children's needs. When your little boy or girl misbehaves, talk to your wife; when you have troubles go to Jesus. Go to Jesus. Do not talk with your neighbours or your parents. Do not go to the bar to drink rum. Talk with each other and talk to Jesus.

I was both impressed and, from my present perspective, I view myself as having been naively surprised by her grassroots feminism. The next day I asked Nurse about her speech, wondering whether what she had said was reflective of what people in the community thought. She responded, "Why don't you ask them? Go out into the town, talk to people. They'll be happy to talk to you." I had known that I would have to talk to people about something, but I had not been clear on what it was that I would pursue. I had managed to secure a small travel grant for the trip and had cast my research as a follow-up on the previous study on crack cocaine use, but in actuality, I did not know what would unfold. I have learned that fieldwork is often like this; you plan to study one thing, but what you actually end up studying depends much on the circumstances you encounter on arrival, access you are permitted and sometimes, as in this situation, what emerges along the way. This was day two, second journey, and I had my work cut out for me.

What did I learn? How has my own changing life status shaped my interpretations of and access to community life as I moved from student to professor, single to married, become a biological mother, in addition to a stepmother? How has travel with students over the past decade shaped Frankfielders' perceptions of my work and thus influenced the nature of that work? These are some of the questions that are the subject of this book. Beyond these, there is a broader framework that guides my discussion of life in Frankfield and the more general conclusions I will draw about life in rural central Jamaica.

FROM SELF/OTHER TO SELF/SELF: THE INTERSECTION OF FEMINIST ANTHROPOLOGY AND CARIBBEAN FEMINISM

What modest contribution does my own study make towards understanding Jamaican gender roles and relationships? Moreover, is there a place in Caribbean research on gender, the family and related topics for non-Caribbean researchers, particularly anthropologists? I raise this latter question in light of the abundant proliferation of Caribbean-generated gender-related research that has produced an indigenous Caribbean body of feminist scholarship since the 1970s. It is important to reflect on how an outsider perspective can contribute to this wealth of insightful, scholarly, insider-produced studies. The answer to these questions depends just as much on the current direction of Caribbean feminisms as it does on this particular historical moment for the discipline of cultural anthropology and feminist anthropology in particular. The two fields have intersected in important ways that have had ramifications for the direction of both. I will provide an overview of these developments to demonstrate how certain strands of feminist anthropology and Caribbean feminisms have become intertwined in the story of *gender as culture* in the Caribbean generally, and in Jamaica specifically.

Both Caribbean and non-Caribbean social scientists have shaped the interpretation of gender both in scholarship and lay understanding, as scholarly conclusions have filtered into the society through policy initiatives and through a variety of media sources. Moreover, these bodies of research have informed one another and have contributed to the national dialogue on gender. I will begin this discussion here providing a brief overview of how the two arenas of research have mutually impacted one another.

Much has been written by anthropologists about our discipline's "historical moment" of crisis that coalesced in the 1980s and 1990s. The crisis was spurred on by criticism of anthropological power relationships and assumptions of ethnographic authority that had been part of the discipline since its formal inception in the late nineteenth century. Historically, anthropological research subjects were approached not because they were deemed inherently interesting, but instead, because they were regarded as specimens of cultural inferiority, subjects of scientific study, examples of the theory of cultural evolution. Moreover, it was once assumed that the ethnographer could generate a "true picture of tribal life" by evoking "the real spirits of the natives", as the inventor of participant-observation, Bronislaw Malinowski, once said (1922, 6). The assumed simplicity of "tribal society" and its "natives" were regarded as ideal study grounds for anthropologists, who, in a year of research, exposed to the cycle of seasons and the ritual calendar could produce "a straight-ahead cultural description based on the firsthand experience an author had with a strange . . . group of people" (Van Maanen 1995, 1). Today, however, anthropologists regard these notions as naïve and "an end to innocence"(ibid.).

Figure 2: Town of Frankfield from hill going to Lampard District. *Photo by Heidi Savery.*

This view, however, did not come without great self-scrutiny inspired by "a new generation of Western-born anthropologists that had played no role in the colonial regimes [and] felt free to denounce its predecessors" (Gledhill 2000, 4). Critics also included professionals from black and Africana studies departments, non-Western anthropologists, and former colonial subjects of anthropological fieldwork themselves. Their condemnation provoked anthropology, especially sociocultural anthropology, into a postmodern critique of its disciplinary "truths" in a period referred to as anthropology's "self-reflexive moment" or "crisis of representation".

Practitioners were inspired to reassess the objectives of the field and to launch explorations into a "new ethnography" which decentred the authoritative voice of the anthropologist rendering it as one among many (Clifford and Marcus 1986). The outcomes, still underway, have produced more internally rigorous evaluations of the methodologies by which ethnographers develop themes for research, implement those themes, and employ their results through discursive representation or policy initiatives involving various applied projects.

In addition and simultaneously, feminist anthropologists experienced their own self-scrutiny. A heightened sensitivity to the politics of representation, fieldwork and research unfolded in the 1980s within feminist anthropology. The critique was in part propelled by self-identified Third World feminists such as Chandra T. Mohanty, whose widely influential essay "Under Western Eyes: Feminist Scholarship and Colonial Discourses" (1991) disparaged the textual strategies harnessed by Western feminists in cross-cultural studies to paint Third World women as monolithically oppressed by patriarchal societies. Such external critiques, and the insights that feminist researchers garnered from local people in the course of their fieldwork, rendered earlier calls for a global sisterhood based on Western, white, middle-class feminist objectives both culturally and politically naïve.

In her forward to the volume *Black Feminist Anthropology: Theory, Politics, Praxis and Poetics*, Johnetta B. Cole, president emerita of Spelman College and anthropologist, acknowledges these shifts in ethnographic practice:

> Black studies in the 1960s and women's studies in the 1970s challenged the field of anthropology with respect to who was traditionally studied, by whom, in what ways, and toward what end. Why were virtually all of the folks studied poor people of color from non-Western cultures and virtually all of those doing the studying white, middle-class men from the Untied States and Europe? Why did the

results of these studies end up in publications that not only were inaccessible to the people who had been studied but made little or no contribution to improving the conditions of their lives? And why was so much emphasis put on the need for objectivity? (2001, x)

Adding to these critiques were the voices of Third World women activists and scholars including the emerging voices of Caribbean feminists. Since its academic and scholarly institutionalization in the 1970s, Caribbean feminism has revisited earlier ethnographic studies of Caribbean family life, gender relationships and roles, produced by European and American social scientists. Many of them have been rightfully critiqued and revamped while others have served as a foundation for further investigation, contributing some valuable insights that remain intact. It is here, then, at this juncture, that anthropologists from outside the Caribbean and social scientists from within Caribbean societies begin to inform one another about their understandings of gender.

The first wave of anthropological research in the Caribbean was conducted from the 1930s to the 1950s, and it was part of a broader wave of social science research that included sociologists and social welfare researchers from the United States (Barrow 1998b, 2). They introduced "family studies" to the Caribbean, exploring the survival of West African cultural patterns and the impact of slavery on Afro-Caribbean family forms, particularly the working class (Herskovits and Herskovits 1936, 1947; Henriques 1949, 1953). Social scientists studied the structure of consensual unions, noting the lack of stability associated with conjugal relationships.

In her detailed study of the nature of social science family research in the Caribbean, *Family in the Caribbean*, sociologist Christine Barrow (1998b, 23) has stated:

> The social welfare workers and anthropologists who set the stage for family studies in the Caribbean came from abroad, mainly from Britain, the colonial mother country. They developed a fixation with lower-class Negro "mating" and family structures. Middle- and upper-class families appeared to be "normal", but those of the lower class were different from anything they had ever known. These "irregular patterns", therefore, required scholarly explanation and, for some, social policies to rectify the deficiencies.

In the 1950s and 1960s, the structural-functional model of family life was introduced, defining the family through the assumed universal nuclear model.

This research explored the impact of poverty on female-headed households, the formation of the "matrifocal" family in which family life was said to revolve around the mother, a strong, independent woman, and the relative absence of nuclear family forms (Clarke 1957; Smith 1960).

Beginning in the late 1970s, Caribbean feminists took on this body of work as part of the purview of feminism in general to assess androcentric and Western-centric biases. Their work was also important because so much of anthropological research conducted throughout the colonized world influenced colonial policy (see Matthews 1953; Simey 1946) and shaped contemporary stereotypes of the Caribbean: social science research had a direct impact on people's lives. In the Caribbean, for instance, colonial administrations drew on anthropological research on matrifocality and male/female partnering patterns to try to transform family structure. Their aim was to generate shifts towards ideal European forms of the "nuclear, co-resident, patriarchal, stable structures, consisting of an adult heterosexual couple, preferably married, and their young children" (Barrow 1998a, 340).

As part of their efforts to create indigenous understandings of Caribbean gender ideologies and social structures that supported them, Caribbean feminists noted the shortcomings of structural-functionalist models that focused on the "abnormality" of the Caribbean family, in contrast to the assumed "naturalness" and "normalcy" of the Euro-American family (Barrow 1998a, 340–41). This initial set of critiques launched ongoing work into the foundations, transformations and complexities of Caribbean gender constructs, as they have been shaped through the historically contingent and interlocking relationships of ethnicity, class and race. In the late 1980s and 1990s, a number of important volumes were issued that explored frameworks for developing a gender-conscious analyses in Caribbean research and teaching strategies (Mohammed and Shepherd 1999; Shepherd, Brereton and Bailey 1995; Leo-Rhynie, Bailey and Barrow 1997; Barrow 1998b; Reddock 2004; Chevannes 2001).

Galvanized by the above criticisms generated by Third World feminists, anthropological researchers began to question Western theorizing in general and Western feminist theory specifically, rejecting wholesale both structural-functionalist training (Bryceson 1995, 258) and the persistence of the evolutionary model. They began to theorize gender in ways that challenged previous assumptions of the neutral anthropologist and instead offered a pluralizing feminism that sought the "diversity, multiplicity, and transformative possibilities of women's politics globally" (Cole and Phillips 1995, 2). As a result, the

1990s saw an outpouring of critical feminist ethnographic scholarship, asserting "a reflexive stance toward one's own social position as a researcher, the frameworks employed and images and discourses deployed" (Montoya, Frazier and Hurtig 2002, 1). The objectives, possibilities and limitations of feminist ethnography were scrutinized. Practitioners grappled with tensions between activist and scholarly ambitions and generated new research methodologies based on participatory models and the potentiality of cross-cultural, activist alliances. Ethnographers also experimented with writing strategies such as mutivocality, personal narratives/life histories, and texts multi-authored between anthropologist and research subject(s).

Feminist anthropology of the Caribbean region followed a similar path. In Jamaica, for example, Marsha Prior retained a revamped notion of matrifocality, but acknowledged the problems with its earlier conceptions in her Jamaican fieldwork (2009). In following Caribbean feminist criticism of matrifocality, Prior examined the coexistence of female-headed households and male domination, whereas earlier studies had overlooked this important relationship. Caribbean social scientists have re-examined the notion of matrifocality, emphasizing its oversimplification and the tendency of scholars to ignore the coexistence of female-headed households and male domination. In other words, the female-headed household has been misinterpreted as an indicator of gender parity. We are now at a crossroads in feminist ethnographic research originating outside of the Caribbean but focused on the Caribbean region: the directions that have emerged since the 1970s, focusing "on questions of subjectivity and identity" (Mohanty 2003, 106), have taken us to a point where we must move beyond documentations and analyses of both essentialized and enshrined "difference" and "universal sisterhood". Non-Caribbean feminist anthropologists cannot assume a facile shared political agenda with Caribbean feminists, but nor should we posit mutually exclusive ones. Instead, feminist ethnography is poised to work towards, in Mohanty's words "ethical and caring dialogues and revolutionary struggles across the divisions, conflicts, and individualist identity formations that interweave feminist communities" (ibid.). Mohanty argues for crafting genealogies of community, home and nation that "envision and enact common political and intellectual projects across these differences" (p. 125). The solidarity these produce should embrace "mutuality, accountability and the recognition of common interests as the basis for relationships among diverse communities [where] diversity and difference are central values . . . to be acknowledged and respected, not erased in the building of alliances" (p. 7). This kind of solidarity appears to be emerging in the field. Black feminist anthropology for instance, seeks to excavate "black women's lives and the theorization of lived experience and culture in the African Diaspora through the lens of feminism" and "posits a comparative (global) perspective as central to its enterprise" (McClaurin 2001, 5, 15). This perspective surfaces in concerns with the similarities and differences they share with their African-Caribbean sisters, producing important trajectories into the ways in which assumptions of shared identity have been simultaneously shattered and reinforced in varying contexts.[7]

Ultimately there has been an important and parallel set of ideas emerging both among gender scholars of the region and non-native ethnographers. They can be summarized as follows: (1) early Caribbean feminists pressed social scientists in general to consider their colonial legacy and representations of "cultural others" within the Caribbean, particularly in the spheres of family studies and gender; (2) heeding their critiques, along with those of black studies and Third World feminism studies in the United States, black feminist anthropologists and feminist anthropologists (as well as the wider discipline) developed responses in theory and methodology; and (3) contemporary dialogues have emerged between feminist anthropologists and Caribbean feminists, sometimes producing collaborative works. This book expands upon these developments by explicitly engaging in a textual dialogue that draws on Caribbean and anthropological gender theory, my experiences teaching and doing research as a Fulbright scholar in both Jamaica and Trinidad, and formal and informal discourse with my Caribbean feminist colleagues. Specifically, it is part of the purview of this book to contribute to Caribbean feminist thought by offering what I hope are novel ways of conceiving, portraying and reflecting on the significance of the dominant Jamaican gender system. In so doing, I am simultaneously asserting an ongoing, important role for non-native ethnography in the study of Caribbean gender dynamics.

FEMINIST ETHNOGRAPHIC METHODOLOGY

My own research methods have been informed by participatory and collaborative models. I have worked with Frankfield residents to develop research topics producing inquiries shaped by mutual interests rather than imposed agendas. My research on HIV/AIDS stigma and education and my work with

American and Jamaican students in the community of Frankfield have been shaped by the ideas of various groups of community members. The involvement of research subjects in the writing and evaluation of ethnography has been another important development, from data gathering, to analysis. I have involved the community of Frankfield in my analyses by sharing with them my data and the conclusions I have drawn at various stages of the research process. I have also sought their comments, criticisms and suggestions. Some of these shared experiences have occurred through informal discussions around dinner tables or while enjoying cool evening air on a veranda, others in church group discussions, at various formal presentations at the Frankfield health centre, and at the Edwin Allen Regional High School where I have occasionally been asked to address students. Personal narratives and life histories have also been important ethnographic developments, and this book includes segments of these throughout. All of these methodologies have emerged to address the conundrums of power dynamics produced by colonial anthropology and transferred to research and writing practices. It is my hope that in addition to addressing an anthropological audience and the Caribbean gender studies communities, this book is clearly written with the people of Frankfield in mind as potential readers, whose daily lives have provided much of the substance for this text.

Finally, the new perspectives born from anthropology's historical moment of crisis have influenced conventional ethnographic methods including participant observation and in-depth, open-ended interviews, producing insights that are unique to the discipline. These insights can be both a corrective on historical inaccuracies, shot through with ethnocentrisms and biases, as well as generative of new bodies of knowledge, perspectives and databases. As I have said elsewhere (Fox 1999, 75), "the value of the anthropological case study is to impress us with the details of people's lives so that we may remind ourselves to reassess and render more complex those generalizations that no longer make sense and that have inspired dangerous stereotypes". This objective of ethnography is particularly important given the relatively small number of studies about rural Jamaica produced in recent decades. While research on Rastafari[8] is prolific, far fewer ethnographies have been produced recently by non-native ethnographers (Austin-Broos 1997; Prior 2009; Sobo 1993), and only a handful by Caribbean anthropologists (see, for example, Chevannes 2001; Ulysse 2007), and these cited include urban anthropology. Nonetheless, ethnographic methods have been widely adopted by gender studies scholars throughout the campuses of UWI, in part because the holistic nature of ethnography – which explores the interconnectedness among the values, norms, beliefs and practices of various peoples as well as their environments and other systemic arrangements (economy, political culture, history) – offers a mode of writing that seeks to captivate, developing an intimacy between author and readers that vicariously transports readers into a new world of images, stories and analyses. Moreover, by focusing on in-depth, local studies, particularly through the collection of personal narratives, we can understand how individuals participate in the creation and reproduction of their cultural worldviews. Finally, ethnography is a useful tool for mobilizing policy initiatives because the medium creates and reinforces a sense of immediacy around the sociocultural problems that are its focus. In these regards, this book is intended for a broad spectrum of Jamaicans, with the ever-present idea that the portrayals rendered here are both recognizable to cultural insiders and provide insight into the role of gender in Jamaican culture that might be useful in policy forums.

Given all of these new forms of ethnography and their important contributions to the politics of gender, race and identity, ethnography from its inception retains a special quality of writing that attempts to bridge the categories of novel, travelogue and monograph. It is not a mere report of data acquired through description and analysis. Ethnography tells a story of the anthropological journey into another cultural world, a journey that increasingly breaks down the self/other dichotomy, and seeks to interpret that world through a blend of anecdote and scholarly analysis. Put simply, storytelling is a key feature of ethnographic writing. Having established the foundation, I now move into the story of the gender system of rural Jamaica, where I will illustrate how it exhibits the paired features of longevity-mutability and collectivity-uniqueness over the course of Jamaican history.

Chapter 2

In Search of Gender Trails

Archive, Folklore and Cultural Memory

STORY GENRES

THIS CHAPTER CONTAINS a series of stories and story fragments about the history of the island of Jamaica, the parish of Clarendon, and the town of Frankfield, origin stories of groups and collectivities that are shaped by ideas about gender ideologies and roles. In particular, I bring to bear the DNA metaphor by exploring the building blocks of my figurative gender molecule, longevity and fluidity. These constitute one base in the intertwining strands of masculinity and femininity that form the "backbone" of the metaphorical molecule that constitutes the gender system in the British colonial slave period. The story of gender in Jamaica is closely interwoven with the island's legacy of slavery that defined and structured race, colour and class hierarchies. The chapter closes by pointing to emerging gender systems, uniquely patterned but part of the broader collectivity created in the British colonial period. This emergent system expressed through gender ideologies, behaviours and roles is another base or rung indicating its particular uniqueness, yet part of a wider group that is the system inherited and informed by the survival of certain features of the gender system under slavery.

These stories of historical, imagined and newly emerging gender systems have become part of Jamaican folklore. As folklorists Leeming and Page have noted, stories that groups of people tell about themselves are noteworthy for anthropologists because they offer insights into those people's primary concerns, values and beliefs. Such views differ, as we will see, because they are influenced by the range of standpoints, the perspectives shaped in part by the social location of people within Jamaican society, as members of the brown or emerging black middle classes or the black working classes, for instance. Stories about past gender systems and how the present systems came to be as they are also serve as forms of contemplation for members of a society, as well as disguises, revealing some truths and masking others. Leeming and Page say that folk stories craft images of "who we think we are, how we believe we should appear to the world and how we think we should perform in it" (1999, 3), and in this way, folk histories are a kind of contemplative negotiation with our past. As anthropologists have long noted, while the beliefs people have about themselves often correlate with the way they actually are, at other times they represent cultural ideals and aspirations, mythologies or even fantasies, which do not necessarily mirror empirical conditions of the past, but which nonetheless influence daily life. Many such stories are rooted in faith. In this chapter, I build on Mohammed's and Barriteau's assertion that gender systems are central to the structure of culture itself, examining how gender tales are metaphors for core meanings about cultural identity. I collected the stories from folktales, archives and cultural memory, sources of insights that emerged like winding pathways, "gender trails", as I wound my way through people's recollections. Metaphorically, I imagined myself in a kind of *Alice in Wonderland* journey, wandering through and around a double helix timeline to pursue foundations – factual, fantastic and ideological strands of masculinity and femininity defined through Jamaican cultural history, to ascertain how historical themes have at once shifted and become coded into the present. This chapter therefore begins a two-part exploration continued in chapter 3 that seeks to situate Frankfield within a national narrative of gender, examining overlaps and divergences.

In an effort to distinguish among the different sources, I have categorized them as (1) oral accounts relying on cultural memory; (2) scholarly and lay-historical writings; and (3) fragments of unanalysed historical data, drawn from the Jamaica National Archives in Spanish Town and the National Library of Jamaica in Kingston. The first category was particularly important for groups of people in Frankfield, such as a group of male Rastafari residents who shared with me their reflections of Frankfield and surrounds during "slavery times". Oral tales were also recounted to me by late-middle-aged and elderly residents of Frankfield, who referred to an indeterminate "better time" somewhere in the more recent past, as they recalled their childhoods and even the child-hoods of their parents, clearly times fraught with financial hardship but bright-ened in memory by close family and community ties and a social order conferring a sense of moral purity. Before recounting them, it will be helpful to provide some definitions of, and commentary on, these story genres.

Folklore narratives include a continuum of story types including mytholo-gies, legends and folktales. All are stories "of the people", narratives that are part of the "collective folk mind" (Leeming and Page 1999, 5) through their telling and retelling across generations and in multiple settings. Stories of Anancy, the cunning and manipulative trickster spiderman, are good examples of folktales that travelled in the imagination of Africans on slave ships as they made their treacherous journey across the Atlantic during the transatlantic slave trade. Anancy stories were reproduced, transformed and moulded to the circumstances that Africans found themselves in as slaves and in their resist-ance to enslavement. Mythology is another type of folklore that "deals with such persistently compelling matters as origins – the beginnings of the world or of a particular people – and they are populated with deities and heroes who more often than not have supernatural powers. Myths, in his sense, are reli-gious stories and they are at the very least metaphorically and psychically true" (Leeming and Page 1999, 3).

A third form of folklore includes legends, stories that are "based on actual events and persons and, over time, are carefully tailored, often exaggerated, and serve to express some group aspiration" (Leeming and Page 1999, 5). Importantly, while the definitions of each help researchers to categorize dif-ferent story types, actual stories are themselves frequently less rigid, incorpo-rating multiple attributes of each, crossing the boundaries of classificatory categories.

The stories of Nanny, Jamaica's only national heroine, are good examples of the merging of folkloric genres: part myth, part legend, with tidbits of his-torical facts about this powerful Maroon[1] general, said to possess the magical powers of an obeah-woman.[2] Nanny was a Maroon leader, a militant rebel, who lived at the beginning of the eighteenth century. Documents maintained by British colonialists who fought against her guerilla army reveal that they were amazed by her intelligence and cunning. Both in her lifetime and today she has been known as a healer and a sorceress, descended from the Asante/Ashante people of Ghana. There is no doubt that she was in fact a real woman who played a key role as a military strategist during the fierce fighting

with the British in the First Maroon War from 1720 to 1739. Yet it is also possible that there were many women leaders and that she epitomizes all of them
as a symbol of unity, resistance and strength, particularly during periods of crisis, immortalized in songs and legends, where her persona and the events and
capabilities attributed to her have themselves attained mythological and leg-
endary proportion. As a result, Nanny is a symbol of "heroic feminism" (Beckles 1998, 46). She is a polemical figure whose social memory is a source of pride
and contention over her specific achievements, her alliances and even the site
of her burial, as exemplified in the story I will share later in the chapter, is a
highly symbolic and contested domain that reveals insights into contemporary
understandings of gender relationships.

Anthropologists since Victor Turner, writing in the middle decades of the
twentieth century, have generally agreed that complex symbols contain contradictory meanings, both generating debate and permitting different segments
of society to coalesce around the symbol, drawing varied meanings that reflect
their own values. Such complex symbols allow for collectivity and uniqueness
to coexist in a culture. As we shall see, Nanny is one such symbol, representing
clashing ideas of the cultural construct of black femininity, one born of a more
recent cultural ideal of black women as strong, intelligent survivors and achiev-
ers, but with great sacrifice and suffering, descended from a noble African past.
This is set against another, more stereotypical, British colonial image attribut-
ing black female power to magic and witchery and hence the savagery of the
African continent and the low status of the black woman epitomized in her
ever-present kerchief tied around her head so that she resembles a poor market
woman or "higgler".[3] Although the sterilized, whitened image of Nanny on
the five-hundred dollar bill imbues her with qualities of dignity and pride not
afforded to higglers or witches, we will see that these traits are reclaimed and
transferred to African femininity by Frankfield's male Rasta population through
the status of a matriarch, the original mythological ancestor of this population.
Both of these symbolic folk renditions of Nanny coincide in one potent image,
embodying the struggle rural black Jamaicans are still engaged in to overturn
legacies of power defined through the crucible of gender, race, colour and class.
Because complex symbols collapse and embody multiple and contradictory
cultural values, and because folklore captures these symbols in its narratives,
in chapter 3 I attempt to unwind these intersecting meanings to piece together
the folk gender system that Frankfield's Rastas claim as their own.

Often posited in opposition to folklore, historical writing nonetheless shares many of the same qualities with its less "scholarly" cousin. Although historical methodology is rooted in empiricism in its search to capture a documented, factual reality while folklore is not (although it often does incorporate empirical facts), historiography, like folklore, involves subjectivity and interpretation. In reconstructing portraits of the past drawn from archival information, historians select particular themes reflecting their own interests and embrace some theoretical explanations over others in the process of developing analytical frameworks. Finally, the archival sources are themselves documents of both fact and interpretations, such as diaries and letters.

In their efforts to inscribe gender into history, Caribbean scholars have not simply included women where they were previously excluded, but instead have posited a theoretical and methodological revamping of the historical process by posing questions about the historical construction of masculinity and femininity. In so doing, there is often an emphasis on the intersections and overlap of historical documents and folklore. In a discussion about how gender can become part of history, Mohammed writes that instead of the proverbial "add and stir" approach to women's history, whereby women's stories are recounted, shifting the attention to *her-story* rather than *his-story*, "the historical construction of masculinity and femininity or the construction of gender identities must itself be the problem" (Mohammed 1998, 20). Personal interpretations, stories about broader societal events, says historian Joan Scott, are "no longer about the things that have happened to women and men and how they have reacted to them; instead it is about how the *subjective and collective meanings* of women and men as categories of identity have been constructed" (cited in Mohammed 1995, 25; emphasis added). Opinion and perspective become central tools of the inquiry, as the historian of gender draws on meaning, value, belief, perception and, in feminist parlance, "lived experience" to ascertain the variability and malleability of gender systems, as well as the derivative impact of historical gender systems on contemporary patterns.

Folklore, as part of these historical streams of ideas, is an important source or "trail" in the feminist methodology of writing gender into history. As Mary Chamberlain contends, in her essay "Gender and Memory: Oral History and Women's History" (1995, 95):

> The issue . . . is not to do with whether oral sources are good or bad, true or false . . . oral sources tell us less about events as such than about their meaning, and their value lies in the areas of language, narrative and subjectivity . . . But if those

differences and problems are recognized not as limitations, but as representative of a "different credibility", then their evidential value takes second place to their potential value of signification.

When these oral accounts are exhibited in collectively shared stories, they draw from "cultural memory", a term referring to conceptions of the past that manifest features of a shared consciousness that become part of social production. As Chamberlain explains it, "the language, images, priorities and expectations which shape memory and give structure and meaning derive from shared, that is social, languages, images, priorities and expectations. In this sense, although the *voice* may be individual, and differs from one to another, the form memory assumes, the ways in which it is collated and expressed, is collective. It is culturally and socially determined" (1995, 95–96). In addition, cultural memory, while part of social production, is not homogenous; rather, it is simultaneously collective and differentiated by the multiple standpoints from which people experience their present day realities. For instance, Nanny is so symbolically potent because she is part of a collective Jamaican historical consciousness. How she is remembered, and for what personally meaningful qualities and historical events, varies for individuals in part because of their own social positioning. As a result, stories change to reflect the teller's social standpoint, and of course they are also subject to the flaws and manipulations of human memory. Nonetheless, cultural memory as a folkloric form provides valuable insight into contemporary views of previous eras, including insight about gender. As anthropologist Jean Besson writes, regarding her fieldwork in eight peasant communities in the parishes of Trelawny and St Elizabeth, "oral history is engendered . . . reflected in accounts of ancestor-heroes and ancestress-heroines", and of course both men and women create and transmit oral history (1998, 140).

The stories recounted here elucidate the gender systems that shaped Jamaican plantation society and subsequent societal arrangements following emancipation. The gender system under slavery is especially significant and richly representative of a pervasive struggle around the meanings of masculinity and femininity in Jamaica today. Historian Hilary Beckles notes (1998, 36), as we have already begun to see in Jamaica's notions of the white lady,

> slavery is conceived . . . as the master mould from which are cast the persistent conflicts among women over definitions and ideological ownership of womanhood and femininity. The contested politics of womanhood, furthermore, has

been accounted for in terms of women's formally differentiated exposure to slave owning colonial masculinities and institutionalized hegemonic patriarchy. These politics have also been explained in relation to the changing gender orders promoted by slavery and expressed culturally through civic institutions and productive arrangements.

While the contemporary Jamaican gender order is not built on slave society alone, the period persists as a "master mould" in its imaginative, explanatory power. Similarly, renowned author Jamaica Kincaid has noted of the people of the Caribbean island of Antigua, in her powerful essay *A Small Place*, that "there is an appropriate obsession with slavery" (1988, 43). Whether or not one agrees that such an obsession is appropriate, in Jamaica it is not uncommon for people draw from cultural memory of "slavery times" to explain many of today's tensions between men and women. Newspaper articles are also replete with references to this period: "slavery-time talk" pervades national and local discourses about gender more than any other period of Jamaican history including two other prominent periods, emancipation and independence, which receive their fair share of devotion.

One explanation for this pertains to the efforts of former prime minister P.J. Patterson, during the 1990s and early 2000s, to promote various cultural nationalist projects whose aim was to centre the history of slavery and emancipation in public discourse. Through this significant racial project, Patterson "sought to displace a multi-racial/nonracial nationalist ideology that dominated the public imagination since Jamaica's independence. This multi-/nonracial nationalist ideology devalued blackness and African culture and history, and placed the history of slavery on the back burner of Jamaica's history" (anonymous reviewer, University of the West Indies Press, personal communication, September 2008). During the Patterson period, African identity was reconceptualized as a source of pride (Thomas 2002, 44), bolstering and mainstreaming values that had been earlier injected into Jamaica through the Rastafarian movement, which emerged in the 1930s (Chevannes 1995, 253). For example, in August 2003 the Patterson administration unveiled *Redemption Song*, the monument commissioned by a national committee to stand at the entrance to Emancipation Park. As Winnifred Brown-Glaude notes (2006, 38), the monument

> commemorates the historical moment of Jamaica's emancipation from slavery [featuring] an eleven-foot nude male and ten-foot nude female standing on a

dome in a pool of water. Under the figures is the message "None but ourselves can free our minds", words inspired by Marcus Garvey and later popularized by Bob Marley. According to the sculptor, Laura Facey-Cooper, the Redemption Song monument represents healing, "the water washes away the pain, angst and suffering of slavery. The figures rise having transcended the past, standing in strength, unity and reverence."

Patterson noted, at the time, that both the park and the monument signified resilience against slavery and the invincibility of the human spirit.

In the 1990s in Frankfield and island-wide, Emancipation Day festivities burgeoned, replete with drumming and "ole time" foods. In Kingston there were major parades and an arts and crafts fair, including items related to African heritage. One finds artists' renditions of African masks and period dolls of smiling black girls wearing petticoats, long dresses and braids, offering an image of black femininity that contrasts with the higgler/market woman.

Another explanation for the pervasiveness of the image of slavery times in the Jamaican imagination may be sought in anthropologist Paul Connerton's notion of "social persistence". Social persistence refers to the ongoing salience of a concept in cultural narratives, which in this case is the ongoing, repetitiveness of the contemporary, informally told slave narrative (Connerton 1989, 38–40).

Connerton elaborates on the significance of "beginnings" in the creation of social memory. He argues: "All beginnings contain an element of recollection. This is particularly so when a social group makes a concerted effort to begin with a wholly new start." He notes that whatever moment is selected as the beginning is relatively arbitrary, but because "the absolutely new is inconceivable": "In all modes of experience we always base our particular experiences on a prior context in order to ensure that they are intelligible at all; that prior to any single experience, our mind is already predisposed with a framework of outlines, of typical shapes of experienced objects . . . The world of the percipient, defined in terms of temporal experience, is an organized body of expectations based on recollection" (1989, 6).

Societies create myths of historical beginnings, which, Connerton suggests, are acknowledged in commemorative experiences and bodily practices. "Slavery times", I would like to suggest, represents such a new beginning in a new land, aided significantly by Patterson's cultural nationalist project, through which "there is an attempt to re-imagine Jamaica as a 'black' nation (not a brown one); hence, the numerous discussions of 'slavery times' . . . Afro-Jamaicans for the first time since Independence, are encouraged to openly discuss and embrace their blackness and black history, including slavery and emancipation" (anonymous reviewer, University of the West Indies Press, personal communication, September 2008). The tales that men and women have shared with me about Frankfield's past are integral to their understanding of contemporary race/colour/gender dynamics on the island and Frankfield's place in that whole. Thus while rural towns throughout Jamaica share many commonalities, and for many casual outside observers one small community may appear to be much like the next, the specific location of communities greatly influences their characteristics. Moreover, islanders will refer to parishes before towns in identifying their origins.

Frankfielders, in identifying with Clarendon, have said on more than one occasion that to know Jamaica one must travel to all the parishes, emphasizing the uniqueness of each sociopolitical locale on the island. What follows, then, is my reconstruction, beginning with the founding of the parish of Clarendon, of one of many threads woven to connect the patchwork of sources: archive, folklore and cultural memory.

THE SETTING: PARISH OF CLARENDON

Engendered Histories

Clarendon was one of the first seven parishes on the island, founded in 1664, and, according to R.J. Lewin, named for Edward Hyde, Earl of Clarendon (*Jamaica Gleaner*, 7 April 1957). Between 1671 and 1841, fifteen additional parishes emerged, but in 1867 they were reduced to the present fourteen. Clarendon is located on the southern part of the island, midway between the eastern and western ends of Jamaica. It is among the largest as well, spanning 468 square miles, and is divided into Upper, Middle and Lower Clarendon, for electoral and revenue purposes. Locals are proud of the farming tradition in Clarendon: the region produces an abundance of agricultural goods through-out the year including citrus, sugar cane, coffee, cocoa, pimento and ginger for export, and food crops such as yam, plantain, carrots, cabbage and potatoes, among many others.

The parish has also been recognized for its physical beauty and geologic

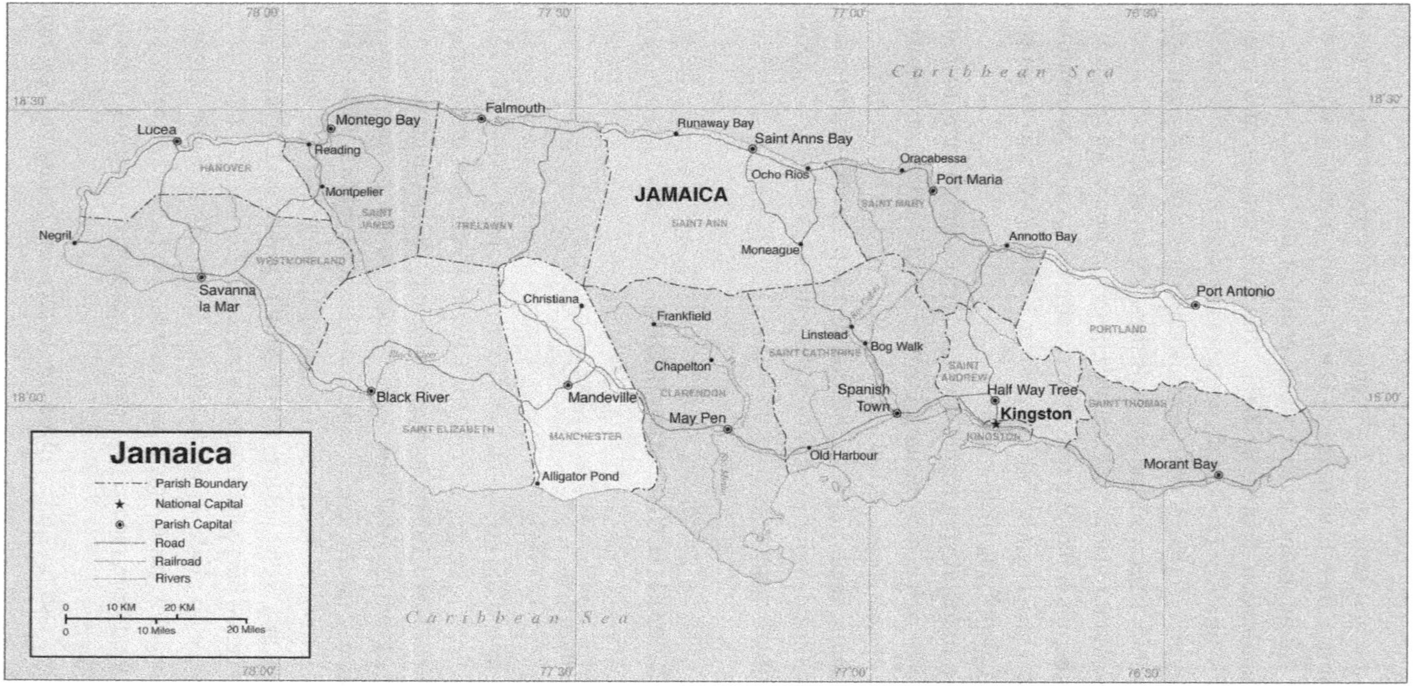

Figure 3: Map of Jamaica with internal political boundaries

diversity. Lower Clarendon, also known as Vere, a separate parish until 1867, includes coastline, plains and hills, with dry vegetation and salt marshes. It contains towns such as Lionel Town and Race Course, as well as historically important shipping ports at Salt River, Carlisle Bay and Milk River. Milk River is the home of the famous Milk River baths, mineral springs known for their "radioactive" healing qualities and the newly renovated Versailles Hotel.

The middle and northern parts of the parish include two mountain ranges, the first which is known as the Mocho Mountains, and beyond them, to the north, is the Bull Head range with its highest point, known as Bull Head, at 2,782 feet above sea level, where the air is cool and refreshing. The Rio Minho (Minho River), in the lower parish, cuts a deep gorge through the Mocho Mountains, where villages and towns lie in the valleys. Middle Clarendon is home to towns such as Four Paths, Hayes and May Pen, Clarendon's capital, under law 20 of 1867, although at various times Four Paths and Chapelton were known as the parish's "chief towns" (Lewin 1957).

Today May Pen is the administrative and political centre of the parish, containing the circuit court and central parish police station as well as the offices of the tax collector, electoral offices and census bureau. It also houses the largest open-air market in the parish, and official market days of Friday and Saturday have lengthened to include most of the week. There are also numerous stores, including large supermarkets selling many imported foods, clothing stores, and the hyped and adored Kentucky Fried Chicken, affectionately known as "Kentucky". There is May Pen Hospital, a chamber of commerce and a central bus depot as well (Institute of Jamaica, Clarendon folder).

In addition to these various assets, Clarendon has also been lamented for its numerous social ills. May Pen's bustling and vigorous appearance belies its real economic condition: it is increasingly the site of crime, prostitution and HIV/AIDS infection. Clarendon has been referred to as a "sleeping giant" with "its breathtaking and tranquil landscape overshadowed by acres of cane-fields and cattle farms . . . [giving] the impression [that it] has not yet evolved from colonial to modern civilization" (*Jamaica Gleaner*, 25 May 1999). Clarendon residents are also the butt of jokes from other parts of the island where people consider themselves more sophisticated. They mock people who are "fool fool" or worse, "dark" (stupid and ignorant), being from Clarendon and the Mocho Mountains especially, because of their remoteness ("Clarendon Plagued with Social Ills", *Jamaica Gleaner*, 30 May 1994). Here we see, in spite of Patterson's black-nationalist agenda, the persistence of negative associations with blackness born in the colonial slave era, even an attempt to explain the problems of Clarendon through the lens of race and colour. Moreover, the parish is noted for its high unemployment (the highest in the country), rapid population growth, teen pregnancy, illiteracy, poor housing and roads, and the low status of women, according to a study commissioned by the Bureau of Women's Affairs, mentioned in the *Jamaica Gleaner* article (ibid.). The study reported that 47 per cent of the population lives in deep rural areas along poor roads, which make travel to school, work and health facilities difficult. Unemployment is particularly high among youth, young women especially. In addition, 57 per cent of households in urban areas are female headed, while in rural areas, 60 per cent are female headed. The study notes that "only 16 percent of women between age 14 and 40 are married but 55 percent of females in the 14–25 age group have at least one child". The study does not comment on what percentage of this latter group is in "visiting"[4] or common-law relationships, underscoring the bureau's normative values, reflective of the dominant gender system, of monogamous, conjugal relationships. These gender dynamics – female-headed households, high female unemployment coinciding with early pregnancy – are part of the configuration of the rural working-class black Jamaican gender system, in place in part because of its geographical location and government neglect reproducing economic hardship. As we will see later, however, many of Frankfield's working-poor population aspire to middle-class status, and choose to commute long hours to the north coast to work in the tourist industry or migrate overseas. Increasingly, women are engaged in overseas migration, changing the dynamics of household constituents. Again, we see the usefulness of the metaphor likening gender to DNA where longevity of a gender situation is epitomized by the bureau's study, yet set against fluidity, sparked by economic determinants and aspirations to middle-class status of rural working-class black Jamaican women.

SOCIO-ECONOMIC PROFILE OF FRANKFIELD

Frankfield is one of the principal towns in north-west Clarendon, referred to by locals as "upper Clarendon", lying in the Rio Minho Valley. The other towns are Chapelton, Rock River and Kellits. Frankfield is built around a traffic circle monument at a crossroads, one leading straight through town, another winding up to the hills. Along the one-mile stretch of road that constitutes the town lie a number of churches: Anglican, Methodist, Seventh-Day Adventist, Baptist, Shiloh Apostolic Church of God, New Testament Church of God and Deliverance Centre, Church of God. There are more churches off of the main road going up into the hills.

During the school year, the streets are jammed with waves of children, their shouts and giggles penetrating the town as they walk to school in clusters, later breaking for the midday meal and flooding one of the many small "cook shops" or restaurants catering to them with box lunches. My adopted family owns one of these cook shops; one wall of the small building faces their yard, another, the street. A sign advertising "stew chicken, pig foot" and other standards of Jamaican cooking is hand-painted on the front of the small building that houses five tables, surrounded by stools, a tiny kitchen and bathroom. During school lunch break, the children stream in for box lunches of fried chicken, salad, and rice and peas. Later in the day, the streets are packed again with children as they pour out of the primary and high school heading towards "Frankfield", the local designation for the centre of town at the traffic circle, to catch taxis or start the long walk home. Children are central to the economy and ambiance of the town.

Shoppers, higglers, hustlers, taxis and loafers, "rude boys" and unemployed men, who stand by the roadside or gather in small bars playing dominoes and drinking white rum and water, also fill the town during the week and on holidays and market days (Thursday to Saturday) and especially on Saturdays. After nightfall, though, the traffic circle is practically deserted except on weekend nights when it jams with blaring reggae, dancehall and, less frequently, American hip hop, until one or two in the morning. On Sundays the town is still and sleepy except for churchgoers who are mostly women, children and middle-aged or elderly men. A few stragglers, men mainly, cluster on roadside corners. Just outside town, men play a vigorous game of football at the Edwin Allen Regional High School field, avoiding the occasional goat or cow wandering through. A donkey or two brays, tethered to a tree at the edge of the field.

There have been many changes in the texture of town life since I began my fieldwork in 1991, perhaps the most conspicuous being the obvious rise in the number of homeless, beggars and "mad" men (drunks and crack cocaine users). During the day, each year it seems, more destitute people dressed in rags, some with wounds, dirty and unkempt, add to the crowd in the streets, begging not only the occasional anthropologist and her students but townsfolk as well. They are sources of great consternation, particularly to shop owners and their

Figure 4: Pots on charcoal fires outside the Frankfield cook-shop owned by Nurse Dunkley's niece.

employees, who shout at them to leave the stores and the shoppers alone. After dark their presence is especially palpable as they remain on the streets, and even on Sundays the town has almost an eerie feel to it as these scorned and marginalized people, men particularly, haggle passers-by for money, mutter incomprehensively or shout out obscenities. There is also an increase in young men looking not at all destitute, with their brand-name clothing and shiny "bling-bling", not hesitating to ask for "a likkle [little] change". Residents differentiate these ubiquitous men and occasional women from legitimately homeless people – a blind man or a mentally ill person too poor for medications – who receive regular help from the community or struggle to do a few small jobs. Today, some say, the lazy and the misguided "tief de job" (steal the job) from others by competing for handouts. A few elderly, impoverished women in true need walk through town with hands held open. One woman in particular stands out: she is tall and stately, yet known as "insane" or "mad" she repeats her mantra to all who will listen, announcing: "I am a Maroon. God bless you. I see that you are intelligent: a donation to me is doing God's work!"

Economic hardship is apparent on many levels, but some hardship is regarded as legitimate while other forms are not, as is the case of young men begging. Exhausted women who have no time for church, held not only on Sundays but Wednesdays and often for various special events throughout the week, wearily set up ironing boards after cooking Sunday breakfast. They starch huge piles of clothes taken down from wire lines propped with bamboo sticks, clothes hand washed either in backyard cement washtubs or in the river. Few residents have the luxury of a washing machine, let alone running tap water in their home. Gospel music drifts through windows, keeping things lively amid endless chores. The sounds of singing, clapping hands, tambourines, and sometimes drums and keyboards waft out of the many churches scattered throughout the town until midday, when the newly saved (mostly women) walk home jubilant, still clapping, their sinning brethren hoping their time will "soon come".

Walking through town on any day, one notices peeling paint and worn down shop fronts. The road is potholed, except for a short strip over a relatively new and long-awaited bridge, built in the mid 1990s by the Government of Jamaica and the Canadian International Development Agency as announced by a plaque on the bridge. A similar green sign is found posted outside rural markets made of concrete blocks and tin roofs: the Government of Jamaica, along with various development banks, is not shy in announcing its meagre contributions to rural town infrastructure. As an example, the old bridge, a beautiful wooden structure, was so dilapidated before the new bridge finally was built that a cow once fell through a gaping hole to the river below.

In spite of the clear signs of struggle, decay and tension, Frankfield emits colour and charisma. In part it is the vibrancy of the people who live there and travel through, to and from school and work, calling out to one another, laughing and complaining, taxis honking and drivers shouting out destinations that contribute to the town's allure. Frankfielders are involved in many occupations, many of which are listed below in data drawn from a recent Social Development Council study of the community.

In spite of this array of work, however, employment is only 70 per cent among household heads, 40 per cent of whom are employed in the field of agriculture, and more male heads are employed than female heads (Social Development Council of Jamaica 2007, 18). In addition, employment for men in general stands at 77 per cent (and 83 per cent within the gender) and 23 per cent for women (and 30 per cent within the gender), indicating that the majority of women are housewives/unemployed.

In terms of union status and family structure, 60 per cent of the male

Table 1: Resource Listing

Physical	Social	Economic	Human	Natural
• Electricity • Telephone service: (land line and mobile) • Transportation: – bus, taxi • Police station • Postal agency • Fire brigade • Health centre • Poor Relief Office • Public sanitary convenience	• 8 churches (along one mile stretch of main road) • 7 community-based organiza-tions • 4 schools – 2 basic – 1 primary – 1 high	• Grocery stores • Supermarkets • Banks • Agricultural land • Market	• Masons (men) • Teachers (mostly women) • Mechanics (men) • Tailors (men) • Seamstresses (women) • Nurses (women) • Carpenters (men) • Plumbers (men) • Pastors (men and women) • Shopkeepers (men and women) • Taxi drivers (men) • Doctors (2 men)	• Rio Minho (River) • Agricultural land

Source: Social Development Council of Jamaica 2007.

population is single because of separation, divorce, death or choice, 30 per cent of households is married and the dominant family structure in the community is extended. The nuclear family type accounts for only 10 per cent. Interest-ingly, 50 per cent of female household heads have attained secondary educa-tion, while only 33 per cent of male household heads have finished high school. Clearly, there are more employment opportunities for men who have not completed high school than there are for women. The Social Development Council study also allocates percentages to types of work done by Frankfielders, identifying agriculture 31 per cent, service 8 per cent, craft and trade 15 per cent, elementary education 15 per cent, professional 8 per cent, and 23 per cent not stated. It is important to note that elementary education does not fall within the realm of the "professional" arena as designated by the Social Devel-opment Council, and the majority of its workers are women.

The lush greenery of the mountains that rise up suddenly out of the town, draped in long, swaying palms, the massive leaves of breadfruit, bending bam-boo and the twisting vines of yams mask the difficulties of daily life in Frank-field for the majority of its residents. It is easy for an outsider to romanticize

this landscape and the echoing of doves, the cawing of the ugly and magnificent John Crow vultures, the braying of donkeys, the bleating of goats, and
the day-long crowing of roosters that blend together in a montage that com-
prises the community. These nostalgic symbols of rural life are accompanied
by its hardships. The difficult employment situation outlined above creates
female economic dependency on males; yet the Social Development Council
study reveals an interesting pattern regarding what it calls the "uncivilized
conditions" of single-parent male heads, with respect to lack of access to multiple utilities. The report notes that

> 50% of single parent male heads are residing in uncivilized conditions. These
> households lack several basic facilities such as toilets, proper domestic water sup-
> ply, electricity and modern facilities to prepare foods. There is however, the pres-
> ence of cellular phones which in some respects is required, but also shows a
> preference in materialistic things over basic necessities. The economic and social
> welfare of children in these households are at risk and the problem is further com-
> pounded by the nature of the household being medium (one male in charge of
> possibly five children). (Social Development Council of Jamaica 2007, 15–16)

While it is typically assumed that men are the ones to be involved with seasonal migration as farm workers, for instance, women too are heading to the
United States on limited work visas to work as maids in hotels, and there are
a number of families I am familiar with in just this kind of arrangement. In
one instance, a father is home with four children and one grandchild, while
his baby-mother of over twenty years is in the American Midwest working in
various motels (field notes, June 2007). In this instance as well, the judgement
of the Social Development Council is misplaced; the baby-father has the interests of his children at heart, not the material accumulation of consumer goods
over family well-being. Nonetheless, clearly the difficulties identified above
may reflect a combination of poor choices overlaying the deeply problematic
distribution of resources. Should individual men be blamed for this, or is it
instead a reflection of government neglect? Clearly the latter plays some critical
role as everyone who lives outside of the centre of town must navigate the
rudimentary roads leading to the various districts to reach places of work. Limited piped water and sanitary facilities, lack of garbage disposal services and
lack of electricity for many render the maintenance of daily life a struggle.
According to the study by the Social Development Council, only 60 per cent
of households have access to modern toilet facilities and 30 per cent use these

in conjunction with pit latrines. While the study states, "households that lack toilet facilities are headed by a single parent male and the household size is medium", it also states that "40 per cent of extended, 50 per cent of nuclear family types and all single parent female heads use pit latrines" (Social Development Council of Jamaica 2007, 13). Any relationship between the gender of the household head and the nature of household facilities would require a specific study focusing on these variables. Nonetheless, these statistics indicate shifting gender roles as women's migration engenders male heads of household who are caring for children on their own. The quest for global capital in this instance is the instigator of gender-role change.

Other resources that are unevenly distributed include cooking facilities and water supply. In terms of cooking facilities, only 60 per cent of households have gas stoves, and the remainder use a combination of charcoal, wood and gas. With respect to water, 70 per cent of households use tanks and drums, and 30 per cent use water from rivers and streams. Only 20 per cent have a domestic supply in their homes, 10 per cent receive water from standpipes and an even smaller percentage receives water from multiple sources. In addition, residents report unsafe water storage and treatment practices, potentially producing significant health risks. Frankfield is clearly a community that suffers from the wider problems that plague much of rural Clarendon parish.

Over the years of my fieldwork, Frankfielders have expressed their malaise to me in various ways. "De yout dem" (the youth) complain that there is little to do, no opportunities, while the established members of the clergy, teachers, business leaders, shop workers and labourers condemn young men for refusing to work the land, turning instead to petty thievery or begging. It is indeed ironic that agriculture remains the highest employer, although residents claim that only a handful of men and fewer women continue to farm. As well, many people decry the decline of community morality, the corruption of the government and its flaccid policies to boost the standard of living. Most do not discuss Jamaica's place in the global economy, but instead argue party politics. In 2007, with the success of the Jamaica Labour Party, hopes for change were raised. Significantly, the global economic crisis has dampened hopes for party success, while a global perspective is on the rise. The town has seen brighter and more prosperous days, and it has proved particularly interesting to note that various groups of people within the town assess this decline in *gendered* terms. Both elderly women and men highlight the degeneration of male behaviour. "Gunmen" and other ruffians, for instance, once thought primarily confined to Kingston, seem to have found their way to Frankfield and surrounding communities of Trout Hall, James Hill and Grantham, where every so often there are murders on the street and in bars. Children express great fear of gunmen since they hear about them on a daily basis, and some have even seen shootouts. Locals and the media talk about how gangs, such as the One Order Organization from Kingston, have penetrated the parish capital of May Pen and surrounding towns, threatening businesses with extortion ("Gangs Flex Muscle in May Pen", *Jamaica Gleaner*, 20 June 2004). While some people are still shocked when bloody violence breaks out due to personal enmity or the great passions surrounding elections, just as many simply nod, suggesting that this is the way things are going.

I became aware of this appraisal of the younger generation of males at a gathering of the community counsel I attended in 2001. A prominent middle-class man bemoaned the loss of community values among male youth, saying,

> There is increasing use of ganja. Many are coming to school sleepy, dazed or charged (they smoke or drink it). This is affecting them. Many boys are not learning too well. Many are without proper supervision. There are quite a few crack users as well. They are influencing others in the use of it. What's happening in the community now is very frightening – youngsters nowadays always stay high, want to feel nice, dance to the music. That's right – whereas in the past they used to work. After school now, children are on the road for hours, *hours*, before they go home. They have nothing to do, or they can't get transport.
>
> They do have counselling sessions at school, but the influence of the community is stronger, in Trout Hall, Park Hall, up hills, where fellows smoke and carry on for the entire day. Children are already gone on trouble everyday. They become quite useless, have no skills, get attached to girls, hook them, and get them pregnant. They are a threat to society. And now, in the government, they are talking about legalization of homosexuality, and legalization of ganja [shakes his head in dismay]. (Field notes, June 2001)

Concurring with this view, the elderly, in greeting one another, recollect earlier times when donkeys pulled carriages to market loaded with produce, when people talked long into the evening, when the Rio Minho ran full and rushing as opposed to its present near-dry-bed condition.

What has happened? How are lives today shaped by the interpretation of lives and circumstances of the past, that is, through cultural memory? And are times worse today then they used to be, or is this the persistent impression of both idealists and older residents whose memories are glossed in nostalgia? To explore these questions, I offer a brief look at the historical context in which Frankfield emerged, detailing what I have learned of its foundation as a slave plantation; its ephemeral post-emancipation (1838) prosperity as a final stop on a trans-island railroad line completed in 1925; and its subsequent slide into economic decline. Yet the story of the community cannot be divorced from the wider patterns of Jamaica's European colonization or the settlement of the parish of Clarendon to which it belongs. I therefore situate key moments in the town's history within this broader framework, weaving together local lore, historical text and archival documents, bringing to the surface the construction of the gender system of the colonial slave system with its intersectional features of colour, race and class, shaping gender role and ideologies. The understanding I hope to convey of contemporary gender systems is predicated on this foundational one in Jamaican history.

JAMAICAN HISTORY IN A NUTSHELL: "DEGENDERED" AND GENDERED

A Caveat

Jamaica's history first as a Spanish colony and later a British colony is richly documented and discussed in West Indian history and literature. Moreover, ongoing archaeological discoveries continue to shed light on the lives of the indigenous peoples who first occupied the island, the lives of slaves living on sugar, coffee and livestock estates, the patterns of the white colonists, and the multiple Maroon communities of escaped slaves, but there is still much archaeological work to be done. Archival research also continues to yield insights into many periods of Jamaican history, including, for example, the complex interactions among Jamaica's many ethnic communities, such as indentured labourers from India, China and Lebanon, who arrived following slavery's demise in 1838 to work on plantations abandoned by the newly freed Afro-Jamaicans. The condensed portrait that follows, therefore, is far from exhaustive. Its central aim is to stress the gendered nature of British plantation society and the ways in which gender was an ideological category, refracted through the intersectional social, political and economic matrix of race, colour, class and sexuality. The section will elucidate how historical constructions of masculinity and femininity, strands of one gender system under slavery, became inscribed in cultural memory, producing an imagined, coexisting gender system of Maroon society, part of the folklore of Frankfield's male Rastafarian population. Thus the features of the plantocracy's gender system shape present-day views that men and women in Frankfield hold about their past, the problems they face today and how they might overcome them. The centrality of the concept of "slavery times" therefore represents a collective new beginning for black Jamaicans, pregnant with gendered symbolism, both historically and in cultural memory. Colonial slave society laid the foundations for subsequent reproductions and renovations of raced and classed gender identities.

Caribbean feminist scholars have emphasized the importance of colonial slave society in shaping gendered narratives, which reverberate throughout the Caribbean region, from national to local levels. Mohammed states, in reference to the effects of the gender systems of colonial societies throughout the West Indies, that "the residual effects of Eurocentrism and elitism of the white planter class on the dynamics of race and gender in each society still inform the ongoing construction of masculinities and femininities" (1998, 8). Similarly, historian Hilary Beckles notes that the emergence of Caribbean nation-states in the postcolonial period reproduced power dynamics through hierarchies of gender. He comments that "the construction of the nation-state as the final victory for anti-colonial forces carried within its very conception and design several layers of enforced agreement that quickly emerged as the new and revised oppressive hegemony" (Beckles 1998, 48). Thus we begin our journey winding our way through the allegorical strands of our gender molecule.

A CONVENTIONAL JAMAICAN HISTORY

The story must begin before the first Africans came to Jamaica in 1517, when Taino Indians inhabited the island they called "Xaymaca", land of wood and water, beginning around 1000 CE. Having arrived over a period of a few hundred years from the Guianas of South America in dugout canoes, the Tainos established a relatively egalitarian society based on fishing, farming and gathering. They collected fruit and grew yams, cassava, maize, beans and spices. When the Spanish arrived on 4 May 1494, as part of Christopher Columbus's second journey to the West Indies, they established a plantation economy, enslaving the peaceful Tainos. The entire population died out within two decades, mainly from imported diseases such as influenza, the common cold and smallpox, for which they had no immunities. The cruelty of the Spanish was so severe that Taino parents poisoned their children with unprocessed cassava juice rather than commit them to lives under Spanish rule. Because of the swift demise of the Taino population, their relatively egalitarian gender system is not woven into the Spanish and later British or African populations, or at least there is no archaeological evidence to suggest it was.[5] In 1517 the Spanish began importing Africans to Jamaica to work as slaves on sugar, coffee and livestock estates, but under the Spaniards, a full-fledged plantocracy was not developed. They were not well supported in Jamaica by the Spanish crown, and the colony suffered ongoing attacks from Dutch, English and French pirates.

In 1655 Great Britain attacked the Spanish colony and won possession of it. Retreating to Cuba, the Spanish freed their slaves; at the end of Spanish occupation, Africans in Jamaica numbered only fifteen hundred (Hart 2002, 3). Many took to the mountains in present day "Cockpit Country", in the parish of Trelawny, to fight the British. Known today as the Maroons (from the Spanish *cimarron*, or "wild one") they established two communities, which were later joined by escaped Africans enslaved by the British. In the seventeenth and eighteenth centuries, Jamaica's mountains were thickly wooded, providing ideal terrain for runaway slaves to escape capture and plan rebellions. By 1661 the British had consolidated the former Spanish colony, greatly increasing the numbers of slaves and plantations. Africans were brought to Jamaica to work as slaves on sugar, coffee and livestock estates established in the late seventeenth century. The largest numbers of Africans came from the Fanti and Ashanti tribes (including the Akan) of Africa's Gold Coast, or present day Ghana. Known as the Middle Passage, it comprised the second leg of the triangular trade.

The triangular trade system linked Europe, West Africa and the Caribbean. It was most prosperous for Jamaica in the eighteenth century when the importation of slaves was at its height, and Jamaica was the largest producer of sugar in the region. A plantocracy emerged in full force after 1655 when the Spanish occupation ended following Great Britain's invasion of the island. British control increased the efficiency of sugar production: The number of sugar plantations increased from 57 in 1673 to 430 in 1740 (Baker 2000). Throughout this period in Jamaica, and the Caribbean region as a whole, the society developed into a three-tiered hierarchy that shaped the social, economic and political structure of plantation society. The plantocracy is conventionally described as a colour/class system, built on the ideology of racism, hatred of Africans and beliefs in their inferiority. In this structure, the first tier was constituted by a minority of free whites comprised of absentee planters, creoles (Caribbean-born British who presided over local politics) and poor whites (descendents of former British indentured servants). They dominated over the free mulattoes, the second level in the triangular social system. This mixed or interracial population constituted a distinct social and political entity (Beckles 1998, 39). Mulattoes owned small businesses, tracts of land and even slaves, emulating the upper tier. Residing at the base of the triangle, the third tier that constituted the vast majority of the population, were the black slaves, both Africans and Jamaican-born persons of African heritage.

STRANDS AND BUILDING BLOCKS: A GENDERED HISTORY

The preceding conventional depiction of the organization of the plantocracy omits gender, race and sexuality as critical intersectional ideological components that defined gender roles and their conditions of possibilities for upward mobility. Feminist revisions that incorporate these axes highlight the structural positions and meanings that race/colour/class/sexuality occupied in shaping gendered relations of the plantocracy. What I will show in the ensuing section is that the culture of the plantocracy was built out of a gender system that collectively included all social locations or standpoints deemed significant by the cultural order. These were ranked hierarchically from the supposedly "pure" white male planter class that occupied the highest position,[6] with women of this class below them, followed by poor white men, then women, followed by a range of types of interracial mixtures. Colour, as one feature of phenotypic variation that constitutes cultural notions of racial categorization, was an important evaluative criterion of class status, which persists today although in weakened form. Moreover, as Kamala Kempadoo argues, race has been constructed as real in Caribbean life through the history of slavery and colonialism, which relied on racial categorization for its justification. Nineteenth-century cultural evolutionary thought harnessed theories of race as a feature of cultural progress, placing Africans in a savage tier and western Europeans in a civilized one. Kempadoo explains how oppressions, discriminations and social inequalities were founded on this theoretical nexus between phenotype (colour/race) and culture. Such thought persists today in Jamaica, "most visibly structured through labour markets and employment opportunities, educational systems, and class relations. Hierarchies marked by skin colour, hair and body type, language, and facial features remain in place, with terms such as *browning, black, light-skinned, dark-skinned,* and *Indio* being commonly used and locally understood" (Kempadoo 2004, 9, 10).

The colonial state also fashioned linkages between the race/culture dyad and sexuality, erotic desires, whom individuals have sex with, and their role in sexual encounters (Davies 2007, 26). These "racialized sexualities" – stereotypes of sexuality tied to race constructs – remain potent tropes within Jamaican thought, and indeed throughout the Caribbean. As Kempadoo also states, referring to contemporary Caribbean society, "sexuality appears as the modality through which race is made and refashioned in specific ways" (2004, 28). Beginning with the conquest of the indigenous population to the importation first of African slaves and later indentured servants from India,[7] racialized sexualities were fermented, generating both stereotypes associated with distinct populations as well as "strategies, policies, and laws around race". These included slave breeding and the "re-creation of race through sex", the whitening of Africans, violent mutilation of sexual organs as forms of discipline and punishment for the slave population, anti-miscegenation laws, as well as sexual fantasies and stereotypes about gendered behaviour based on race:

> Slave women were cast in colonial imaginations as promiscuous, "cruel and negligent as a mother, fickle as a wife", and immoral. Black femininity was often represented as naturally "hot constitution'd" and sensuous in an animal-like way . . . white womanhood represented the pinnacle of femininity, couched in assumptions of fairness, purity, frailty, and domesticity . . . The mulatto woman . . . represented the erotic and sexually desirable yet was outcast and pathologized and emerged during slavery as the symbol of the prostitute . . . stereotypes of a "docile, insipid, tractable shadow of a being with no mind, personality of significance of her own" dominated Caribbean understandings of Indian womanhood, an Orientalist representation of her – as a highly sexual being and a temptress – followed close behind. (Kempadoo 2004, 29–29)

Race, class, colour, sexuality and ethnicity were established as "structuring powers" creating social positioning, access to resources and the command of political power (Hawkesworth 2006). As Ulysse points out, drawing from Henriques, the race/colour dyad was drawn up in the following way: "The offspring of a white man and a black woman is a mulatto; the mulatto and the black produce a samba; from the mulatto and white comes the quadroon; from the quadroon and white comes the mustee; the child of a mustee by a white man is called a musteffino; while the children of the musteffino are free by law and rank as white persons, for all intent and purposes" (Ulysse 2007, 28, citing Henriques 1953). The ideology of white power as exhibited in this racial/colour terminology was also classed and gendered, shaping behaviours and aspirations, although individual personality differences cannot also be ignored. For example, mulatto women "occupied a space on their own as reluctant or willing concubines of white males" while other mulatto women strove to emulate white women through their appearance and conduct. Nonetheless, brown women (a colour/gender term) were rarely accepted into white society (Ulysse 2007, 30–33).

As Beckles (1998, 39) notes,

> The majority of mixed race women remained enslaved, worked in field-gangs and were not differentiated from African women in terms of life experiences. Few escaped slavery, and most remained consigned to labour gangs alongside their black mothers. They lived in the plantation villages created by their African family and shared their experiences . . . it was common for most mixed race women to be socially absorbed into the dominant African mainstream, thereby negating the impact of the colour coding system that characterized the hierarchical order of colonial society.

Moreover, although mulatto and black women worked in the fields and were subjected to the same oppression, the racialized, gendered division of labour was such that most domestics and urban slave women were mulatto, while field labour was the main location for black women. And as historian Cecily Jones points out, "black women's bodies belonged neither to themselves nor to their partners and husbands, but ultimately to white masters and mistresses" as they were subjected to sexual exploitation as breeding workers, satisfying white male lust and discipline (2003, 216).

Thus the tiers of the plantocracy are significantly more complex than conventional, degendered histories depict in terms of a mere colour/class hierarchy. Understanding the various work roles, interests and experiences of its members as they were positioned within it based on the confluence of gender, race, class, colour, sexuality and ethnicity is a project unto itself. Moreover, it is important to point out that the hierarchy of the plantocracy was not static but emergent and shifting, as is all culture. Thus the gender system of one historical moment was never fully stable. The system had malleability and the lower two strata were home to various combinations of gender and colour. For example, black women engaged in strategic miscegenation to bargain for their freedom, performing one feature of the gender systemic: the roles between men and women.

The general demographic, however, was maintained through continuous shipments of slaves into the early nineteenth century, followed by "slave breeding" (Mair 1995). The specific journey of the triangular trade that included Jamaica began its first leg in English ports such as Liverpool or Bristol. Slave traders left England and sailed to West Africa, including a port in Lagos, Nigeria, or along the Gold Coast, to trade textiles, iron and other commodities in exchange for human cargo. The ships would travel up the West African coast, collecting slaves held in enormous dungeons after their capture. On the second leg, the slavers left Africa, transporting their chattel across the Atlantic to Port Royal, where they were sold at auction to plantation owners. After emptying the ships of slaves, crews filled them with sugar, molasses and rum, produced by earlier shipments of Africans, to bring back to England (Ruddock and Robinson-Glanville 1996).

The Africans who survived the appalling conditions of the Middle Passage met lives of great hardship and cruelty on British plantations. Slave society, built out of the varied cultural heritages of slaves, withstood systematic violence based on stringent legal norms and exercised through the ownership and operation of the white planter class. Beckles notes that "chattel slavery, an institution built upon private property rights in persons was thoroughly gendered in its design and functions" (2004, 230). The mulatto population was born out of the sexual exploitation of black female slaves by white male slaveholders, who were expected by their peers, fellow patriarchs, to boast about the numerous rapes and other forms of sexual torture they forced on slave women. Perceived as licentious and overly sexed, black women slaves were portrayed in part as forbidden sexual desire. Adding to Kempadoo's depiction above, Barbara Bush explains that they were simultaneously painted as a worker, a "defeminized neuter unit . . . passive, downtrodden, subservient", and as "cruel and negligent as a mother within the black slave family" (1990, 11–13). As evidence of the longevity of cultural definitions of femininity, Bush demonstrates that "the composite image of the slave woman, built on popular myths and stereotypes, has proved durable, despite the existence of contradictory evidence in contemporary writings which shows it to be inaccurate" (p. 14). These images came out of European contact with West Africa in the fifteenth and sixteenth centuries as the slave trade emerged and grew. European male traders stressed African women's physical differences with European women and their "impudent nakedness", linking their relative nudity in comparison to European women with immorality and sexual promiscuity, born out of Christian notions linking sexuality and blackness with evil and the devil. By the late eighteenth century fallacious ideas about black women's sexuality were "loosely bandied about" (p. 14).

The gender system of the plantocracy demonstrated qualities of longevity and malleability. Racist ideologies emerged from earlier European contact with Africans; however, the gender/colour/class hierarchy was not fixed throughout the years of the British colonial slave period. In the early years of the plantocracy, white indentured Irish women (poor whites), considered "secondary whites" because of their poverty, were permitted to engage in sexual affairs with enslaved, free black or free coloured men, indicating a particular permutation of the material status of gender relations, following Barriteau, as one component of the gender system. However, as material conditions changed, the sugar industry expanded and the period of white indentured labour ended after 1700, white supremacist ideologies were harnessed to cement the small white population, reinforcing its dominion over others. White women, subjected to patriarchal authority, were thus forbidden sexual relations with black and mulatto men.[8] The control over their sexuality by the white male planter class elevated them within the system, placing them above black and mulatto women, and enabling them to "aspire to the leisured, pampered position of higher status women" (Bush 1990, 12). Hence, through the confluence of racist ideology and the burgeoning wealth of the plantocracy, the material conditions of poor white women shifted, impacting on the nature of their sexual relationships. The contradictory nature of gender systems is apparent here, as the control of these women simultaneously permitted their upward mobility.

White masters maintained their positions of superior masculinity *vis-à-vis* black and brown men and all women through "systems of violent terror", writes Beckles. The records of an English slave manager/planter in Jamaica exemplify this system of abuse:

> – Wednesday, 28th January, 1756 – Had Derby well whipped, and made Egypt shit in his mouth.

– Friday, 30th July, 1756: Punch catched at Salt River and brought home. Flogged him and Quacoo well, and then washed and rubbed in salt pickle, lime juice and bird pepper; also whipped Hector for losing his hoe; made New Negro Joe piss in his eyes and mouth. (Cited in Beckles 2004, 234)

Black males were doubly emasculated through violence to them and to black women, as white planters asserted their dominance through sexual exploitation. In the face of these forces of emasculation, used to set examples and deter uprisings, revolts nonetheless occurred. As Richard Hart (2002) argues, slave resistance, including uprisings and other forms of rebellion (refusal to work, runaways), was largely responsible for the end of slavery. James Ferguson concurs, stating that "the history of black resistance runs parallel to that of slavery itself. The brutality of the plantation system never succeeded in crushing the spirit of the millions of Africans who were transported to the Americas" (1999, 122).

The plantocracy reinforced ideologies of race, colour, class and gender asserted in political and economic power, legal rights, social relationships and institutions, as well as self-identity. Most slaves worked the land, men *and* women, clearing, planting and cutting sugar cane or processing cane at sugar mills. Fewer numbers worked as domestic hands in plantation great houses. Moreover, slave resistance to this system, Hart contends, should be considered as the most powerful force for change. It was ultimately a series of rebellions concluding in the 1831 rebellion of Samuel Sharpe, a Baptist preacher, who led a five-month-long insurgency involving burning and destruction of plantations, which contributed to the end of slavery on Jamaica. Sharpe was hanged in Montego Bay, proclaiming before he died, "Rather death than life as a slave." The slave trade was abolished in 1807, but slavery itself did not officially end in the British West Indies until 1838 (Bayer 1993, 15).

Although Jamaican society has undergone many upheavals and transformations throughout its turbulent history since abolition, the structure of the plantocracy established the parameters against which future power struggles would continue to engage, along with emergent forms of patriarchy (Beckles 2004, 234). Yet even prior to their enslavement, argues Beckles, there is evidence to show that black women's resistance began in Africa and continued through the Middle Passage such that "anti-slavery mentalities, therefore, preceded the plantation" (1998, 45). Once they were enslaved, black women resisted both white and black male domination in their lives. Lucille Mair identifies a range of strategies, including unwillingness to work in order to hinder the economic viability of plantations; outspokenness in voicing complaints about their owners and overseers and in filing their complaints in colonial courts; plotting and conspiring to poison their owners or burn the estates; running away, engaging in guerilla tactics and many more rebellious acts. Enslaved black women were considered "equal under the whip" and thus they suffered torturous punishments for their resistance, including the stocks (from three to six hours as a mild form of punishment), flogging and even hanging. Yet as Mair says, "by refusing to accept slavery like dumb animals, by regularly raising their voices, women, in their way, forced their presence on the consciousness of many: this was the thin end of the wedge in undermining the system of slavery" (1995, 25).

Following their freedom, in their post-emancipation flight from estates, the new proto-peasantry settled in free villages. Between 1838 and 1842 over two hundred free villages were established, organized around a church and creating a vast black peasantry, the lowest tier of the colour/class system. Others occupied unused lands, "captured" plantation lands as squatters, settled in post-treaty corporate Maroon societies, such as Accompong (Besson 1998, 135), or established communities out of former plantations purchased by missionary societies, such as the Moravians and the Baptists. The three-tiered hierarchy of the plantocracy did not collapse with the end of slavery but emerged, reconfigured into a three-tiered colour/class system. The white minority became an upper class, the mulattoes emerged as a small middle class and the emancipated population occupied the lowest stratum of rights and privileges.

In the post-emancipation period, other Jamaican towns were formed from the slave quarters and services that were built on the periphery of estates that had large work forces. With the collapse of slavery, many peasants remained in these houses, a small number continuing to work for low wages on the plantations, in an apprenticeship programme soon to fail; others sought to establish their own small farms, or shops and services. These included boot and shoemakers, tailors and dressmakers, tinsmiths, blacksmiths, bakers, house and sign painters, among others. Some communities built schools with clergy assistance while others built hospitals and post offices too (*Jamaica Almanack* 1811–40):

> In Clarendon, the former slaves settled on land in the Mocho Mountains (chiefly on the northern side), on the southern slopes of the Bull Head range and in the

upper part of the Rio Minho. In the bottom of the valley, some of the estates that had gone out of business rented land to tenants. Of course, these tenants did not build houses on their rented land or plant permanent crops. Instead, they planted catch-crops there, and lived on the holdings which they thought of as their own. (Taylor 1976, 38)

In addition, the nonconformist churches, including the Baptists, Methodists and Quakers (all of which played an important role in the abolition movement, shaping public outcry against slavery in Great Britain and teaching slaves about their rights and freedoms), were central in the village life of the emerging peasantry, establishing key institutions of elementary education. Emerging from this consolidation of religion and education were trained "community leaders, or elders as well as local clergy and school teachers" (Ferguson 1999, 183). Moreover, the social structure of such villages was modelled on African societies: "Cooperative and communal work groups performed labour-intensive or arduous agricultural tasks on a rotating basis . . . In the absence of credit from banks, communities set up mutual loan schemes, sometimes known as *su-su*, which collected savings and issued loans" (ibid.). Yet following the end of slavery, life continued to be extremely difficult. The wider economic conditions of Jamaica were severe, and unemployment in rural areas was high.

> Sugar's decline brought hard times to Jamaica's black population. As the estates failed, the free peasantry could no longer earn wages or find a market for its food crops . . . Neither individuals nor the colonial government had the money to pay missionaries, teachers, or medical doctors . . . From the 1860s, there were really two Jamaicas. Along the coasts, the remaining white and coloured planters elected the legislative assembly and maintained limited public services. In the interior, free villages originally built next to active estates now were totally isolated. The villagers struggled to survive on the produce of their tiny and often eroded plots. Hunger, disease, and theft became common. Prejudice on both sides intensified the division between the races. (Rogozinski 1999, 185–91)

As the free peasantry emerged, the island continued to experience an economic slide, from its eighteenth-century heyday when sugar was king. In the 1860s the banana industry took hold and export to the United States began in the 1870s. In 1870, Jamaica became a Crown colony, acquiring a new constitution. At this time, important public works projects began in the building of new roads and bridges, which would eventually connect towns such as Frankfield to Chapelton and May Pen to Kingston. In 1885, a railway station was built in May Pen, linking Clarendon more directly with Kingston. It reached deeper into the interior in 1913 when an extension was built from May Pen to Chapelton, and then from Chapelton to Frankfield in 1925. The main reason for this extension was to increase the efficiency of transporting bananas to Kingston, as they were now Jamaica's chief export crop. There were six bridges on the new line, as well as a viaduct at Crooked River, which was 400 feet long and 120 feet high, the biggest at that time in Jamaica. As a result, upper Clarendon became an important banana-producing area, and Frankfield and Spaldings grew into important towns (Taylor 1976, 43).

The opening of the Frankfield extension was so important to the community and the island that it was noted in the *Jamaica Gleaner* ("Ten Miles of Line from Chapelton to Frankfield Was Built Through Difficult Country", 17 March 1925) as follows:

> The District of Frankfield, in Upper Clarendon, was in gala attire yesterday. It was the day fixed for the formal opening of the Railway between Chapelton and Frankfield and the day had been long anticipated. The cry for the Railway has been loud and long, and yesterday saw the realization of the efforts that have been made for several years past. Indeed, not only Frankfield, but the districts covering the ten miles of track from Chapelton to Frankfield, bore evidence of the enthusiasm of the people and their gratification at the completion of the Railway.

After the railway was constructed, many roads were also built in the next decade, and small farmers began to purchase mass-produced cars and trucks in greater numbers. Even at the opening of the railway, there was concern expressed by members of the legislative council about the potential impact of "motor traffic". Thus, Mr Smith, a member of the parish, stated: " 'If they wanted the Railway to pay, they must have two trains.' Already he had heard that there was some plan for motor traffic to run between Frankfield and May Pen" (*Jamaica Gleaner*, 17 March 1925). Moreover, at a meeting of the council, comprised completely at the time of white landowners, concern was also expressed over a land settlement scheme. Many residents, Mr Smith continued to report, referring to the former slave population, "had been living on rented lands for 30–40 years" and these residents did not plant permanent crops for fear of being turned off from the land at any time (Frankfield was then a peasantry propriety district). "Mr Smith then stated, to marked support – 'hear, hear' – the council members cheered", that the governor should purchase the lands and resell them to the peasantry, thus increasing government revenue, contributing to the development of the parish and even supporting the success of the railway (ibid.). Yet the railway did not transform rural life the way cars did. Before the 1930s, most people travelled only as far as the nearest market town; however, the pervasiveness of the automobile increased regular travel to Kingston in particular, as young people from around the island migrated there to seek economic opportunity.

In 1929 and throughout the 1930s, Jamaica was not immune to the global economic depression. Malnutrition, high unemployment, declining schools and increasing unrest gave way to the labour riots of 1938, when workers went on strike:

> After a series of strikes and violent episodes in Westmoreland [on sugar planta-tions] dockworkers and street cleaners stopped work in the capital. The situation rapidly deteriorated when mobs attacked shops and trams, blocking streets with barricades. During a week of unrest, troops killed eight protestors and wounded 171, while over 700 Jamaicans were arrested and charged with public order offences. It was perhaps the worst outbreak of disorder to be experienced in the British Caribbean and one which was to have lasting effects. (Ferguson 1999, 245)

Out of this crisis arose new social, political and economic movements in the country. Alexander Bustamante emerged as the leader of the labour movement, founding the Bustamante Industrial Trade Union. In 1938, Bustamante joined with the People's National Party, a party founded by his cousin Norman Man-ley. Later, in 1943, Bustamante left the People's National Party to found the Jamaica Labour Party. He later went on to become the country's first prime minister after independence in 1962.

In 1944 adult suffrage was granted, giving both males and females twenty-one years of age and above the right to vote. Throughout the 1950s, there was increasing diversification of the economy in the bauxite industry and expor-tation to the United States where aluminium production would take place. US companies such as Alcoa and Reynold Metals, although controversial, con-tributed to the movement away from sugar (Ferguson 1999, 282), as did the growth of banana plantations when the US company United Fruit, which had been operative in the country since the early 1900s, became a major exporter of Jamaican bananas. In the 1960s, the tourist industry also began to flourish, with wide ranging effects on employment, construction and international rela-tions, particularly with the United States.[9]

In January 1962, a draft of the independence constitution was debated before both houses of parliament and subsequently approved, unanimously. On 5 August 1962, at midnight, the Jamaican flag was raised, and on 6 August 1962, Jamaica attained independence from Great Britain, with a multi-party parliamentary democracy in place, following the Westminster model. The constitution established a separate judicial system and protections against dictatorship. Jamaica became a member of the British Commonwealth (Ferguson 1999, 280).

The last three decades in Jamaican history have introduced new concerns, particularly political tensions and so-called tribalism between the Jamaica Labour Party and the People's National Party, although the decline of violence in the 2007 elections lead some political observers to reflect on Jamaican democracy coming of age. The US involvement in the "war on drugs" and the continued rise of the tourist industry are also significant topics that continue to be addressed in great detail elsewhere; it is not within my purview to consider a detailed history. However, it is important to emphasize that these conventional social and political movements are significant to Jamaican history, and of equal value is the rise of Jamaican feminism and gender studies, outlined in chapter 1. As I have sought to demonstrate, the engendering of Jamaican history is an outcome both of the contributions of feminist scholarship and of the important insights of Jamaican people who perceive their history as gendered, largely because of the centrality of ideologies of gender to the construction of Jamaican cultural life. Jamaican feminism, as an activist and scholarly movement, can be regarded as one of the forces of fluidity in the Jamaican gender system, since such systems are constituted by ideas as well as roles, hierarchies, and cultural notions of masculinity and femininity, among other things (see Mohammed 1998, 2002b; Barriteau 1998, 2003).

I have presented this condensed overview of two versions of Jamaican history, one conventional and degendered, the other gendered through the colonial slave society's matrices of race, class, colour and sexuality. These analytical descriptions lay the foundation for the ensuing exploration in the next chapter, where I will present a more detailed exploration of Frankfield's gendered history. Here I delve into Frankfield's folklore, examining how residents construct their own tales of continuity and change, pairing the two in a conceptual "rung" of the rural black Jamaican gender system.

Chapter 3

Laying Foundations

A Patchwork Gendered History of Frankfield

THIS CHAPTER CONTAINS TWO central goals. The first is to pursue the same analytical framework outlined in the previous chapter, developing a gendered history of the community of Frankfield by stitching a patchwork narrative drawn
from archive, folklore and cultural memory. The gendered features of this
reconstruction are shaped by the nexus of ideological features of Jamaican life
outlined in the previous chapter, focusing particularly on race, colour and class.
I follow this approach because as I sought to understand the ways in which
gender informs Frankfielders' views of themselves, I realized the centrality of
their own folklore in relation to national narratives of the past and archival
data. Here, then, I offer a parallel gender system, one that is imagined by Frankfield's Rastafarian population, stressing the longevity of a nostalgic African
past. The second goal presented at the conclusion of the chapter is to assess
how the metaphor, gender is to culture as DNA is to biological life, shapes
understanding of rural black Jamaican gender systems to this point, including
the impact of the gender system of the plantocracy and emerging knowledge of other competing and intersecting gender systems that I have thus far
identified.

FROM WHENCE IT CAME

Frankfield's origins are elusive. The archives at the Mona campus of UWI, in
Kingston, contain scanty information, an assortment of newspaper clippings

from the *Jamaica Gleaner* (Jamaica's oldest newspaper); a report by an anonymous author about the history of the parish of Clarendon, in which the town
is situated, all compiled rather haphazardly in a manila "Clarendon folder".
The National Library of Jamaica has a similar folder with more clippings, a collection of speeches delivered by a once-prominent citizen, and other odd items
requiring any narrator of the town's history to piece together fragmentary
parts. Local residents themselves are not much clearer. Stories vary consider-
ably and are segments, rather than full narratives. Ironically, in spite of the
spotty records, townsfolk nonetheless have strong sentiments and images of
the town having changed from something better – more communitarian,
orderly, cleaner – to its present condition. What follows is an effort to share
the oral accounts of Frankfield's origins from Frankfielders themselves, as well
as residents' characterizations of the present-day community in relation to
visions of its past. Some of these stories are rooted in "slavery times" while
others draw on the more recent past. Through this retelling, which involves a
weaving together of residents' patchworks with historical documentation, I
demonstrate how assumptions about gender are embedded in Frankfielders'
ideas about what the town used to be versus what it is today. Moreover, it is
clear that residents regard the community as situated within a broader gendered narrative about the Jamaican nation, which is factual, mythical, allegorical and, of course, influenced by ideologies of race, class and colour. The
community of Frankfield and neighbouring towns that are included in some
residents' understandings of Frankfield's history and the nation often overlap
in stories of the past and sometimes even merge into one space, demonstrating
the ways in which ideas themselves come to constitute "community". Shared
representations of collective selves, in as much as actual physical spaces and
clusters of individuals, signify "the community" (Anderson 1983).

Frankfield consists of eight districts, communities that are part of the
municipality of the town. They include Commissary District, a collection of
homes and small stores about half a mile outside the centre of town on the
road known as the B4; "Frankfield", the centre of town; Lampard, lying up a
winding hill north of town; Waterworks, further west on the B4, running parallel with the Rio Minho, on the way to the Edwin Allen Regional High School;
Cow Pen, beginning with group of houses and "shacks" accessed from the centre of town by a stone foot bridge on the Rio Minho; Nine Turns, a district
north of Frankfield on the way to the town of Grantham; and the last two,
Etrick Hall and Andrew Hill. If Frankfield has a "poorer" district, it is Cow Pen,

known as a community where drugs are more rampant than elsewhere, unemployment is high and descendants of Maroons are said to live, shrouded in legends of their magic and self-insulation.

In discussing the town's origins with residents, a number of people have pointed to Cow Pen as an original space, deriving its name from a cattle plantation that used to be Frankfield. The district occupies "hill and gully" terrain, appropriate for cattle to wander and graze. In fact, according to archival records, Frankfield was a livestock plantation. Yet there are other notions of Frankfield's beginnings. One now retired history teacher informed me that many people are interested in how the town derived its name, linking the name with its foundation. She told me that one of her high school students had written her a report about a man named Frank who owned a field, but she was unable to remember the references – nor did the student identify who Frank was or how his field came to be a town. Another resident identified the family of McKenzie, who still reside in Frankfield, as long time residents, also an important clue, as there was a McKenzie who owned livestock in the area of Frankfield in the nineteenth century. People frequently shared these kinds of fragments with me, followed by apologies and regrets that the old timers who once knew the history are all gone now.

THE ARCHIVES: SCATTERED REMAINS

Since Frankfielders themselves do not know exactly when and by whom the town was founded or under what circumstances, and the library at UWI Mona was only marginally helpful, I extended my search to the National Archives. On a burning hot day in March 2005, I hopped in a taxi and took a ride from Kingston[1] to the National Archives. Housed in Old Spanish Town amid stately, elegant, crumbling colonial buildings, the archives safeguard colonial documents of land grants that were made by the British Crown to British citizens, permitting them to become landowners in Jamaica. The collection also contains almanacs from the 1700s, crop records and other proceedings detailing the economic and political aspects of the colonial period. I informed the archivist about the nature of my inquiry ("How was the town of Frankfield, Clarendon parish, founded, by whom and when?") and began looking through an assortment of documents searching for any mention of the name of the town. With the help of the librarian, we located a blurry microfiche of land grants dating to 1666. Slowly scrolling through with the aid of a magnifying glass, I learned, with great excitement, that a man named Thomas Rodon was granted 201½ acres from King George II of England in 1666 in the existing parish of Clarendon. The land grant records identified Thomas Rodon as one of the original British owners of land in Clarendon, yet I still did not know where this land was located or if it had anything to do with Frankfield.

Consultation with other records revealed an exhilarating link. With further help from the archivist, we probed through the crop accounts, records of the yields produced and sold on the market from estates across the island. The name of Frankfield emerged first in the crop accounts of 1788 (volume 14) as a sugar estate that also produced rum. Thumbing through original documents, not microfiche this time but oversized volumes of pages stiff and yellowed, written in beautiful cursive script, I read the following entry: "Frankfield Estate 211 acres. 58 Tons sugar; 11 puncheons of rum. Personally appeared before me, Wheeler Fearson, Mr James Fleisketh, overseer on Frankfield estate and made oath that the above is a true and just account of the crop made and brought to market from said estate for the year 1787." The entry indicates that the town was in fact a plantation, visited by a colonial bureaucrat named Wheeler Fearson to record the market yields as indicated by the overseer of the estate, James Fleisketh. An estate with an overseer indicates an "absentee landlord". Was it possible that a descendent of Thomas Rodon was residing in England? I looked ahead to the 1789 crop account where a similar entry was made, indicating that Frankfield was a small plantation. Big sugar estates produced far more than sixty-six tons of sugar, the recording for that year, suggesting that some other economic venture was at hand. "Perhaps livestock?" I asked myself. In 1789, James Fleisketh was still overseer of the estate. But there was no mention of the name of Rodon. Did the Rodon family own the land?

Next, I turned to the 1811 *Jamaica Almanack*, since there is no mention of Frankfield in later crop accounts. The almanacs, initiated in 1751, only began to indicate property owners by parish, their occupations and the nature of their property (slaves and "stock") in 1811. Consulting the document a shiver ran up my spine. The entry read: "Frankfield, George Rodon proprietor, occupation: Attorney." In 1811, 145 years after Thomas Rodon was granted land by the King of England, George Rodon, perhaps Thomas's great- or great-great grandson, owned slaves and livestock, as recorded in 1811 until his death in 1824, *on a property named Frankfield*. In the 1826 almanac, a new Rodon appears, Henry Rodon, presumably George's son. An "F" Rodon is also listed.

Perhaps this is Henry's wife, who, because she could not own property, was not considered significant enough to mention by her full name. Then, turning to another archive, the almanac of memorials, I learned that in 1835, Henry Rodon died. In 1838, when slavery officially ended in Jamaica, Henry Rodon is still listed as the owner of the estate. Yet at this time, the almanac lists "apprentices" instead of slaves, and there are 183 according to the record book, indicating that Frankfield participated in the failed apprentice system that emerged throughout the island. Then, in 1840, the Rodon name disappears in connection with Frankfield and an O. McKenzie is identified as the property owner. And here, archive meets folklore.

This patchwork constitutes much of the historical documentation of what is available in Jamaica of Frankfield's history. I never learned how the town acquired its name although it was common for the British to name communities after place names or people from England. Nonetheless, it is clear that Frankfield, like many other Jamaican towns, began as a plantation. Perhaps that plantation included the housing of the slave quarters, their kitchen gardens, and various services and shops.

Who are Frankfielders today? Some are likely to be descendents of the slaves who worked on the plantation, but they are also a community of migrants from towns throughout the island and perhaps other plantations, incorporated through marriage, patterns of work (including indentured servants from China and India, making Frankfield home to one prominent Chinese family who owns a large grocery store and an East Indian family who runs a doctor's office). Many people also identify themselves as "mixed", including African and East Indian and African and English. Some children attending the primary school have referred to their parents as "Coolies", often a pejorative term for East Indian migrants, but in common Jamaican usage, simply a descriptive term. Frankfielders also include "escapees" from Kingston seeking a more stable and sane life in the country, and even one locally well-known case of a soldier absent without leave from the army.

RASTAFARI, NANNY AND "THE EARLIES": AN IMAGINED, *GENDERED* COMMUNITY

Local Rastafari have constructed their own version of Frankfield's earlies,[2] connecting the community and surrounds to Maroon activity to the south at Mocho Mountain. In their rendering of it, Frankfield is afforded an important status in its reconstruction of historical gender relationships between men and women, although, as I will show, this unique imagining is firmly rooted in another building block of the allegorical gender molecule, the collectively shared history of Jamaica's resistance to slavery and the role of Nanny of the Maroons in this history. In their version of the way things were, Frankfield is linked to the centre of Jamaica's most important stories of rebellion against slavery and colonization. Theirs is "truth" as they say, "nuh just a story". While some of their ideas resonate with historical documentation emphasizing the significance of Clarendon in resistance to slavery, they also assign a place for Frankfield which is not documented. Rastafari is a movement that rejects Western capitalist hegemony as well as any force perceived to be oppressive, including the police, the Catholic Church and so on (all Babylon, in Rasta terminology), looking instead to the African peasantry as an idealized source of moral values. By connecting Frankfield to that source, they relay a morality tale linking the present decline with a glorified past, when, even beleaguered by slavery, those true to their roots behaved nobly. They are now a model for those who emulate them: the Rastafari.

Frankfield's Rastas are a loose community of men[3] – and, as with many small rural towns, there are no visible Rastafari women who are sexual or economic partners to these men living in the community. This is important to keep in mind as I proceed because their image of the past is also a tale about the relationship between men and women, a gender system they reconstruct, held together by local Rastafari notions of masculinity and femininity. How the male/female dynamic has changed from their imagined collective past is offered to explain current gender relationships between Rastas and local women. Also, the Rasta interpretation of the history of Frankfield as a morality story is a commentary on the community today, in relation to their beliefs about what actually happened long ago. In what follows, I intertwine the pieces of the past presented to me by the Rastamen with archival data and historical reconstructions.

In 1690 there was a rebellion at Sutton's estate in Clarendon, which lies south-west of Frankfield. This is a well-known rebellion, referred to widely, including in both Rasta lore and in the *Journal of the Chapelton Historical Society Newsletter* (Chapelton is located about ten miles west of Frankfield), as "Cudjoe's Rebellion" (1982, vol. 2). In the newsletter, this famous rebellion is written about in a tone of great pride, revealing local sentiments and its connection to the event, demonstrating that society members share Frankfielders' own interests in ascertaining the relationship between their town's background and the broader story of the nation. Since the newsletter is primarily a collection of essays and stories, it, too, is part of local lore – literary lore – rather than documented scholarship.

Cudjoe, believed to have been born in Jamaica of Akan descent,[4] is recognized as the elected leader of the Maroons who lived on the eastern part of the island in the Blue Mountains, known as the Windward Maroons. He was known at the time by colonial historians to be "a bold skilful and enterprising man, who on assuming the command, appointed his brothers Accompong and Johnny leaders under him and Cuffee and Quaco subordinate Captains" (cited in Hart 2002, 43).

In the words of James Knight, a historian during the colonial period, "Capt. Cudjo who Commands Them, is the son of one of Mr Suttons Negro's, who was at the head of that Conspiracy and Governed the Gang to the time of His Death" (cited in Hart 2002, 43). The following is also recorded about the Sutton's rebellion in a set of anonymous letters known as the Long papers:[5]

> On the 29th July last all the Negroes on Mr Sutton's estate in the mountains in the middle of the Island broke out in rebellion, to the number of more than five hundred, forced the dwelling house, killed the caretaker and seized fifty fuses and other arms with quantities of ammunition. The marched to the next plantation, killed the overseer and fired the house, but the slaves therein would not join them. (Cited in Hart 2002, 17–18)

The article in the *Journal of the Chapelton Historical Society* asserts unequivocally that Cudjoe led this rebellion and also that he continued to lead fellow escaped slaves in attacks against the plantation administration and government. They would hide in the hills of Cockpit Country in what is today the parish of Trelawny (1982, vol. 2).

According to Frankfield's Rastas, though, the hills above and beyond the area that became Frankfield – not just Cockpit Country which lies further to the west – were important hideaways for Maroons. As Hart has noted, prior to the first Maroon War,[6] there were "numerous settlements of escaped slaves and their descendants in parts of the island to which the plantations had not been extended" (2002, 44). Historical documentation supports the view, shared by Frankfield's Rastas, that Clarendon harboured many escaped slave communities. In notations about the first recorded slave rebellion in 1673, which took place in the centre of the island in the parish of St Ann, the records state, "200 retired to the Mountains & secured themselves in difficult places betwixt the parishes of Clarendon, St. Elizabeth and St. Anne" (ibid., 14).

As part of their argument placing Frankfield and its surrounds as important sites of Maroon activity, the town's Rastas posit that it is highly unlikely that all hideaway communities were documented by the British, the record keepers of the time. Their central point is to insist that rebellion against slavery and against "Babylon", which had its roots in European colonialism, was central to the lives of the Maroons, whom Rastas view as their direct ancestors. It seems apparent to them that since the whole region incorporated hideaways for Maroons, and since Cudjoe's rebellions drew from slaves living on plantations from east and west, that slaves on the estate that was Frankfield would also have been part of these rebellions. This point is key to the Rastas' understanding of their community today, but I will suspend elaboration until after I relay a second component of their story, which is perhaps more controversial but of utmost importance to their gendered view of history. At this point, we have a rather straightforward, male-dominated view of the gender order in Rasta folklore: Rastamen can link themselves to a powerful black male slave, Cudjoe. But this is only part of the story. The other strand, femininity, enters in surprising ways that indicate that strict associations of Rastamen with ideologies of male dominance may be overly simplistic.

In their oral history, Frankfields' Rastas tie the town's earlies not only to Cudjoe and Maroon resistance in general but, much more specifically, as neighbour to the burial ground of Nanny. To reiterate what was briefly stated in chapter one, Nanny was a revered chieftainess of Ashanti/Akan origin who was one of the great resistance leaders from the 1690s till her death somewhere in the 1750s (Mair 1995). She is said to have used magic, cunning and intelligence to trap British troops and to stage many revolts: "In Maroon oral tradition Nanny has a reputation of being not only a great military tactician but also personally invulnerable" (Hart 2002, 80). Tall tales have been spun of her tremendous capabilities, including the parody of defraying bullets shot at her by using her buttocks. She is at once magical, cunning, dignified, revered, fearsome and endearing – qualities represented in affectionate and respectful names such as Granny Nanny, Grandy Nanny and Queen Nanny.

In an article exploring the multitude of representations of Nanny, American studies scholar Kimberly Brown writes that Nanny is "situated somewhere between mystic and martyr, rebel and myth". Brown cites literary critic Jenny Sharpe who insists, "the story of Nanny is the story of contending forms of

knowledge: written versus oral histories, colonial versus national cultures, institutional versus popular ways of knowing" (quoted in Brown n.d.). Hart (2002,
44) expresses a similar view:

> Oral tradition has it among the Accompong Maroons that the famous Nanny,
> after whom Nanny Town in the Blue Mountains at the eastern end of the island
> was named, was Cudjoe's sister. Whether this was a blood relationship it is impos-
> sible to determine. Nor is it known to what extent if any Cudjoe exercised control
> over the military operation of the Maroons in the northeast. All that can be said
> with certainty is that the liaison, whatever its form, was close.

Nanny is officially buried in Moore Town in the Blue Mountains. However,
according to one Rasta named Moses, a hard-working farmer and owner of a
roadside store named "Poor Man Struggle" in Frankfield, the Moore Town
stone marks a false burial ground. Moses and other Frankfield Rastas tell a different story of Nanny, reflecting a local permutation of this heroine in
Jamaican national consciousness. In this folklore, Nanny represents the centrepiece around which a unique conceptualization of the local gender order is
perceived. Importantly, theirs is not the only local rendition of Nanny's burial.
Jean Besson found in her work among Accongpong residents that "Nanny, the
ritual ancestress-heroine appropriated from the Windward Maroon polity in
the eastern mountains of Jamaica, is said to be buried next to her 'brother'
Cudjoe at Old Town, where stories likewise mark her reputed grave" (1998,
144). Taken together these stories suggest the possibility of more local versions
of Nanny's burial, such that her symbolic appropriation offers insight into one
of the ways local gender systems are constituted. Local people harness dominant national symbols, weaving them into their own reconstructed folk histories, instigating conceptual systems that ultimately impact on behaviour.
What is imagined does not necessarily remain in the imagination but can
impact on day-to-day behaviour. We shall see that this is the case for some of
Frankfield's Rastas in relating a mythological story of their matrilineal descent
from Nanny, thus rendering the source of their own gender system through
this route.

Moses and other Frankfield Rastafari contend that that Nanny is buried on
Mocho Mountain and that their version is "de truth and we should nuh be
afraid of it". Our conversations about Nanny took place over a two-year span,
and Moses encouraged me, after a brief hesitation, to use his name in sharing
his story: "Nanny is buried on Mocho Mountain, about ten miles south-west

of Frankfield." While telling me this one day in his shop, another Rasta was present, and he chimed in saying, "I seen her grave wit me own eyes on Mocho." "Why, then," I asked, "do people say she is buried in Moore Town?" Moses responded, "You see, de people dem, up in Moore Town not *real* Maroons. You see, *dem sold out* to the British when the British offered dem some land for some money. Dem *manipulate* the truth" (personal communication, 15 February 2005; 9 March 2005).

Moved with curiosity about the conflicting accounts, I travelled to Mocho Mountain first in March 2005 and again in August 2006. During the first visit, my husband, daughter and I were driven by a friend from Frankfield nick-named Blacks, describing his dark black skin, which he says is an indicator of his Maroon heritage. Even though he does not wear dreadlocks, his ostensible Maroon connection, an ethnicity tied to race and colour, elevates him to a near-revered status; hence, he was trusted to take us to the site, since Moses was unable to leave his shop for the afternoon. Once the symbol of low rank in the slave-owning plantocracy, black manhood now occupies a new location in this locally created, Nanny-inspired gender system.[7] Entrusted with directions from Moses, Blacks drove us to a town on Mocho Mountain named Thompson in the district of Ten Miles. On arriving in the town, Blacks asked residents for the location of the burial site: "Where Nanny buried?" he queried, clearly assuming people knew what he meant. Everyone we asked pointed to the thirteen-mile marker on the side of the road. At a local restaurant/bar where we stopped to chat with residents, a Rasta offered to accompany us, and we hopped back in the taxi. We parked in a driveway by the side of the road and got out to walk the rest of the way up a steep hillside until the Rasta declared: "This is it", pointing to an old, unmarked gravestone.

The site of the stone is located about thirty feet above the road's surface up a steep incline covered with scrub, vines, roots, loose rocks and some implanted boulders. Turning to the group of children who had followed us to the site from the parked car, I asked, "Who is buried here?" "Nanny," they all chimed in. "What do people teach you about this place?" I continued. The eldest responded, "They teach we Nanny buried here." "Who is Nanny?" I asked them, and again the eldest in the group answered, "Nanny is national hero."

Inquiring further at a local grocery and bar, some residents said they did not know if it was Nanny or another important "slave woman", but most said that they had learned, through stories passed down, that this simple, unmarked stone was Nanny's real burial place and that the rocky hills and caves in the area were sites of Maroon hideaways and strategic planning for attacks on the British colonists.

On the next visit I returned with some research assistants, Heidi Savery and Ron Dalton, both archaeologists, as well as Moses himself. Blacks drove us again. Standing at the grave, and later that night and over the following few days, Moses recounted a more detailed story about what he contends is the "true history" of the Maroons in Mocho, what is known as "Nanny Gravel", referring both to the name of the history and the specific place of her burial:

> Every first of January there is a meeting in Smithfield. People come from all over de world talkin' the real history of Jamaica. Every year I go and listen to de real history. This meeting moves around to the fourteen parishes. You have men that show up not wearing clothes like this [*Moses pats his own clothes*]. They wear bark from trees, the plants, the shoes. You have to look at them like this all night; you look and wonder if they are real. Them drum and sing and tings. A man named Joshua who studied in England go around with the show, the meeting, and gives different views to the people. There is lots of different views. First time I go up there I was about thirty-two. This is the straight history of Nanny: Nanny used to live in Chapelton in the earlies. Chapelton is an ancient town, earliest town in Clarendon. Nanny used to walk forty-something miles: me check it out. From Chapelton to Kingston is about forty-five miles. [The Maroons] were getting a threat so they went to the highest mountains, Mocho Mountains, to Ice Mountain the second highest mountain in Jamaica. From the top, you can see the sea. This was a hiding place for them. You see it from where Nanny buried, surrounded by mountains.
>
> There were a lot of people against Nanny. The brainwash squads leading them towards a different life. So Nanny lived in Mocho many years. The British tracked them down and bring some of dem to St Elizabeth. The Maroons that were not captured stayed in Mocho, plant lots of tings, banana and the cane and tings.
>
> One man at meeting, I listen to him talk, him ninety-three, him grandfather.[8] He said Nanny grave there. No road never was there. Since then, them need a road, so I saw them cut that road, around 1983/4, right past the grave. Her grave was a secret. Anywhere you live, you are buried. The camp was just behind the grave. Nanny was the most powerful of all national heros.
>
> Why me believin' story of Nanny in Mocho? Today, they talk about a foolish set of people coming from Mocho. This is something coming from history. Like the holidays. We ask, what is the meaning of this day? We no live in those days, how can we know? It's in the name. Mocho. Nanny Gravel. Why do we have

these names? History has to have evidence. Mommy may die, but she tell her son; he tell him son. As long as we live around history it cannot die. The treaty with the British was written to include Moore Town and Accompong where Nanny's brother lived. But not Mocho.

Moses's legend underscores the significance of slavery times and the power of Nanny as features of a mythic origin story that orients the present, and those who recognize its truth, in a continuum of moral strength and descent tied to the African past. His story links together a Rasta network that weaves "through the parish and beyond" (Besson 1998, 144), coming together in the annual New Year's Day gathering. He describes those in attendance at the annual meetings as "dressed in bark", almost not real; "you have to look at them all night" as if they are spirit beings, ancestors returned to report to those who will listen. Their bodily practices are part of the commemorative social remembering, along with the talismans of the African continent that Rastas wear around their necks, their red, yellow, black and green tams or white cloths enclosing the dreadlocks of the Rastafari – the mane of the Lion of Judah, symbol of Haile Selassie I, the former Emperor of Ethiopia. Additionally, Rastafarians believe themselves to be one of the twelve lost tribes of Israel. These bodily inscriptions of identity are reinforced through "education" and "history", which Moses says are learned at the gatherings. They are symbols of the truth of the past, of the strategies of manipulation and cunning adopted by the Maroons, the tools of survival eventually liberating Afro-Jamaicans from colonial powers. Yet when Moses says that "they talk about a foolish set of people coming from Mocho", he reiterates the negative folklore surrounding Clarendon, what was written in the *Jamaica Gleaner* article cited earlier in the chapter: "they joke about people who are fool fool or dark being from Clarendon, Mocho especially because of its remoteness" (*Jamaica Gleaner*, 30 May 1994, 25). For Moses, this belief is held by those who are not "free from mental slavery", as Bob Marley sings, but it is also perpetuated by those from Mocho themselves, not as a belief in its reality but rather as part of their re-enactment of the past. The myths of Mocho as a backward place are part of a ruse, a story harnessed to mask the truth, a rumour spread to hide their secret of the cleverest of all, Nanny and her fellow Maroons. Here we see how stories are both forms of contemplation for members of a society as well as disguises, revealing some truths and masking others. For Moses and his fellow brethren who contend Nanny lived and died in the Mocho Mountains, they have seen through the disguise.

As Moses said, "Nanny was the most educated, that's why she was the leader. She teach those around her to share her power." Some of this power is conferred on those who accept the story, connecting those alive today with the early, formative and noble past that was Frankfield and surrounds, linked to the most powerful African in Jamaican history: a woman.

OF ARCHAEOLOGICAL REMAINS . . .

Of the stone itself, my research assistant Heidi Savery provided the following description of the "grave":

> The place where Moses took us exhibits what can be called a marker of sorts, made of quarried chunks of limestone stet in a mixture of concrete tempered with small- and medium-sized gravel and sand. The limestone chunks vary in size with the lower courses carefully laid in horizontal rows. The upper courses are laid-up with progressively fewer stones and placed with less form giving the overall appearance of a small mound. Upon initial investigation, it appears as though this structure sits on natural bedrock and may be built into the mountainside. Also, there is a modern, painted cement road marker positioned at the roadside at this exact location. The place is well known as is evident from the fresh and scarred over machete marks on the young tree that now grows directly behind the structure. It is not overgrown, as is the common fate of forgotten elements of the Jamaican landscape, but intentionally kept. The structure is certainly older than the road, but then again, roads were often built right over cart paths and well-travelled routes. (Personal communication, 9 January 2007)

The above archaeological description does not aim to confirm or reject Moses's story. Rather, it acknowledges the importance of the local claim that this stone is Nanny's burial marker. Such a claim emerges out of the experience and cultural memory of the local Rasta population. Both experience and cultural memory are phenomenon mediated within cognitive, spatial and material realms. The stone and its spatial location indicate two such realms, the story a third (Brumfield 2003). The material reality of the marker posits the potential opening of a dialogue between folklore and history, requiring that we take seriously Moses's story for its contemporary interpretive possibilities as well as for what it may reveal about a hidden past, encoded in crumbling remains. This latter task I leave to the archaeologists. As for the former, we now proceed.

COMMUNITY AND NATION IMAGINED

The central trope that runs through this narrative about Nanny is the idea of a glorified past set against contemporary moral decrepitude, or, in the language of the metaphor, one noble gender system of the past that sat alongside the corrupt gender system of the plantocracy. This nobility and glory, embodied in Nanny, symbolizes the purity, power and wisdom of the African mother. Imani M. Tafari-Ama, a Rastawoman who has critiqued Rasta patriarchal ideologies, writes the following: "The Rastafarians regard themselves as inheritors of the Maroons' freedom-fighting tradition, and the Rastafari woman is appropriately characterized as a 'lioness', positioning rebel woman against the Babylon system" (1998, 90). Seen in this light, Nanny is the original "lioness" creating a direct line between herself and contemporary Rastafari. Moreover, both a morality tale and a tale of redemption are contained in the relationships posited between Nanny and Cudjoe, Quaco and other male leaders. Her purported brothers share many of the same characteristics as Nanny (bravery, intelligence); yet as men, they are not afraid of her or her power. How is such a relationship possible in contemporary Jamaica where tension and mistrust characterize relations between men and women? More particularly, how is such a story possible emanating from a group of men who are linked to a tradition of Rasta that views men as the natural, spiritual heads of household and community, more likely linked to Cudjoe than Nanny in a conceptual line of descent?

One explanation may be that Nanny is not a sexualized figure, and so not positioned/fantasized by today's Rastas in any imagined sexual relationship.[9] In fact, as Brown notes, "According to historical reports, Nanny was believed to be well into her sixties when she led the Maroons. And as Jenny Sharpe suggests, it is unlikely that Nanny would have held such an important position in Maroon society had she still been of childbearing age" (n.d.). As with many women leaders around the world today, and certainly an Akan woman in Nanny's time, status was accrued in their post-menopausal years, when they are free of the responsibilities of child rearing and when they are no longer under the sexual regulations imposed on younger women, during periods of maidenhood, from menarche to marriage (Ward and Edelstein 2005). For Moses and others who share his interpretation of events, their story is revealing of the meanings they attribute to their present place in history. Benedict Anderson reinforces this idea, arguing that communities exist largely in the imaginations of their residents, from town to nation: "All communities larger than primordial villages of face-to-face contact (and perhaps even these) are imagined. Communities are to be distinguished, not by their falsity/genuineness, but by the style in which they are imagined" (1983, 15). Anderson's ideas are helpful here for thinking about the Rasta narrative connecting Frankfield to the Windward Maroons, even though his focus is the nation as the imagined "community". He probes the many ways that the rise of the printing press and other discursive forms created cognitive bridges for people occupying the disparate space of a nation, generating strong emotions of connectedness and belonging in spite of great divides, not only geographically but also in ideas and identities among its members. These bridges connect people in a common struggle to assert their unity; village, town and city are imagined in relation to the nation largely through the ideology of nationalism, permitting people within their localities to feel connected to a greater whole. The stories of Nanny's burial and the role of upper Clarendon in Maroon resistance imagine Frankfield as a participant in regionally important events that were instrumental in creating the nation. The stories also establish a set of criteria against which the present can be evaluated: Frankfield on a trajectory of moral decline against a more distinguished past, built on a different gender order.

This theme of a fall also runs throughout the conversations of the community's established middle-aged and elderly residents, both men and women as well as poorer, hard-working churchgoers. This is ironic, in the sense that the Rastafari occupy very different social positions, and each group often maintains misunderstandings about one another. Many of the community's business and professional establishments and the larger peasantry tend to be fearful and somewhat ignorant of the tenets of Rastafari, linking them with violence and the drug trade, as well as low moral values, which they associate with marijuana smoking, squatting on lands and, of course, their unruly dreadlocks. Many Rastafari also stereotype middle-class churchgoers as perhaps more rigid and conservative than they actually are.[10] Nonetheless, both groups share a common notion of Frankfield's past as existing on a higher moral order than it does today, and both locate themselves as observers rather than participants in the decline. Both tell tales of Frankfield's fall from grace, part of the biblical narrative that shapes the worldview of a large majority of Frankfielders and many Jamaicans in general.

Frankfield's established middle class does not associate Nanny with the moral apex of Jamaican history, nor do they deny her importance as Jamaica's only cultural heroine. Instead, they stress the importance of women in family life, who are seen to connect households and generations across time. The role of women as stable figures, occupying positions as mothers as well as wage earners is particularly important (Barrow 1998b, 75–77). For example, Nurse's living room wall is graced with pictures of four "matriarchs", including her auntie who raised her for much of her childhood, her mother, her sister and herself. Their portraits represent women as the connectors of family ties, generating another form of community across households and towns, for the women lived in different homes but raised a common family.

The current state of moral decrepitude is assigned mostly to the misplaced values of grown men and male youth, yet also to increasing numbers of young women who are rejecting notions of femininity linked to "moral Jamaica" (Castello 2004). Their revealing dress is frowned upon and their behaviour considered disrespectful by the two groups who consider themselves to be upholding part of a set of disappearing standards: one being Christian morality, the other the Rastas, maintainers of the idealized values of a nostalgic African peasantry. Examples are cited of mothers coming into the primary-school yard, raising their voices at teachers, encouraging their children to fight those who disrespect them; or women walking through town with curlers in their hair, unkempt, and even physically threatening others to settle disputes. These behaviours of self-representation are part of a syndrome that appears to reject the historical striving of the brown female population towards white ladyhood during the plantocracy, and which was later adopted in the post-emancipation and independence periods which still embraced British values, not yet embracing Africa, blackness and resistance to slavery with pride. Perceived by the brown middle class and upwardly striving black working class, such behaviour is regarded as a rejection by poor black women of outward symbols of purity, European cultural ancestry and Christian morality. These qualities locate Frankfield, in middle-class imaginings, as a place where things used to be proper, when men and women had more clearly defined roles, when homosexuality was not openly discussed or sung about in popular music, when dress and hairstyles reflected modest femininity, and when the youth followed a script that would transform them into responsible, hard-working adults. Unlike the Rasta image of the past, Frankfield's middle-class elderly residents do not link this script with an idealization of Africa. If anything, when they were young, they denied and looked down on these connections, influenced largely by British colonial views of African inferiority.

Yet today, as earlier noted, this pejorative perception has begun to fade through the influences of Bob Marley and the reggae movement and the black nationalist agenda initiated by former prime minister P.J. Patterson. Even Nurse Dunkley, who, as I have noted, is a relatively conservative Methodist, sometimes refers to herself, with a smile and a twinkle in her eye, as "Mama Africa",[11] a title she would likely have rejected in her youth. Even amid societal "fall", there is faith in redemption and salvation, tied, however subtly, to the dignity and regality of an idealized African womanhood.

This psychological, symbolic component of Patterson's racialized agenda, tied to Africa and the centrality of slavery in Jamaican history, could not on its own offer an opening for a reconceptualization of blackness. The new ideology of race that aimed to implode the three-tiered race/colour/class hierarchy of Jamaican society was coupled with a neoliberal economic platform that claimed to elevate racial identity by including blacks in the enterprise of capital accumulation and consumerism. Citing David Scott, Deborah A. Thomas notes, "For the liberal and left brown middle classes of the 1970s, blackness was part of an abstract principle of social change. For the black middle class of the 1990s, by contrast, blackness is part of an individual (even individualistic) identity politics of the new People's National Party of P.J. Patterson, or the new consumer egalitarianism of the liberalized market" (2002, 44).

Thomas contends that for lower-class blacks, "what may look like crass (and perhaps imitative) materialism" is instead a "racially vindicating capitalist consumerism", a "radical consumerism" that is urban, migratory and based on youth popular culture (ibid., 39–44), which is in some sense imitative of African-American hip hop culture and sports paraphernalia. In rural Frankfield these urban trends take hold both through overseas seasonal migration and regular travel to Kingston. The brown and increasingly black middle class condemn the visible outcome of these trends, what I have described as the presence of male youth in the streets and immodest young women. Middle-class Frankfield perceives this as a misguided youth culture that begs instead of works, or works intermittently, rejecting agricultural labour. They spend what money does come their way on flashy, "bling-bling" accessories: for males, large gold chains, baseball caps worn to the side and brightly coloured tunics with emblems of American sports teams or multinational companies. The Nike emblem was so pervasive in Frankfield among youth in the mid 1990s that a hatter produced his own duplicates emblazoned with the Nike swish, and graffiti artists decorated the side of a building with one that still remains – just the symbol alone on a white-washed wall. Young women spend their money on fancy hairdos and revealing dresses, appropriating capitalist consumption by finding "ways to resignify dominant ideologies and practices in order to resituate themselves as powerful actors within their own transnational spheres" (Thomas 2002, 45). Thus the racialized class conflict in Frankfield is in many ways about what it means to be a black man and a black woman; set against the post-independence brown elite, it is a conflict about the emergent gender system and how masculinity and femininity should be constructed to frame it.

MODELS OF MANHOOD AND THE JAMAICAN NATION

Perceived and actual shifts about Frankfield's transformations by its middle class can be more specifically tied to ideas about the Jamaican nation and the place of Frankfield within that nation. These ideas revolve around negative associations with emerging roles and patterns of behaviour particularly associated with masculinity. For at least the last decade there has been an ongoing, national search for models of manhood that can "redeem" the current predicament. There is emphasis among both men and women of the need for enculturation and socialization of boys away from a culture of violence and crime, a general perception of boys' low performance in schools, and the tendency towards early fatherhood as the key marker of manhood, into new identities, based on different values. Questions about the challenges of manhood are frequently raised in the media, and sought after in workshops, conversations, conferences and other highly publicized events around masculinity. One example was in 2004 with "men's conference", which sought to promote national discussions among men and women from all walks of life. In forums such as this, citizens are exposed to scholarship on the topic, largely generated by Jamaican feminism and the rise of masculinity studies within this genre. Since Jamaicans of all backgrounds are avid newspaper readers and talk show listeners, these media help to disperse common themes throughout the society. For instance, an article in the *Jamaica Gleaner* entitled "Rites of Passage for J'can Males" (20 June 2004), discusses many of the publications on the topic of masculinity, including the oft-cited Errol Miller book *Men at Risk* (1991). The article is representative of a general concern in the press that the public become aware of the debates and recent scholarship surrounding "male marginalization". It summarizes Miller's thesis about male underachievement (without including recent controversies that revisit his "male marginalization" thesis). The article introduces readers to the Belgian anthropologist Arnold Van Gennep, who coined the term "rite of passage", to discuss the lack of rites of passage in Jamaican society for adolescents. The absence of such rites has been deleterious for Jamaican males, according to the article, leading to confusion about responsibilities and adult roles such that "sexual activity and childbearing have become . . . symbols of transition into adulthood". Recent scholarship has confirmed how important fatherhood is for men, primarily in terms of producing offspring, pointing out that "men boast about having children, not about their contributions to raising them" (Brown, Anderson and Chevannes 1993, 198).

The loss of rites of passage for Jamaicans of African descent, according to the *Jamaica Gleaner* article, is a contributing factor to this predicament which limits male adult-identifying characteristics beyond sexual activity and childbearing. Notably, the article also states that rites of passage disappeared through "the process of colonialism and slavery which disrupted the transmission of such practices from our ancestral roots in Africa". Here, as elsewhere, the article accomplishes two objectives: first, it links the present with "slavery days", which, as I argued earlier, is the dominant historical trope in Jamaican cultural memory, shaping popular perceptions of current permutations of gender conflicts. Second, the article contends that the problems faced by individuals are magnified onto the entire society and are problems for the entire nation. Individual struggles are part of the tensions of the collectivity. An outgrowth of the men's conference, the article proposes a mission for men to "transform male culture" because "the future of our families and communities depend on this". Local communities present unique "snapshots" of relations between the sexes and are connected in a national narrative, a collective gender pattern that ties the present with a shared ethnic past, an idealized African past. Mohammed (1998, 8) comments on this process of idealizing an ethnic past in the negotiation of contemporary, problematic gender relationships:

> The dynamics of gender in each society or region operate not through grand revolutionary upheavals but through the ongoing negotiations between men and women both at the individual and collectively organized levels. Masculinity and femininity exist not simply in opposition but, I argue, equally in relation to each other. *In this process of reconstructing gender identities, the rhetoric – either nationalist or cultural – has generally been toward reinforcing an "ethnic" ideal which predates the disruptions of colonization.* (Emphasis added)

Thus the current state of decline is largely envisioned as a slow fall from an initial standpoint of courage, bravery and independence tied to Africa, with Nanny, a woman, as its representative.

One folktale about Nanny portrays her as a spiritual-magical being, recounting that when the slave ship arrived carrying her, she marched down the gangplank, standing proud and tall, and walked away into the Blue Mountains. Nanny symbolizes Africa and her diaspora redeemed, the power of womanhood, mother of the Afro-Jamaican people, including Jamaica's male national heroes. She is beautified and memorialized in art and on the five-hundred-dollar bill. She is the African Mother (Mair 1995, 1), Mama Africa, and she symbolizes the imagined, idealized, original balance between men and women that has long since disappeared, and likely never existed within the Jamaican cultural landscape. Perhaps most important for Frankfielders, the two imagined versions of the past that I have discussed in this chapter generate hope for the future amid a troubled present.

VISUALIZING GENDER "MOLECULES" AS SYSTEMS

Given the historical overview of Jamaican history, Clarendon and Frankfield that the last two chapters have conveyed through the lenses of folklore, archive and cultural memory, it is now possible to visualize, in diagrammatic form, parts of two of the gender systems that existed during slavery and in the present-day. Conceived as an emblematical gender "molecule" just as DNA is a molecule, I have discussed attributes of two parallel slavery-time systems, one that has been historically documented as the plantocracy model and the other that is likely to have existed in historical form in Maroon society and imagined by Frankfield's Rastas, in which Nanny is the original matriarchal ancestor. There were certainly other gender systems that coexisted during this period as well. For example, as the abolitionist movement gained strength in the nineteenth century, alternative models of black masculinity and femininity clashed with the stereotypes of the plantocracy, although as Bush points out, the abolitionist image of the black woman "was equally a distortion of reality, based on racist images of African culture" (1990, 13). The plantocracy model is encased in the outer strands of masculinity and femininity which are given cultural meaning, defining the social, sexual and reproductive behaviour of men and women through the intersecting axes of race, colour, sexuality and class. The gender system was a product of the multiple interactions of these axes built on the political economy of plantation society. This was shown in a number of ways, one example being the changing rules regulating the sexual conduct of poor white women in relation to black and mulatto men as the sugar economy boomed. Tightening the reigns of their white supremacist ideology, the white male planter class imposed restrictions on these women regarding their sexual partners and they were forbidden to engage in affairs with free black or mulatto men. Another example is the emulation of white-lady status by mulatto women, who, in spite of their efforts to aspire to leisure-class status, were mainly barred from the order of white privilege due to their colour/class. This system was not static, but mutable like the DNA molecule. Its various members were involved in attempts to manipulate the material and ideological dimensions of the gender system for their own ends. The case of black women's selective miscegenation could lead to their emancipation, freeing their children from the plight of slavery, for a slave woman's child was always born into slavery, even if its father was the master of the plantation (Beckles 2004, 230–35).

Moreover, this system, both durable and in flux, emerged out of at least two other intersecting systems. On the one hand, African slavery disrupted the gender systems of the many societies that the enslaved were torn from, through initial demographic imbalances that shifted sex ratios of African societies by importing higher numbers of males to "systems of political and labour organization, living conditions and access to other groups" influencing everyday interactions and the unfolding nature of masculinity and femininity under the new system (Mohammed 2002a, 264). Mohammed notes, drawing from Elizabeth Fox-Genovese's study of nineteenth-century African slave society in the United States and Mair's study of Caribbean slavery, that "disruptions to the original gender systems from which slaves were drawn had and would have an impact on the gender dynamic between men and women of this group for centuries to follow" (ibid.). Yet on the other hand, African gender systems did not go extinct, as Bush notes. Instead, Africans injected some features of their previous gender systems into their own interactions, drawing from religious beliefs and subsistence patterns (Bush 1990) and, as we will see in the next chapter, through practices such as dancehall, which has a long historical presence in Jamaica.

Thus, while it is not my aim here to analyse the specific nature of these intertwining systems, I do want to indicate this as an arena for future study;

that is, all gender systems have precursors that are carried over in varying degrees into newer manifestations. To understand the nature of particular gender systems, we cannot only look at the specific historical period but must understand something of previous historical cultural configurations of gender. Another example underscores the point. As I stated earlier, Great Britain introduced its perceptions of a homogenous, savage Africa into its construction of black womanhood and manhood in the Caribbean. White femininity in Jamaica was defined in relation to this identification of black womanhood which revolved around sexually depraved, passive, downtrodden workers, and cruel and negligent mothers. The treatment of slave women and the nature of their resistance were formed partly in relation to such an image. For white male planters, the image, derived from earlier contact of the British with Africans, was harnessed and carried over into the plantocracy to further political and economic objectives and rationalize sexual molestation of black women by male slave owners. For slave women, resistance against these assigned characteristics was to protect their own notions of their gender identities (Mohammed 2002a, 265), born out of daily interactions and features of earlier gender systems that they sought to maintain. These dynamics are represented in the gender molecule by the paired characteristics of longevity and mutability.

In addition, the dynamics of longevity and mutability interact with the other rung of the gender molecule: collectivity and uniqueness. We have seen that the raced and classed components of gender in the plantocracy were lived in particular ways by its members. The earlier example of the diary of the white planter illustrates this through the punishments he inflicted on his slaves. They each were individuals experiencing their own suffering – their own "social unmanning" – at the hands of a cruel slave owner (Fox-Genovese, cited in Mohammed 2002a, 265). Their horrendous subjective experiences viewed in relation to the slave owner's pathological sense of punishment (*his* own subjective experience) are both rooted in the plantocracy's ideologies of race and gender, a collective attribute of the system that portrayed black males as subhuman, devil/beasts. The system's collectivity is evidenced also in the structural positioning of each member within the hierarchy.

The second parallel and contradictory gender system we have seen was presented by Moses and company. This system is folkloric, existing in cultural memory, likely with some historical precedent, as Hart's work implies. It conceptualizes black femininity and masculinity in opposition to the characteristics assigned by the plantocracy. These liberating characteristics are embodied in the representations of Cudjoe and Nanny and include intelligence and cunning rather than stupidity and evil; fearlessness and strength rather than cowardice and weakness. These positive qualities are assigned generally by Frankfield's Rastas to male and post-menopausal female Maroons as they reconstruct their past, as well as to their descendents. Our taxi driver, Blacks, for example, uniquely embodies the longevity of this collective, cultural notion of Maroon masculinity in the contemporary imagination. These features of an imagined gender system of Maroon society, while far from comprehensive, are instead suggestive of the larger point I am trying to make: in line with Mohammed's earlier claim, there exist multiple, coexisting and contradictory gender systems. I add to this the idea that these systems can be imagined, just as Anderson showed that communities can be imagined, impacting everyday life, providing explanations for existing problems and shaping present-day interactions (1983). This is true not only of Moses's portrayal of Nanny as a matriarchal ancestress for Frankfield's Rastas, but also of the plantocracy. While a real system, it is one that was built on ideas that were false, notions of black femininity, for instance, that stemmed from European cultural constructs of Africa. Its reality was produced out of mythologies: while the intersectionality of race, colour, class and sexuality coming together in a gender system were real, the ideologies that constituted these axes were not rooted in actual qualities of persons they were attributed to. Not only are there coexistent gender systems, emergent while simultaneously carrying with them strands of the past, but their existence in the material world is matched by their existence in the world of the mind. Thus, any search for additional gender systems must combine research into archive, folklore and cultural memory.

Chapter 4

The Rural Black Jamaican Gender System

Case Study, Frankfield

THE ETHNOGRAPHY OF SYSTEMS: COLLECTIVITY-UNIQUENESS

In this chapter I offer a descriptive analysis of the contemporary, rural black Jamaican gender system as I came to understand it by pursuing fieldwork in Frankfield. As such, my general aim is to focus on what is shared by this particular demographic. Such an enterprise, however, is fraught with methodological and conceptual challenges. In particular, beginning in the 1980s poststructuralist and postmodern anthropology proffered a legitimate critique against descriptive analyses of systems, precisely my undertaking. One critique that I pointed to in the preface pertains to the problem of reifying analytic models of systems. The analytical tool came to replace the dynamism of cultural life, in essence replacing the reality. I have attempted thus far to avoid this particular pitfall by reminding readers that the DNA model is a metaphor, a figurative analogy, for thinking through the complexities of the concept of gender and its conflicting characteristics. The descriptive features of DNA are what elucidate the relationship between gender and culture. A second critique of systems analysis has to do not with the models used to analyse systems but the concept of a system itself. Classical social theorists analysed social systems through principles of social organization, creating a series of labels to identify concepts based on "principles of categorization like gender, generation, and rank and with groupings, such as lineages, clans, age sets, and associations" (Wolf 2002, 228). Postmodern and post-strucuturalist anthropology have asserted that these analytical tools are unable to capture the fluid, emergent, dynamic, contradictory and transnational qualities of cultural life. Wolf (ibid.) has noted the following:

> We can now see in retrospect that this labeling was too static, because organiza-
> tion was then grasped primarily as an outcome, a finished product responding to
> a cultural script, and not visualized in the active voice, as process, frequently a
> difficult and conflict-ridden process at that. When the main emphasis was on
> organizational forms and principles, it was all too easy to understand organization
> in architectural terms, as providing the building blocks for structure, a reliable
> edifice of regular and recurrent practices and ideas that rendered social life pre-
> dictable, and could thus be investigated in the field. There was little concern with
> tactical power in shaping organizations, maintaining them, destabilizing them,
> or undoing them.

Since my use of the term "gender system" clearly points to integrative features of gender, it is important to clarify how I have avoided Wolf's well-warranted concerns, echoed throughout the discipline, and how I will do so in future chapters. My key methodologies have been to capture the simultaneity of continuity and change within gender systems as well as the unique expressions of their collective features. The insights of self-identified Third World feminists, African-American womanists, native ethnographers (a term used to identify ethnographers who study their own society) and action anthropologists have been particularly instructive in identifying the value of ethnographically producing life histories and personal narratives to portray the representativeness of individual lives, as well as how such local understandings are embedded in larger-scale historical systems, as physician-anthropologist Paul Farmer has achieved with his own fieldwork in Haiti.

Gloria Anzaldua, an influential, self-defined "Third World woman" writer, has also addressed this relationship between individuals and the wider systems that shape their life-choices. In her piece, "Speaking in Tongues: A Letter to Third World Women Writers", Anzaldua crafts a collective letter, a call-to-arms, or, more accurately, a call to the pen, to her fellow "mujeres de color, [women of colour] companions in writing". She begins by "trying to visualize" them:

> Black woman huddles over a desk in the fifth floor of some New York tenement.
> Sitting on a porch in south Texas, a Chicana fanning away mosquitos and the hot

air, trying to arouse the smoldering embers of writing. Indian woman walking to school or work lamenting the lack of time to weave writing into your life. Asian American, lesbian, single mother, tugged in all directions by children, lover or ex-husband, and the writing. (2004, 93)

In this passage, Anzaldua achieves something unusual, simultaneously capturing both the unique and the shared – the struggle to express oneself amid the structural inequalities that have silenced women of colour generally. This is an accomplishment that the ethnographic enterprise struggles to attain in its longstanding preoccupation with what is common to a group of people, set against more recent critiques. Feminist ethnographer Lila Abu-Lughod, who has studied Bedouins in Egypt has offered such a critique, arguing that

for the anthropologist . . . [a] serious problem with generalization is that by producing the effects of homogeneity, coherence, and timelessness, it contributes to the creation of "cultures". In the process of generalizing from experiences and conversations with a number of specific people in a community, the anthropologist may flatten out their differences and homogenize them. The effort to produce general ethnographic descriptions of people's beliefs or actions risks smoothing over contradictions, conflicts of interest, doubts, and arguments, not to mention changing motivations and historical circumstances. (1993, 9)

Abu-Lughod articulated her fears about over-generalizing "culture" as a shared entity at the height of anthropology's "crisis of representation" in the 1980s and 1990s, when the anthropologist's ethnographic authority came under both internal and external critique. She ultimately strove to disentangle herself from the conundrums of generalizing by "writing against culture" and construing "ethnographies of the particular". Her own stories of individual lives acknowledge that "a story is always situated; it has both a teller and an audience. Its perspective is partial . . . and its telling is motivated" (1993, 15). She reminds ethnographers that the contexts in which individual stories are told have shifted since their telling and urges ethnographic narratives to trouble the homogeneity of cultural representation. She hopes her readers will focus insistently "on individuals and the particularities of their lives" both to find similarities in all of our lives and to train "our gaze on flux and contradiction" (p. 27).

Adopting this middle route, in the remainder of this chapter I will aim to capture what is shared among Frankfield residents without flattening, but also without getting lost in particularities such that structural limitations are overlooked. An overemphasis on individual variation negates the role that structural inequalities and shared privilege play in shaping opportunities, access to resources and decision-making power – what Farmer (2005) has called "pathologies of power". For instance, we have already seen in chapter two that women in Frankfield suffer from higher unemployment than men and that there are fewer job opportunities available for them. We have also seen that emerging migration patterns leading women to seek overseas employment affect the composition of single-headed households, such that single male heads are increasingly common, suffering from the "uncivilized conditions" (for example, pit latrines) that the Social Development Council has cited. Both of these examples, migration and shifting household composition, are two kinds of shared circumstances that the ethnographic personal narrative helps to flesh out and render tangible through the lens of individual lives.

In addition, my conceptualization of a gender system, based on Mohammed's and Barriteau's earlier analyses, incorporates the idea of malleability as one of the "rungs" of the metaphorical gender molecule. The changing nature of household composition in Frankfield, shaped by emerging migration patterns, which in turn are influenced by the opening of seasonal work for Jamaican women as motel and hotel housekeepers in the United States, are examples of gender system malleability – changing gender practices which will in turn affect concepts of masculinity and femininity in Frankfield. The system itself by definition is inherently dynamic. Change emerges from many sources, including political and economic conditions as well as conscious and unconscious efforts to destabilize political and economic hierarchies (as the analysis of dancehall culture indicates) built on longstanding elite control which distributed authority on the basis of colour, race and class. Even my interviews with adolescent girls at Edwin Allen Regional High School, who assert confidence in their sexuality with adolescent boys, suggest a shift in culturally prescribed feminine identity away from passivity towards active agent. I continue this focus on the emergent qualities of gender systems in the chapters to come, identifying additional destabilizing factors – but not forgetting how they are paired with efforts to retain the longevity of hierarchical race, colour and class codes. This chapter and the next will also emphasize individual variation to understand how gender systems are internalized and refracted through the lives of specific persons. I will seek to avoid cultural portraits that homogenize differences in a snapshot of an ethnographic present.

Thus the systemic qualities of gender must be understood as both collectively and uniquely manifested in various groups and individuals. Gender systems are at once unfolding processes of emergent culture and tactical efforts of social elites to affix the qualities that privilege them onto the cultural landscape.

The ethnographic challenges in presenting the fluid qualities of systems are significant, but they have been addressed methodologically by feminist anthropologists largely through the venue of the personal narrative. I remind readers that one of my central aims in this work is to interrogate the methods of ethnography, to demonstrate how feminist ethnography has addressed the old quarrel with anthropology as a top-down outsider/insider approach that retains the anthropologist in a more powerful position than the community and research subjects. Static systems analyses accommodated an authoritative, outside ethnographic voice by constructing the notion of bounded social entities that anthropologists stood outside of, peering in and grasping persistent truths. On the other hand, acknowledging the instability and emergent qualities of cultural life exacerbated by globalization has required anthropologists to recognize themselves as part of a host of destabilizing features, arriving "on the scene", so to speak, and intervening in everyday life. The mechanisms of transportation and communications create channels for the movement of people, thoughts and things that challenge any notion of social systems and cultural life as bounded by invisible impermeable membranes. The methodology that captures these ruptures must position the anthropologist within them, carefully negotiating opportunities to participate in people's lives. This requires relationship building and maintenance as part of fieldwork. When approached honestly, building relationships requires the anthropologist to be vulnerable, open to questioning herself and self-reflexive. Cellular telephones and email permit ongoing links between anthropologists and research communities, thus stretching the boundaries of the field. This process is part of the undoing of the rigid anthropological self versus the informant other that I have sought to accomplish both in my fieldwork and in this writing.

This chapter is organized into subheadings that identify various components of this gender system, drawing once again from Mohammed's and Barriteau's definitions. As I examine its particular attributes, I point both to elements that have been inherited from the plantocracy system and ways that the current system is in flux, demonstrating the qualities of longevity and malleability. Where it is useful, I provide examples of the expression of systemic features in individual lives in order to mitigate the production of stereotypes, showing variations and discrepancies that challenge a simple portrayal of a monolithic gender system. This effort lays the foundation for chapter 5, which focuses on the unique ways the system is understood and lived by a number of residents of Frankfield.

SYSTEMIC ATTRIBUTES OF THE RURAL BLACK JAMAICAN GENDER SYSTEM

It is useful here to reiterate both Mohammed's and Barriteau's definitions of gender systems, since the ensuing sub-headings follow from them. Under each subheading I describe the feature of the gender system identified in its title. Mohammed (1998) defines gender systems as constitutive of the rules governing social, sexual and reproductive behaviour of men and women in any given society; these include the social roles assigned to men and to women, the cultural definition of masculinity and femininity, the sexual division of labour, rules surrounding marriage and kinship behaviour, and women's position relative to men in political and economic life.

As stated in the preface, the metaphor that gender is to culture as DNA is to biological life underscores the systemic nature of gender. The DNA molecule creates the organism, reproduces it and generates the transformation of an organism into new species through mutations. Similarly, as a system, each gender "molecule" or manifestation of a gender system at one point in time is shaped by paired building blocks of longevity-mutability and collectivity-uniqueness. These qualities of gender systems are part and parcel of human cultural life, contributing to the actual reproduction and nature of culture. Over time, one gender system can generate into a new system that will also reflect longevity-mutability and collectivity-uniqueness.

As I attempt to construct a conceptual gender "molecule", emphasizing the centrality of gender systems to Jamaican culture, I want to point out that the outer strands of the twisted ladder, the molecule's backbone, are constituted by cultural definitions of masculinity and femininity. These definitions, like other features of the system, shift; the twists of the molecule therefore conceptually indicate emergent notions of masculinity and femininity. The other features of gender systems stand in relationship to the pillars of masculinity and femininity, including alternative gender identities.[1] That is, people formulate their notions of gender selves within and against existing parameters of what it means to be a man and what it means to be a woman in a particular setting. It is critical, therefore, to know how a group of people defines what manhood and womanhood are to understand gender system features such as the norms of kinship behaviour, the sexual division of labour, and men's political, economic and religious power *vis-à-vis* women and the like, which shape daily behaviour and interact with people's understandings of themselves.

THE CULTURAL DEFINITION OF MASCULINITY, FEMININITY AND ALTERNATIVE GENDER IDENTITIES: NORMS OF SEXUALITY AND EMERGING DIFFERENCE

The sub-heading of this section incorporates an important feature of both Mohammed's (2002) and Barriteau's (1998) elements of gender systems[2], culturally defined male and female identities, as well as Barriteau's additional alternative gender identities. I also include "norms of sexuality" to flesh out how sexual norms are tied to these definitions and how new, different norms are emerging. Because of its significance as an alternative gender identity, at the close of this section I designate a specific section to dancehall culture, its challenges to the norms of modest femininity as well as its reproduction of heteropatriarchal dominance, even amid this challenge.

Rural black Jamaicans subscribe to what I would call a "folk" biological reductionism in their attribution of meaning to masculinity, femininity and alternative gender constructs. Biological essentialism has been written about and critiqued in the scholarly literature, hence I contrast this body of thought with community notions pervasive in everyday life. Such a reductionism rests on the notion that men and women belong to dichotomous gender categories – masculine men and feminine women – rooted in physical differences. Many believe that these were established at a time of creation. Moreover, men and women are linked through a system of compulsory heterosexuality reinforced through heteropatriarchal norms. There is little room for sexual ambiguity: the gender identities of "chi-chi man" or "batty boy" and "mama-man" or "mama-boy", for instance, are marginal and represent subordinate masculinities. Chi-chi man and batty boy refer to homosexual men, who are generally despised, although venues for discussion about the realities of human sexual variation do in fact take place in the elite hallways of Jamaican universities and at scholar-activist conferences. The HIV/AIDS pandemic has accelerated the importance of these discussions, bringing them into the discourses of government ministries such as the Ministry of Health and through the activism of such organizations such as the Jamaican AIDS Support Group. On the Jamaican street, and in letters written to the *Jamaica Gleaner* and the *Jamaica Observer* newspapers, however, heterosexism and homophobia remain the norm. Mama-boy/mama-man are essentially labels that extend these heteropatriarchal norms to boys and men whose sexual identity is suspect as a result of their movement into female spaces. Boys and men who are seen to trespass too frequently into the domestic realm (cooking, doing laundry, particularly female underclothes) and who are coddled and protected by female relatives into adolescence are likely to be referred in this way. At the same time, Rastamen often cook what is called Ital foods (natural, vegetarian and salt-free) and men who are single heads of household and therefore must care for children and engage in domestic work are generally not labelled as mama-men.

Men are regarded as sexual beings who must engage in sex with women merely to live (Robinson, Thompson and Bain 2002). Multiple sexual partners are therefore regarded as a natural part of the expression of hegemonic masculinity, a belief that poses enormous challenges to those engaged in HIV/AIDS prevention methods that seek to instil the values of abstinence and faithfulness to one partner. It is ubiquitously known that men frequently demand "skin-on-skin" contact in sexual intercourse while women often remain powerless to insist on men's use of condoms. Women are well-aware of their limited negotiating power as evidenced at a "pregnant women's clinic"[3] at the Frankfield health centre in 2006. Women of all ages rested on wooden benches in the waiting room, most of them having heaved their growing bodies up the incredibly steep hill to the one-storey cement building which houses the health centre. The morning began with an opening prayer delivered by one of the head nurses. As she prayed, eyes closed and fists clenched, for the women to have strength, courage and good health throughout their pregnancies, many of the patients began to wipe away tears and nod along as the head nurse, known as "Nurse" as all nurses are, touched on points they could relate to: "you didn't expect this one"; "you wonder how you're going to feed another". When she was finished, she informed the women about the availability of the female condom in the nearby town of Spaldings. Although Nurse heralded it as a tool of empowerment for women, she nodded empathetically as the women shook their heads in dismay when they learned the cost, which at the time was eighty Jamaican dollars. It cost as much to buy a condom as a few large tomatoes at the market, a dozen ackee or a litre of gas.

Nurse then introduced me as a visitor who had returned many times: "You have probably seen Dr Fox around town. Please give her your time and attention." I then met with some of the women individually in a private room, to interview them about the circumstances of their pregnancies. I learned from one woman that her partner donned a condom, only to remove it, in an intended surreptitious act, prior to intercourse, as she pleaded with him to keep it on. Another told me she became pregnant even though she was receiving Depo-Provera shots. She was living with her baby-father and this would be their third child together. A third woman told me that she knew her baby-father was involved with other women, but because he was a mechanic and would be able to help provide for her new baby, she did not want to risk losing him by conveying her obvious displeasure about his promiscuity. In this public venue, pregnant women's experiences of sexuality were firmly tied to their gender identification as mothers, revealing their lived experiences of these collective definitions.

Definitions attributed to masculinity and femininity, and their associated sex-segregated parental roles, are tied to notions of appropriate sexuality and widely accepted beliefs about male and female "nature". Men are expected to display toughness, sexual aggressiveness and independence/autonomy, reflected in economic stability and "breadwinner" status. These traits are encouraged early on in the socialization process. In rural communities, fathers residing with their children encourage boys in their early teens to wake up early when it is still dark and "feel the dew" to prepare them for a life of hard work, financial independence and providing for women (Chevannes 2001). Chevannes asserts that financial independence, rather than age, marks the onset of manhood, as does the birth of a child, demonstrating the potential for fecundity. Since financial independence is ideally a precursor to the fatherhood role, it also marks the establishment of sexual maturity. Moreover, once adult status is conferred, men are expected to display dominance in the household, independence, male camaraderie and sexual promiscuity. Upper-class men, typically white descendents of the British, may also be regarded as sexually promiscuous, but they are predominantly viewed as caring, faithful family leaders (Douglass 1992), demonstrating the definition of masculinity is shaped by class status and race.

Many rural women are ambivalent or negative about men, regarding them as untrustworthy and primarily interested in sex, yet working-class women seek multiple partners too. Much of the literature contends that women's multiple partnerships are connected to their need to secure financial support from men, one man to "pay the light bill", another to "buy school uniform" and perhaps a third to help with groceries. Transactional sex rather than sex for pleasure characterizes analyses of female sexuality so that the enhancement of sexual dimorphism, mainly through dress, hairstyles and comportment, is especially important in securing these relationships. Differentiation in dress begins early, and its importance is publicly established for children through school uniforms. Schoolboys, from the "infants" – the youngest group of schoolchildren, age four – through high school, wear khaki uniforms while schoolgirls wear variously coloured jumpers (depending on district and age). Boys are encouraged to dress themselves at this stage but girls are still dressed by their mothers, in part because it takes time for them to learn how to plait their own hair (Chevannes 2001). When they reach adolescence, rural girls are encouraged to comport themselves as ladies, aspiring to persistent norms of white femininity by walking erect and moving in a way that shows sexual modesty. It is not uncommon to see women, both young and older, walking past cat-calling men, their heads held high, looking straight ahead, ignoring the whistling and "hissing" sounds ("tsss, tsss") of the men trying to get their attention. While walking through Frankfield with a group of women, I was reprimanded when I turned my head and responded to one of the men. "Shhhh," one woman said, looking straight ahead, "don't talk to him!" This was one lesson on how to behave as a proper lady. Again, a lady is the ultimate expression of elite white femininity achieved through education, refinement, attention to a well-groomed appearance and unobtrusiveness (Douglass 1992). Many rural brown and black women continue to perform their gender in this way, indicating, as Butler has pointed out, that behaviour or "performance" is critical in defining gender identity. Definitions come into being as they are enacted. Individuals are aware of this, so that the same brown or black teenage girl who comports herself like a lady in the presence of her parents might transform her gender identity into something else in another context.

For example, increasingly, teenage girls are eschewing the norms of modesty, even in the middle of the day, wearing school uniforms as they initiate transactional sexual relationships by seeking out "sugar daddies". These are older men, many of whom drive taxis, who provide the girls with gifts and money in exchange for sex. A phrase that many teenage girls repeated to me was "school boy have pocket change but big man have salary", indicating the importance they place on the economic transaction. Another phrase adolescents cite is "school boy money end on Friday", to indicate their interest in working men. Transactional sex, viewed as acceptable for women with children seeking support from baby-fathers is deeply disquieting to Frankfield's middle-class residents. This is an emergent, alternative definition of femininity condemned in public forums and in personal communications. At the same time, while this description of the sugar daddy/teen girl phenomenon represents an increasingly common new configuration of the conventional "men look sex; women look money" mould of sexuality, it does not address the possibility that adolescent girls may seek sexual relationships that involve pleasure and/or love, or that there may be some situations where adolescent girls may exert greater agency in shaping their sexual conduct than is typically attributed to them.

In February 2005 I conducted some interviews with a group of twelve young women in grade nine at the Edwin Allen Regional High School in Frankfield as part of a wider study on gender based violence arranged through the Centre for Gender and Development Studies at UWI Mona. The girls offered some insights into potential configurations of their own sexual behaviour when asked a series of hypothetical question about a teenage girl named Ramona. When asked whether Ramona, who had a boyfriend, would have sex with him, under what circumstances and why, I received the following responses:

- "Girls will have more than one boyfriend. It is possible she would have sex. Girls are involved in fights over boys, and girls will have sex to trap them, to keep them."
- "Some girls don't want sex because of diseases going around, but some do to trap a boy."
- "No sex, no money."
- "Girls sometimes force boys. Boys may want to keep their virginity if their parents are in a prominent position. Girls use seductions."
- "Females can be very seductive."
- "Ramona might be ready to have sex, but sometimes girls can't say that because people will think something's wrong with them."
- "Her parents might tell her not to get pregnant and lose opportunities."
- "She want a boy who has money; school boy money end on Friday."
- "He should have a light complexion; people will say he's good looking."
- "He doesn't need education, only money, kriss [nice] car, name-brand clothes."

- "Most cute guys have STDs [sexually transmitted diseases] because they're not with one partner."
- "It depends on what kind of girl she is and who the boy is."
- "If she has good self-esteem she won't have sex, but sometimes she would have sex to keep him or the boy might threaten her."

In another set of questions, students were asked if a hypothetical boy named Ricardo would have a girlfriend, and if so, what would be the nature of his relationship with her:

- "In most cases, Ricardo would have a girlfriend and have sex."
- "He would have more than one girlfriend."
- "If his girlfriends didn't want sex, he would leave them, disrespect them."
- "He would pressure her a lot; invite her to his house. School guys only want sex from school girls."

The former scenario indicates a range of possible situations that influence these young women's decisions or inability to make decisions about sexual conduct. Multiple and conflicting factors shape their notions of appropriate female sexuality, including propriety about female morality, health concerns, the link between money and consumer goods, male/female power dynamics based around male strength, gossip, the power of female seduction, and skin colour.

A number of the young women expounded on their appreciation of female seduction powers when they were asked how they would respond to Ramona if they knew she was a lesbian. One young woman stated: "I would never be alone with her. I'd be scared of her, that she would try anything on me." Another pretty, brown young woman, with an elaborate hairdo, confidently said of herself, "If we were changing for PE [physical education] and I'm look- ing so fine and sexy, 'cause I know I'm *all that*, I know she would look at me!" All the participants burst into laughter when she said this, agreeing with this young woman's self-appraisal. It is interesting to note, given this clear display of self-confidence, that girls may pressure boys to have sex, challenging sim- plistic, homogenous descriptions of school girls as victims. At the same time, a number of their responses and the latter scenario, particularly those in which Ricardo was the agent, also reveal their vulnerabilities.

DANCEHALL CULTURE: ALTERNATIVE GENDER
IDENTITIES OR HETEROPATRIARCHY?

The phenomenon known as dancehall is a dominant feature of Jamaican popular culture. Its influence in Jamaican society is complex and multifarious, but
for my purposes I am particularly interested in addressing its role in shaping
cultural definitions of masculinity and femininity. Dancehall involves a series
of practices that illustrate both the continuity and malleability of gender systems: it both contests dominant racialized and classed gender ideologies and
at the same time reinforces existent ones about black female sexuality. Dancehall dramatically breaks with and reinforces slave society's polarities between
black women and white ladies, highlighting the role of behaviour, or performance of gender, as a condition of possibility for attaining the status of a lady
for middle- and working-class brown and black females. Focusing here on concepts of femininity and masculinity in dancehall therefore helps to illustrate
the value of the DNA model, particularly the intertwining strands of masculinity and femininity that construct its "backbone". I remind readers that the
main role of DNA in biological life is the long-term storage of genetic information, information that is passed down through reproduction and recoded
through mutations, thus transforming the organism. The metaphor permits us
to see these features of the production and reproduction of gender at work
when we realize that dancehall has existed in the Jamaican cultural landscape
for many centuries – albeit with different musical and visual particularities –
as a site of contestation about the ways in which gender, race, colour and class
attain intersectional meaning. "Genetic information", or ideas and practices
about masculinity and femininity, reoccur over long periods of history while
new information generates new possibilities for gendered expressions, recon-
figurations of power and redistribution of resources. Dancehall is one aspect of
Jamaican culture that helps us to understand how gender is built into the fabric
of culture as a system – a system that, by definition, is in process, unfolding
and in flux.

Dancehall's capacity to shift the gender norms and practices of Jamaica's
youth and to challenge the island's colonial legacy of white supremacy through
its race/class/colour/gender hierarchy has been debated by scholars and the
elite, whose anxieties have been piqued by dancehall's transformational possibilities. Given its profound influence, my concern here lies with the following
question: Does dancehall primarily reinforce existing sociocultural hierarchies

or transform them, challenging continuous features of the gender system (definitions of masculinity and femininity, relationships of power in political, economic and religious realms, kinship roles, and so on)? Indeed, scholarly inquiry demonstrates that it does both, exhibiting features of continuity and malleability.

Mainly an urban phenomenon that emerged from the inner-city yards of Kingston in the 1980s and 1990s, the culture of dancehall has spread throughout the island. As Norman C. Stolzoff contends, dancehall is not only the most popular form of youth entertainment throughout the island, but "a field of active cultural production, a means by which black lower-class youth articulate and project a distinct identity . . . to deal with the endemic problems of poverty, racism and violence" (2000, 1). Dancehall lyrics and style permeate Jamaican culture, from live concerts in clubs and outdoor dancehalls to fashion spreads in newspapers and advertisements. In so doing, it "plays a deeper role in shaping notions about personhood – that is, the motivations, values and worldviews of young children" (p. 2).

I have seen this influence, although in more muted form, in Frankfield where outdoor dancehalls occur every few months. Soundsystems come to town for all-night parties beginning late in the afternoon and turning out large crowds. Even if residents had glass windows, which most people do not, the parties would keep the entire town awake until four or five o'clock in the morning as the lyrics boom through powerful speaker systems. The dances often begin as community-wide parties, where people of all ages gather to socialize, drink and eat from jerk stands. As the night wears on, the parties change in character, becoming a montage of "melody, rhythm, the body in dance on the dancefloor itself as a space of spectacle and display" (Cooper 1995, 5) replete with heightened sexual innuendo and increasingly scathing cultural commentary by the deejay "toasting", cutting through the songs with his own lyrics. In this venue, where oral performance and bodily displays intersect, dancehall femininity stands in marked contrast to upper class and upwardly mobile middle-class sensibilities. As Carolyn Cooper explains: "Jamaican, the preferred language of orality, assumes the burdens of the social stigmatization to which the practitioners of afrocentric ideology in Jamaica are continually subjected. Upward social mobility in Jamaica requires the shedding of the old skin of early socialization: mother tongue, mother culture, mother wit – the feminized discourse of voice, identity and native knowledge" (pp. 2–3).

The characterization of femininity stands in contrast to literary, colonial forms of expression which, because they are elite,[4] are also deemed "masculine" reinforcing the demasculinization of black male lyricists of dancehall through simultaneous association with orality and African heritage. Yet it is precisely these qualities that render dancehall so powerful a force for resistance. Stolzoff comments on the link between dancehall and these expressions of African cultural memory, quoting Hedley Jones, former president of the Jamaica Federation of Musicians: "Dancehall has always been with us because we have always had our clubs, our marketplaces, our booths . . . where our dances were kept. And these were known as dancehalls" (2000, 3). Stolzoff further states that dancehalls have existed in Jamaican society for over two centuries: these spaces where syncretic African and European music forms have blended and cultural production has unfolded are sites of "interdependent domination and resistance, change and continuity" (Comaroff 1985, quoted in Stolzoff 2000, 4). Dancehall spaces, as venues for working-class black Jamaicans, have always both renewed and reconfigured the Jamaican social hierarchy built out of divisions of race, class, colour, gender, sexuality, religion and political affiliation, and they are thus threats to Jamaica's powerful elites and "central to the society as a whole, because Jamaicans of all races and classes define themselves in relation to it" (Stolzoff 2000, 6).

For many, the presentation of the female self occurs in relation to dancehall styles. The middle-class, modest look of "good girls" who wear discreet jewellery and conservative hairstyles contrasts significantly with what dancehall researcher Donna P. Hope (2006, xi) describes as "the beauty of fat, large-breasted, big-bodied, dark-skinned women who revel in their overtly sexual displays of legs, thighs and breasts as part of their economic and sexual freedom". Similarly, Bibi Bakare-Yusuf (2006, 5–7) offers a detailed description of dancehall fashion worth quoting here at length:

> The style appears anarchic, confrontational and openly sexual. Slashed clothing, the so-called "lingerie look" (such as g-string panties, bra tops), "puny printers" (showing the outline of the genitals), Wild West and dominatrix themes, pant suits, figure-hugging short dresses and micro hot pants infamously known as "batty-riders" are favored. Revealing mesh tops, cheap lace, jeans designed as though bullets have ripped into the fabric and sequined bra tops became an essential part of dancehall women's wardrobe in the 1990s. At the close of the 1980s, the dancehall female body was wrapped in bondage straps and broad long fringes or panels attached to long dresses to accentuate the fluidity of the body's movement in dance. Incompatible materials and designs were juxtaposed – velvet, lace,

leather, suede, different shades of denim, rubber and PVC, as well as animal prints such as mock snake, zebra and leopard skin, to produce an eclectic personal statement. Seemingly irreconcilable colours are combined to produce a refreshingly audacious, motile canvas on the dance floor. . .

Hairstyle, make-up and jewelry are a key part of the dancehall look. In the late 1980s to late nineties, huge cheap and chunky gold earrings with razor-blade designs, as well as necklaces with dollar signs were worn on the ears, nose, nails, waist, and belly button as status symbols. More recently, the style has moved towards "ice" (slang for diamonds) and "bling-bling" (code for expensive jewelry and accessories). Hair is either dyed in bright colours or covered in metallic-coloured wigs, weaves and extensions (platinum blonde, orange, turquoise, aubergine, pink). This style disrupts the Jamaican elite notions of "good" and "natural" hair versus "bad" and "processed" hair . . . In opposition to the Jamaican elite preference for understated beauty characterized by lightly applied make-up highlighting flawless skin, dancehall women's make-up is deliberately bright, glittery and brash.

Shoe styles continue the sexual fetish theme of the clothes: laced or zipped up stilettos, knee or thigh-length boots in patent leather or "pleather" are favoured for their emphasizing effects on the crotch and thighs. High-heeled strap shoes that coil round the calves towards the knees complete the image.

Scholars argue that dancehall fashion at once challenges received ideologies while simultaneously reinforcing them. As such, dancehall styles are a prime example of the way in which continuity and mutability pair together within gender systems. Mutability occurs as the dance literally fashions opportunities for the expression of lower-class black female agency and identity. Through creative style, Bakare-Yusuf contends, dancehall women employ their bodies as symbolic displays against patriarchal codes of female morality: "dancehall clothes cannot be said to promote feminine weakness; on the contrary, dancehall women are clearly not to be messed with" (2006, 13). In addition, dancehall women invest their identities with "meanings and processes which link them to both the spectacular fetishism of global consumerism and mass media semiosis as well as the African love of ceremonial pomp and pageantry" (p. 2).

These dynamics play out in Frankfield, although the fashions are muted on a day-to-day level. While I have been present at the early stages of a dance, as darkness draws near, I have retreated to Nurse Dunkley's home, conforming to the social requirements of her middle-class household. Had I chosen to stay late, I would have risked their hard-won trust and family loyalty, something I have cherished and would not be willing to relinquish. Thus it is only in another parish, St Elizabeth, where I have travelled for weekend breaks while doing fieldwork, that I have been to rural outdoor dancehalls past midnight to witness the transformations that take place as the composition of the crowd changes, the dancing becomes increasingly sexualized and the song lyrics become increasingly provocative. While I have not been present at this stage in Frankfield, I have nonetheless heard the music as clearly as if I were there, lying in bed wide awake at three o'clock in the morning, earplugs completely useless.

Following these all-night spectacles, sleepy churchgoers rouse themselves to pursue their life of respectability, while dancehall participants remain in bed. On one such morning, I spoke with two groups of adolescent black females, one group at the Methodist church in the centre of Frankfield and later a few whose families belong to an evangelical Church of God in Lampard district. Both groups of young women strive for modest femininity in their comportment, dress and behaviour. I asked them whether they attended the dancehall and received negative responses. One young woman told me with clear disdain, in agreement with their mothers, with whom I had already spoken, that they do not attend those "crazy dances" and referred to the "vulgar" language of the lyrics and dress of the female participants. When I asked why they thought the dances were so popular another young woman shrugged saying, "Me nah know. The people love it" (field notes, July 2007). Both statements may appear to express a derogatory dismissal of a colour/class of women whom they try to distinguish themselves from, but it is a conscious rejection to assert the upwardly mobile self. It is not only the lighter-skinned middle and upper classes who distinguish themselves from dancehall as a marker of their moral and cultural superiority and thus their "right to govern" as Stolzoff indicates (2000, 6), but rural working-class blacks and their adolescent female children in particular, aspiring to the middle class through behaviour and education, who distinguish themselves from those rural youth who like to act as if they are "from town". While colour and class are markers of identity, so is behaviour or performance of self. Performances of class, as Ulysse (2007) has pointed out, mediate these divisions, allowing the transcendence of colour categories. Thus, as Stolzoff explains, dancehall serves as a symbolic venue that people define themselves in relation to. Cooper asserts: "Their 'noise' can be simply dismissed as yet another example of the increasing vulgarity of both rural and urban life in Jamaica. Or it can be recognized as a profoundly malicious cry to upset the existing social order. Night noises that pollute middle-class neighbourhoods, disturb a neighbour's sleep, are a threatening challenge to those uneasily awake in comfortable beds" (1995, 5). Given these gender/colour/class disruptions, how does dancehall also reproduce heteropatriarchal norms amid shifting notions that encourage the open expressions of lower-class black female sexuality? Are the latter in fact liberatory acts within the context of their performance or, as Hope (2006, 69) argues, expressions of female sexuality firmly entrenched within "the promotion of a capitalist-influenced sexuality for the benefit of men" produced through lyrics? Hope, in a multiple-part article entitled "Courting and Conquering the Feared P——ny" (*Jamaica Gleaner*, 3 and 10 February 2002), analyses two kinds of dancehall lyrics written and sung by men that position women as sexual objects to be conquered, on the one hand, and, on the other, as mothers to be revered, their struggles noted and respected. Moreover, she points to the conflicting notions of masculinity in dancehall lyrics. The sexual symbolism revolves around "courting, conquering and/or dominance of female sexuality, femininity and women . . . [where] the female sex organ, the p——ny[5] (vagina) becomes the focus of intense lyrical attention. Arguably, this is an instance of patriarchy's operation at its elemental, basest and most sexual level, oftentimes labelled misogyny" (*Jamaica Gleaner*, 3 February 2002). Hope then shares a number of lyrics that speak to the violent conquest of the female sex organ such as Spragga Benz's song "Jack It Up": "*Jack it up, cock it up, dig out di red* (Lift it up, hoist it up, dig out the red[ness])". Hope also quotes from Red Dragon's "Agony": "*Mi have di agony, man mi have di agony, mi have di agony girls dem remedy* (I have the agony, oh yes I have the agony, I have the agony, the remedy [cure] for the girls [women])".

Hope, however, contends that "the misogynistic label" is a distraction from the true site of dancehall, away from reflection on the "negotiation of multiple masculinities as part of the lived realities of the actors in the dancehall. Instead, it seeks to reorient it around an invalid/inconsistent feminist discourse on the overt and covert use of violence against women as part of the symbols that are encoded in the dancehall":

> The selective usage of language/lyrics to court, conquer, subjugate and defeat the feared p——ny, i.e., the partner in intimate relationships, on the one hand, is coupled with language/lyrics that revere and uplift the perception of the womb, mother as a site of positive femininity whose role is to nurture and uplift masculinity. This duality of the male-female discourse in Jamaican dancehall music

speaks to the simultaneity of the love-hate relationship that is an ongoing part of the masculine engagement with the feminine "other" in Jamaica. (*Jamaica Gleaner*, 10 February 2002)

My intention here has been to point readers to the debates that scholars are engaging in, even with themselves, as Hope's own shifts in focus indicate. Dancehall is a site of cultural challenge to hierarchically ordained meanings associated with particular configurations of gender/race/colour/class. It is imbued at once with conflicting meanings, as are all complex cultural symbols. In this case, lyrics range from misogyny to mother-respect, dominant and conflicting masculinity as well as black female agency through fashion and sexual expression, breaking away from constrained "modest" femininity. Whether or not, as Bakare-Yusuf (2006) argues, the women who wear these fashions are consciously aiming to transform gender relationships, the in-your-face styles and in-your-ear night noise reverberate with confrontation. Bakare-Yusuf notes that many of women she interviewed did not intentionally aim to challenge hegemonic structures, but instead were "dressing for themselves" and expressing themselves. Dancehall, like other collective/cultural phenomena, is internalized and expressed uniquely. Even if the intention to resist gender definitions is not consciously embraced by individuals, they nonetheless embody an image of change through their performance of gender. It is questionable whether or not these collective expressions ultimately transform other features of the gender system outside of definitions of femininity (including greater decision-making power in political, economic and religious realms), and whether or not they generate shifts in the sexual division of labour that improve the earning potential of working-class black women and lead to a reduction of violence in everyday life. As I raised in the preface, I am sceptical about the viability of Butler's view that mocking performances of dominant gender norms lead to real change. Bakare-Yusuf (2006, 20–21) is more hopeful: "It is important to remember that Jamaican women have a long history of resisting oppressive regimes and articulating their existential positioning using a variety of media. I locate dancehall women's sartorial expression as a continuation of this history of resistance and cultural production." I would add that symbolic behaviour is a critical dimension of social change that opens the imagination to new potentialities, but it ultimately requires concrete transformations in economic and political opportunities. In rural settings such as Frankfield, the Afro-Jamaican gender system is challenged by this originally urban phenomenon, as competing and contradictory notions of femininity and masculinity are expressed through the dancehall space itself, taken up and disseminated in popular media, refracted through the scholarly gaze and worried about by town elites. It is both a rung of longevity-continuity and collectivity-uniqueness in the gender spiral.

GENDER SOCIALIZATION THEORY: STRENGTHS AND WEAKNESSES

Gender socialization of children by adults constitutes an important set of practices that stress the dominant definitions of femininity and masculinity acquired in daily life. This adds a third layer of influence to the two I have previously discussed. To reiterate briefly: the first is the impact of historical gender systems on gendered identity, and the access to political and economic resources it generated. The most significant of these was the plantocracy upon which notions of intersectional gender/race/colour/class were built out of the political, economic and cultural evolutionary perspectives of colonial slave society. The competing systems that shape the gendered identities of Frankfield residents include the role of the imagined, mythological gender system of Frankfield's Rastas and the nostalgia of Frankfield's elderly middle-class residents for the more rigid and ordered system of their youth in post-independence rural Jamaica. While the plantocracy generated structures of inequality around specific axes of identity including race, colour, class and gender, contemporary *imagined* gender systems also play a powerful role in shaping perceptions of self that give rise to individual and collective agency. We see this in Moses's and Priest's decisions, for instance, to pursue Rasta lifeways, including mentoring youth in the community, particularly male youth, in values of responsible manhood.

The second influence on gender identity formation that I have discussed is the force of popular culture as indicated in dancehall fashion and lyrics, some of which challenge persistent ideologies of masculinity and femininity. Nonetheless, an important mitigating factor that highlights the longevity and collectivity features of the rural black gender system is gender socialization. Gender socialization refers to the process through which children acquire the characteristics of masculinity and femininity defined by the wider society. For scholars of socialization, the social roles assigned to men and women begin with specific teachings and practices in childhood that seek to inculcate children into the dominant values of the society that pertain to masculinity and femininity. Childhood is therefore considered the most significant period in the life cycle for shaping gender-role behaviour and the identity that emerges later in life. As feminist sociologists Stanley and Wise point out, however, gender socialization theory is problematic in that it "postulates a pre-formed and almost autonomously unfolding ego which develops independently of the social . . . it sees what happens in social reality 'outside' of the child as independent of these processes and irrelevant to them" (1993, 101). It is also overly deterministic, presenting an over-socialized conception of people, presumed to be as overly passive without self-reflexivity, and the choices people make are assumed to be the outcome of their childhood experiences. I would argue that the process parents are engaging in with their children in Frankfield does embrace an awareness of the social, and children are regarded as deeply embedded within a matrix of relationships that the socialization process aims at either maintaining or intervening in, depending on whether or not parents regard the relationships as supportive or detrimental to their core values.

In the ensuing discussion of gender socialization, I outline the various factors that shape the process, including parents and the wider kin group, teachers, peers, religious institutions and the media. These agents of socialization, particularly parents and teachers, seek simultaneously to enculturate and socialize, endowing children not only with appropriate behaviours but with the cultural ideologies of masculinity and femininity that they believe will produce heterosexual, hard-working, upwardly mobile community members. Even though gender systems are in flux, it is possible to identify a set of generally shared cultural notions about how girls and boys are different and how they should mature, drawing on the pervasive biological essentialist model that parents and teachers seek to convey to children about gendered behaviour.

SOCIAL ROLES ASSIGNED TO GIRLS AND BOYS: SOCIALIZATION THROUGH THE LIFE CYCLE

From infancy to around age five, the rural, outdoor yard remains the domain of young children and their mothers as well as other female relatives residing in the household. There is an attempt to construct the yard as a bounded sphere, protected from conflicting and emergent concepts of masculinity and femininity that more easily penetrate the primary school environment because of its proximity to other spheres of cultural life. Within the yard, women seek to shield young children from those competing values and norms about gender that might threaten the ideals that adults hold for their children. Within this gendered space, small boys and girls are watched closely until they are old enough to go to school, and when gender differences begin to be increasingly emphasized. At this time, boys and girls begin to live in increasingly gender-separate worlds. While some men prefer to have boys, Chevannes's study (2001) underscored that there is a strong preference for daughters, at least among women in the inner city. This seems to be generally true in the rural areas as well, particularly as young men eschew farm work, leaving middle-aged and older men to the physically demanding labour of work "in the bush". Some reasons cited for this preference include the following: boys are more anti-social and likely to get into drugs, gangs, and crime; boys are hard to control; girls help more around the house; girls do better in school; and girls are less likely to abandon their parents in old age.

Around age five, explicit role differentiation begins, influenced by the strong identification that women feel with their daughters. By treating their sons in opposition to their own femininity, boys begin the process of taking on masculine roles and dispositions. Boys acquire gender-appropriate identity both through separation from their caretakers and active association with older boys and men. When coeducation begins, boys are encouraged to run errands, congregate with other boys and, in adolescence, acquire sexually aggressive norms of behaviour. Girls play with other girls, continuing to identify with their mothers and other female kin, taking on greater household responsibilities and aspiring still to the traits of a lady (Justus 1981; Douglass 1992). They are encouraged to go directly to school and return to the yard immediately after classes. Girls are expected to perform well in school, and they are increasingly outpacing boys academically in Jamaica. Still, girls have many household chores including cooking, cleaning and tending younger siblings, so they learn to work hard and manage significant responsibility early on. Girls take pride in their household responsibilities but are also resentful of the position of boys, who have fewer responsibilities and much greater freedom for play, leisure and observation of the world of men outside the home. Mothers and daughters are often emotionally close, but adolescence brings tensions as girls seek more freedoms. Mothers give their sons some household chores, so they can learn to take care of themselves, but not to the same extent as girls. If a chore requires leaving the yard, or if it is "rough work", then it will be given to a boy. By the age of nine or ten, a farm boy will look after livestock and go to the field with his father (Chevannes 2001).

Children are generally believed to be "rude" and are subjected to harsh discipline to teach "manners". Discipline takes the form of verbal threats, "bad words" and "floggings" by the mother, father or other adults in the household. Mothers are generally responsible for the discipline of young children and girls. Older boys are believed to be particularly "rough" and therefore in need of the father's discipline. Although boys may have little contact with their fathers, who may not live with or near them, they receive significantly more punishment than girls, and physical abuse is a problem, particularly with stepfathers (Bailey 2004).

BEYOND THE YARD: GENDER SOCIALIZATION IN ADOLESCENCE

The socialization of boys and girls diverges more sharply in adolescence. Girls are still confined to the home, mainly because at the onset of puberty they are at risk of rape and pregnancy. As is true in many parts of the world, parents worry especially about their daughters' safety and fear early pregnancy because of financial burden, the long-term effect on their schooling, and the shame it brings on the girl and her family. Pregnant high school girls still must leave school; if they are fortunate, they may be able to continue their studies at homes for pregnant teens. This separation is a clear indication of symbolic and actual ostracism and sexism.

Boys, on the other hand, are now hanging out on the street, the domain of men, and becoming independent. Mothers know they should not be too "soft" on boys. If a boy stays in the home and does household chores, he risks being labelled a sissy or "mama-boy". Men are expected to be strong, tough, dominant providers. Boys need to move to the streets to develop these characteristics and become men, particularly in the absence of significant fathering. It is generally believed that girls attend school more often than boys, perform better in school and receive more education, for a variety of reasons. First, school is essentially a feminine institution where the majority of teachers and principals are women; therefore, boys often believe that doing well in school is for "sissies". Second, teachers have a gender bias: they believe girls are generally serious and attentive, whereas boys are simply not (Bailey 2004). Not surprisingly, teachers are more lenient with girls and punish boys more often, frequently employing corporeal punishment. Third, parents believe that education will offer more career opportunities for girls than for boys, so girls receive more encouragement and support to go to school. Fourth, school is for children, and boys are anxious to become men. Fifth, by this age boys have learned that men should dominate women, and boys do dominate girls on the playground (ibid.), but not in the classroom. Finally, by adolescence, if not sooner, boys have learned that a man's role is to become the breadwinner and head of household, both roles that do not depend on schooling.

Statistics collected from the Frankfield Primary and Infant School and Edwin Allen Regional High School bear out some of these ideas. At the primary level for the 2006–2007 school year, 608 boys were registered at the school as opposed to 568 girls. In all of the classes, infant through grade six, with the exception of grade one, there were more boys than girls (Attendance Data, Frankfield Primary School, 26 February 2007). At the high school, for the 2006–2007 school year, there were 999 boys registered as opposed to 1,194 girls. Significantly, starting in grade eight, the numbers begin to show significant differences in enrolment. In grade seven there were 223 boys and 241 girls; in grade eight, 208 boys and 251 girls; in grade nine, 161 boys and 240 girls; in grade ten, 193 boys and 219 girls; in grade eleven, 204 boys and 243 girls (attendance data 2006–2007, Edwin Allen Regional High School).

There are few economic opportunities for adolescent boys who drop out of school, at least in the formal sector. Younger adolescent boys are frequently seen around town working in shops, pushing wooden carts loaded with various goods, or outside of town, working on citrus farms, toting large bags of oranges on their heads. Older boys may gather in peer groups, on street corners or at "rum shops", talking, joking, drinking, dancing, gambling, playing games such as dominoes and making advances to girls who pass by. If they have money or relatives overseas who send them care packages, they might dress up in flamboyant, brand-name fashions, attending dancehalls and bars in the evening. The lack of jobs and pressure to have money lead many in the inner city into drug dealing, gangs, hustling and theft at a surprisingly young age. Increasingly, as I pointed out in chapter 2, fears of gang activity are being felt throughout the rural areas, as gangs disburse to cities throughout the island, closer to rural communities.

The most pressing concern of adolescence is becoming sexually active.

Becoming a man or a woman is connected to sexuality. Children grow up in a sexually paradoxical world, where double standards abound. The church and middle-class morality constrain sexual expression of women, while sexually explicit lyrics permeate reggae, hip hop and dancehall music, referring particularly to women's vaginas as the proper locus of male attention and to chi-chi men as societal scourges. Softly pornographic girly pictures are also rampant in advertising and public spaces. Yet parents and teachers rarely discuss sex with their children. Instead, they learn from older peers, cable television and, increasingly, the Internet. While protecting their daughters, parents ignore or at least tolerate the sexual activity of their sons. Male sexual prowess is idealized in the culture. In order to be a man, a boy must become sexually active, preferably with several girls, and he is under pressure from his peers to display his manhood through heterosexual activity. Violent threats against homosexuals are also an assertion of masculinity, ensuring that those who display their anti-gay sentiment are not characterized as such. Boys generally become sexually active between the ages of fourteen and fifteen, and girls between sixteen and seventeen (Chevannes 2001), although sexual activity itself is not representative of adult status.

Once a young woman has completed her schooling and a young man can support himself, then having children is considered to be a normal, natural and necessary part of life. In fact, a childless woman is sometimes referred to derisively as a "mule". Working-class children grow up in multi-family yards in the cities and towns or extended family households in the countryside. Children are cared for not only by their parents, but also by older siblings and adults, kin or non-kin.

Women's space is the yard or home and associated buildings (outhouse, wash basin, animal pens, fruit trees and garden). Across race/colour/class lines, women are largely responsible for the care of children, and they acquire significant status through mothering activities, many of which take place in the yard. The yard is considered to be the safe space where such nurturing occurs, while the world beyond is seen as dangerous, especially in the inner city. Many working- and middle-class women without children take in the children of others, caring for them as their own. Motherwork, which extends to aunts and grandmothers, includes nurturing and affectionate behaviour, mild scolding and instruction in gender-linked household chores. Girls learn feminine tasks such as cooking, laundry, sweeping and sewing. In rural areas, boys help their fathers with farm activities, hauling water and collecting wood. In practice, this ideal of sex-role training is more fluid: boys and men do help with house-hold chores while girls may also work with their fathers in productive activities outside the home (Fox 1999).

Men's place is beyond the home, in the fields, the town squares in the country, city streets, bars and the workplace. Fathers are defined predominantly as breadwinners and disciplinarians of children across class lines. Mothers flog their daughters, but leave the threats of "wicked floggings" to fathers (Chevannes 2001). Although households are mother-centred, fathers maintain social dominance even in absentia. Fathers are more likely to be stable members of households in middle- and upper-class families, but their activities also take them away from the household, and they are rarely available as emotional resources for boys. Boys therefore identify with fathers who are unable to assume fully their functions (Justus 1981). In Rastafarian households and communities, which strive for economic self-reliance and subsistence, fathers are known to take on more affectionate roles; however, here, too, they remain disciplinarians and women retain the primary role of nurturer. In a random survey of men in Frankfield Square one day in the summer of 2006, they responded to the question "What does it mean to be a man?" in the following ways, demonstrating the persistence of the frequently competing ideals of responsibility, economic success represented in acquisition of material goods, and sexual dominance that pervade gender ideologies of manhood:

- Doing what life and people expect from him (age 46)
- Taking responsibility in the home (age 24)
- Taking responsibility in the home and takes care of his kids (age 35)
- Thinking for yourself (age 36)
- Having a house and a car (age 26)
- Being in charge (age 40)
- Being the leader (age 33)
- Setting the example for the youths (age 37)
- Having responsibilities (age 27)
- Being the head of the house (age 33)
- Having many women (age 39)

One unusual comment in its self-reflection and view of women was made by a forty-year-old single man working as a store manager. He said that a man is "someone who understands himself, because some men are abusive because they lack understanding". He also expressed that women are "perfect, gentle and stronger than men".

For most, a boy becomes a man when he is able to support and defend himself, dominate women, and be sexually active. He can then enter into a regular sexual relationship publicly. He is formally an adult when he earns enough money to establish a household and support himself, a woman and his children. This is particularly difficult for working-class men, owing to a lack of good jobs. Consequently, adolescence is prolonged, for many men, well into their twenties, during which time they may continue to live with parents (Justus 1981).

A girl starts to become a woman with her first menses. In order to be considered an adult, though, she must become independent of the often-severe restrictions imposed by her parents. In the middle class, this is often accomplished through marriage. In the working-class majority, however, it is generally achieved through pregnancy, which could be viewed as an act of rebellion or defiance (Brody 1974). I conducted a similar series of random interviews among women in Frankfield who were walking about town in the summer of 2006, asking them the question "What does it mean to you to be an adult woman?" They responded in a variety of interesting ways that suggested the emerging ideals of independence, equality and financial self-sufficiency as well as the ongoing persistence of female subordination. The responses included the following:

- Working hard to get whatever you want (age 20)
- Being unhappy at times and undergoing pain and stress (age 25)
- Understanding that life is not equal especially when one faces gender inequality as a never-dying obstacle in the search for success (age 23)
- Doing hard work and having responsibilities (age 30)
- Being different and your own unique person (age 25)
- Being on your own (age 22)
- Being independent (age 40)
- Having a good character (age 41)
- Being recognized equally as men (age 25)
- Being treated with respect (age 25)
- Living a good life (age 21)
- Having children and know their responsibilities in the home (age 29)

The goals of independent womanhood, including financial security, are initially thwarted by an early first pregnancy. If living at home, parents perceive this pregnancy with strong disapproval, causing the girl to seek refuge with kin or friends, who intercede with her parents on her behalf so she can return home. After the birth of the child, the girl's mother assumes full control over it, but it is understood that the daughter will be responsible for the care of subsequent children (Chevannes 2001).

Subsequently, a young woman is freer to enter into the world of the street and adult life and form relationships with men, both casual and long-term, including co-residential unions. Typically, a working-class woman will have several "visiting" relationships in her late teens and twenties, resulting in children from several fathers. Pregnancy sometimes seems to be an attempt to "cement" a relationship (Brody 1974). The illegitimacy rate is high – 87 per cent in 1995. Of those born out of wedlock, the father was legally registered in only 41 per cent in 1995, although a majority will acknowledge paternity informally and offer some support.

MARRIAGE AND KINSHIP BEHAVIOUR

Another feature of a gender system is marriage and kinship behaviour. In Jamaica, particularly among the working class, legal marriage is a rare but highly prized status, reflecting conjugal and economic stability, as well as conformity with church morality. Since 1887, when civil registration for marriage was first institutionalized, marriage rates have remained low among Jamaica's working-class majority. In 1988 the rate was 4.4/1,000 (Douglass 1992). Three forms of partnering prevail: legal marriage, common-law marriage and visiting arrangements. Multiple partnering is also common. It is culturally acceptable for a man to have more than one woman since men are expected to be promiscuous by nature. Women seek multiple partners as well, as sources of economic support.

Marriage tends to occur near the end of childbearing years rather than before or during childbearing. Eighty per cent of the total population is legally single, including 69 per cent of those over the age of sixteen. On the other hand, many adults are involved in relatively long-term, often stable, co-residential common-law unions. The marriage rate has been increasing of late, rising from 4.7 marriages per 1,000 people in 1989 to 10.3 in 1999. The average

age at first marriage is thirty-three, and takes place when a couple can pay for the ceremony and a separate household, and have already produced offspring from previous non-legal unions. According to a recent report in the *Jamaica Gleaner* (20–26 December 2001), Jamaica has the latest age of first marriage for women and the second latest age for men in the world. These patterns are reflected in household composition. According to the *Jamaica Survey of Living Conditions 1998*, "[72] per cent of the female-headed households had no spouse present" which contrasts to male-headed households where women were present 73 per cent of the time (PIOJ/STATIN 1999). The survey also notes that there is considerable variation in the proportion of female-headed households both with and without children, from parish to parish, ranging from 36 per cent to 56 per cent for the former and 73 per cent to 87 per cent for the latter. Notably, it is Clarendon parish with the highest percentage. Interestingly, there is also "a marked difference in the amount of elderly females (41 per cent) who live alone compared to their male counterparts (19 per cent)", yet among the working age population, 81 per cent of males lived alone as compared to 59 per cent of females. This trend simultaneously reveals the increased risk of poverty for elderly women and the continued dependency of women on men for economic support.

Marriage is more common, and occurs earlier, in the brown and black middle classes and the upper class dominated by whites, where it is hypergamous and occurs earlier in life with women in their early twenties and men in their late twenties (Douglass 1992). Among the black working class, older adults often become parents again when they are grandparents, when women who have migrated to the city or abroad send children home to the country to be raised for a time by their own mothers.

Christian, working- and middle-class marriage ceremonies take place in churches with wedding receptions often occurring outdoors at a relative's home. Amid music arranged by a soundsystem, toasts are made and "box lunches" of fried chicken or curried goat are served. Among the upper classes, church weddings are followed by lavish receptions with extravagant meals, and men make toasts in honour of their wives.

When working-class women marry they do not expect romantic love, although it does exist. Instead, they "look money" and status, while men "look sex" (Sobo 1993). Many men and women avoid marriage because of lack of trust, poor communication and economic wariness. Women believe men will avoid financial responsibility and men fear women's control over them. Common-law arrangements indicate a common household without legal sanction, while visiting relations involve neither legal sanction nor a common household. Common law is by far the most popular conjugal bond of the working classes. Working-class women first enter into visiting relationships in their twenties, but tend to move into common-law arrangements after they have their first child (Brody 1981). Both for common-law and married relationships a system of bilateral kinship exists, through which children's descent is reckoned through both parents. Besson also points out that "serial polyandry" and "serial polygyny" (sequential husbands and wives) are common practices (1998, 138).

Visiting relations are a form of extended courtship with a sexual component, involving frequent meetings when couples live close to one another. Men are expected to help financially with a woman's children, particularly if the man is her baby-father. During visiting meetings couples go on outings together to clubs, parties, sports events, the beach and church (Roberts and Sinclair 1978).

Children are taught by early adolescence that men initiate courtship through the use of their bodies and that women who do so are considered "bad" women, without sexual control. Based on my interviews with adolescent girls attending Edwin Allen Regional High School, it appears that this particular norm is shifting. Certainly, the teenaged girls discussed in chapter 3, who initiated sexual unions with adolescent boys and sugar daddies, did not consider themselves "bad", even though this perception is maintained by adults. Before dancehall, initial sexual contact was likely to occur when a man conveyed his interest in a woman with sexual comments or "lyrics", leading to the woman accepting advances by permitting the man to hold her hand (Chevannes 2001). Smith (1960) maintained that chaperoning, where a third party should be present, is the ideal form of courtship for working-class parents, who assume that sexual intercourse is inevitable if the pair is left alone. My own fieldwork experience indicates that this ideal is no longer a reality. In addition to conversations with adolescents who readily indicate that sexual activity is the norm, there are multiple pathways for initiating sexual conduct outside a parent's gaze, in addition to dancehall. On one occasion, as I walked down a rural road with a farmer who was going to show me his farm, we passed a group of three or four adolescent boys and girls playfully laughing and walking closely together. My farmer friend turned to me and said, "They're on their way to have sex." I asked him how he knew, and he pointed to a house up the hill, indicating that was where they go and suggesting this was a known fact. Sexual rendezvous are also initiated by clandestine communications. An individual who wishes to have sex with another will wait until a third party informs him or her that it is safe to go to a particular place to meet up. The prevalence of cellular telephones is also creating opportunities to connect outside the watchful eyes of adults.

The ease of multiple sexual engagements encourages one of the key characteristics of working- and middle-class male/female relationships prior to marriage: mistrust. However, affection between men and women grows, especially with age, as reproductive roles become less significant and trust increases (Fox 1999). Still, a man's influence extends over his family and wives are supposed to listen to husbands. Both legal and common-law marriages are regarded as economic arrangements to share sexually divided work, although this ideal is not as rigidly adhered to as it is described and husbands and wives often assist one another in their respective tasks. Because marriage is a symbol of respectability, legally married couples, in particular, work to maintain an image of stability, legitimacy and propriety by participating in community life. Love and status are important motivations for marriage for the upper classes. Middle-class families strive to emulate husband-wife relationships in elite families.

Jamaica ranks tenth on the list of lowest divorce rates in the world. In 1999, there were 4.4/10,000 divorces. Women more often than men instigate divorce for all classes of Jamaicans. Between 1989 and 1997 all divorces fell under the grounds of irretrievable breakdown of the marriage. Divorce remains a stigma for women, many who move abroad or away from the community to avoid social isolation (Douglass 1992). There is a "cultural promiscuity of violence" perpetuated by men who regard wife-beating as an acceptable form of chastisement for what they regard as insufficient domestic or sexual services or lack of respect. Men also identify women with children, using violence as form of punishment for disobedience (Bailey 2004).

GENDER ROLES IN ECONOMICS: THE SEXUAL DIVISION OF LABOUR

According to the International Labour Organization, in 1999, 10.3 per cent of men and 22.3 per cent of women were unemployed, referring to those without paid work. In 1999, 73 per cent of men and 55 per cent of women were economically active. Women predominate in the informal sector as informal traders or higglers. The upheavals of the mid nineteenth century – the abolition of slavery, the failed apprenticeship programme that had intended to keep former slaves on plantations while ostensibly transitioning them into wage labour, as well the arrival of Chinese, Indian, Lebanese, Syrian and Jewish immigrants – created competition for work. In this difficult climate, women entered higglering as a substitute for unavailable income for black men, who turned increasingly to migration, a pattern that continues today. Throughout the twentieth century, higglering has played a critical role "to replace the absent family wage of the male breadwinner and to fulfill societal expectations of their gender" (Ulysse 2007, 69). Scholars have also noted different forms of higglering, generating various typologies that indicate rural versus urban higglers, the frequency of trading as well as the kinds of goods sold, in addition to farmers' produce which they have purchased (p. 70). Some higglers, for instance, sell homemade sweets, clothing, household goods or school supplies at small stands outside school buildings. Besson (1998, 146) has noted that in the parish of Trelawny, a trend towards gender differentiation in dry-goods higglering, with men selling items of clothing, matches, cookware and the like, is increasing as a "transnational, postmodern method of sustainable development". As produce from the United States and goods from China increasingly flood the Jamaican market, there is some interchangeability in male and female roles among the peasantry. Flexibility in this particular arena of the gendered division of labour is necessary for survival. Hence, long-term adaptability to shifting economic conditions is the driving force behind this increased rate of change in gender roles, rather than shifts in gender ideology. It is also possible that some of these women have become informal commercial importers, travelling to Miami to buy cheap goods and back again to sell them, as Ulysse's ethnographic study has demonstrated (2007). However, I did not investigate this potential aspect of the gendered division of labour in Frankfield.

Frankfield's community market reflects similar patterns seen in rural areas throughout the island. Most of the vendors are women, although increasingly men sell dry-goods commodities. Notably, the head of the market is a man, who explained:

> The market operates three days of the week: Thursday, Friday and Saturday. The vendors, mostly the women, carry their products such as yam, banana, onion, pear, coconut, et cetera. These produces are called ground provision. Others, men

and women, carry cloth, plates, shoes, et cetera. These are called haberdashery. The men are the butchers who carry meat such as beef, pork and goat meat. There are women vendors selling fish too. There are about sixty vendors or higglers in the market on market days. There are more women than men who sell in this market. Higglering is a main source of income in Frankfield. (Field notes, May 2007)

Notably it is female higglers, typically black working-class women, who play a central role in Jamaican folk culture as strong, independent women. They are, nonetheless, low status along with other female-linked, informal sector positions such as domestic workers and prostitutes. Nonetheless, female higglers, as sellers of ground provisions, have constituted the "backbone of Jamaica's domestic economy since slavery days" (Besson 1998, 148).

Another historically prevalent adaptation to limited financial means among the working class, derived from West Africa, is the informal savings institution known as *pardner* (partner). In this arrangement, people pool their money to a common fund, either maintained informally or in recent years, through banks. Members take turns drawing from it to pay for major expenses such as a car, school fees or large appliances, or the establishment of microenterprises. A third key strategy for getting out of poverty is migration for both men and women. In 1999, 47 per cent of migrants travelling to Canada and 49 per cent travelling to the United States were male. The female majority obtains positions as domestics, nannies and cooks. Migration also occurs from parish to parish within Jamaica, particularly to work in the tourist industry on the north coast, and to the United Kingdom. Increasing numbers of Jamaicans migrate to work in tourist communities along the north coast. Women work as vendors of souvenirs and crafts, and as maids. Women may manage small resorts for their husbands and sons, but it is men who benefit from the big money in tourism derived from land speculation and enterprise, as well as drugs. Men also produce and sell woodcarvings and jewellery (McKay 1993).

The growth of the electronics and textile manufacturing sectors in the 1960s and 1970s, and again in the 1990s, spurred on by so-called free trade agreements, led large numbers of young women to relocate to urban areas to work in factories for low wages, few benefits, cramped work conditions and long hours in insecure jobs. This feminization of the labour force is partly due, according to Barrow (1998a, xxii), to the preferences among employers for women, "based on patriarchal assumptions of a labour reservoir of daughters and wives". Women therefore work in greater numbers on the factory floor in free-trade zones overseen by male managers. They have not been encouraged to join labour unions, even though they are the most exploited workers, receiving the lowest wages, and the fewest opportunities to increase their skills. Even when women have joined the labour movement, they

> have internalized gender stereotypes and suffered the effects. They have little confidence in themselves or each other and are frustrated and critical of their own involvement in what they know to be highly patriarchal associations. They are bypassed in critical contract negotiations, deprived of resources and training, and what influence they have had has been confined to routine matters of office management, social welfare, and support services. A woman who challenges this is an "upstart", who "must be put in her place". (p. xxii)

Nonetheless, as Bolles points out, the labour movement across the Caribbean has survived in large part due to women's persistent participation (cited in Barrow 1998a, xxii). However, male dominance in managerial and executive positions within in labour unions is also reflected in the work force. Both men and women work long hours with little pay on agricultural plantations (for example, banana, cane, coffee) and throughout the economy, constituted by agriculture (23 per cent); industry, such as bauxite mining (0.6–0.7 per cent); manufacturing (10–11 per cent); wholesale, retail, hotel and restaurant services (21.1 per cent) and community, social and personal services (25.2 per cent) (all statistics from 1996; see Alleyne 2000).

RELATIONS OF POWER: GENDER AND POLITICS

Both Barriteau and Mohammed speak to the importance of power dynamics structuring relationships between men and women as a component of gender systems. While I have already alluded to power relationships in household life and the assertion of heteropatriarchal power in defining sexually appropriate behaviour, politics is another explicit domain of male power. Political position is viewed as an unfeminine realm (Senior 1991) although with the election of Portia Simpson as prime minister in 2006 and the appointment of women in ministerial positions across the Caribbean, this pattern is slowly changing. At the same time, there are restraints to change. The campaign to oust Simpson from power in 2007, mentioned in chapter 2, reinforced a race/colour/class ideology of gender, suggesting that Simpson, a black woman, had overstepped her bounds in achieving national political leadership. On a daily basis, women, particularly those from the working class, are overburdened with domestic responsibilities, leaving them with little or no time for politics, and they often eschew political discussions because of the violence and divisiveness associated with elections and party politics. I found this to be common in Frankfield. Nurse Dunkley and her friends often waved their hands or shook their heads in dismissal when I would raise political conversations, asking for opinions about particular party platforms and candidates. Nonetheless, during the 2007 campaign, some women refused to wear red or orange, the colour of the People's National Party, in favour of green, the colour of the Jamaica Labour Party, symbolically displaying their political preference. In fact, initially ignorant about this practice, I gave some women reddish-orange T-shirts as gifts on my arrival in June 2007, only to be told that the shirts would be consigned to a drawer until after the elections. Openly sharing one's political views, however, is regarded as divisive of the more important bonds of kinship, friendship and church sisterhood, particularly among women who may not share similar views.

Men, on the other hand, being largely free from domestic responsibilities, can dominate the political arena. Middle-class women are active in political parties, especially in campaigns, but serve mainly in supportive roles, at the lowest levels, as in other spheres of Jamaican life. Women are, however, beginning to gain greater influence in politics and other public arenas. As feminism has become an active force in the region, its proponents have generated research and raised issues of special relevance to women, including domestic abuse, sexual harassment in the workplace, equal opportunity in the labour force and the like. Numerous organizations advocating the advancement of women have emerged. In addition, women are moving into middle- and upper-level managerial and professional roles. Nonetheless, women are still mainly valued as mothers, not only by men, but by many women themselves.

RELATIONS OF POWER: GENDER AND RELIGION

Religion is a second arena of power relationships between women and men. As I stated earlier, bodily differences are understood by many rural Jamaicans to be foundational to gender-role differentiation, expressing a kind of folk-biological essentialism. Many regard the relationship between the sociocultural world and human biology as divinely ordained, the body as the vessel through which gendered meanings and power relationships, laid forth in scripture, are "read" and performed (Ortner 1996, 441).

Indeed, no newcomer to Jamaica can overlook the pervasiveness of the church in daily life. Tour guides and locals alike inform visitors that "there are more churches per square mile in Jamaica than any other country in the world". This piece of trivia symbolizes the extent to which church life and religious beliefs permeate so many aspects of daily life, both reflecting and shaping gender ideologies and relationships. As in other areas of Jamaican life, the leaders of most churches are men, performing public, status-accruing roles such as preaching and collecting the offering. However, the majority of members are women, who are responsible for more inconspicuous, typically domestic, tasks and they are more highly represented in church organizations. Men and women believe that women are more "spiritual" than men, which is to say, more likely to become ecstatic in a service, a notion that reflects the role of the church with respect to women's "suffering, malaise, and healing". These issues are as real, "and sometimes more real, than issues of class interest and conflict" (Austin-Broos 1997, 157–58).

There are four significant forms of religion in Jamaica today. The traditional Christian churches, including the Anglicans, Baptists, Methodists and Presbyterians, were established in the early nineteenth century and hold the allegiance of 25 per cent of the population, according to the 1991 census. Their membership has declined drastically during the twentieth century. Revival, an indigenous, folk or Creole religion (also known as Zion and Pocomania) that developed in the mid nineteenth century, is not recorded in the census. The Pentecostal Christian churches, which date to at least 1918, have grown steadily and are now the most popular, at 29 per cent. Finally, the famous messianic, millenarian Rastafarian movement, which originated in Jamaica in the 1930s, has had a dramatic impact on Jamaican culture even though it accounts for less than 1 per cent of the population.

Pentecostalism and Rastafari both developed in the early twentieth century and are markedly gendered; indeed, each of them has redefined gender roles in ways that are at odds with each other. According to the 1991 census, 57 per cent of Pentecostals are women, and the percentage of women at services is generally much greater. In contrast, Rastafarians are overwhelmingly (81 per cent) male (Sir Arthur Lewis Institute of Social and Economic Studies).

Pentecostal churches attract young, single, working-class mothers in particular. Although Pentecostal congregations are led largely by men, women can attain positions of leadership, including that of pastor. The ideology of these churches is essentially a protest against male domination and exploitation of women, particularly male "promiscuity" and "irresponsibility". Diane Austin-Broos has noted that churches play a central role in women's conception of themselves in relation to their circumstances. They "provide one way in which [women] can directly respond to a larger hierarchical order that intersects with their gender relations" (1997, 156). Many women in attendance, for instance, are raising children either without a male partner or with a partner in absentia due to migration. Pentecostalism offers them an opportunity to be "cleansed" from fornication and make them "brides of Christ" with the support and protection of the congregation. Jesus is the faithful, dependable husband (a type apparently lacking in "the world") as well as an alternative role model for male converts who have been "saved" from the world of sin.

Because Jamaican churches blend both hegemonic elements and opportunities for creative expression, women are also able to redefine their social positions negotiating leadership in church organizations, asserting their independence from men. However, women follow strict rules of dress and demeanour associated with modesty (Austin-Broos 1987). June-Ann Castello has also noted that within many denominations in Jamaica, women must satisfy specific criteria if their performance of Christianity is to be accepted. Among these, "women must not expose arms or legs or provide a hint of cleavage. They must not wear 'male' clothing; that is, trousers . . . they cannot shake their 'booty' in Jesus' name because to come into the presence of perfect holiness is to leave the 'booty' matter behind" (2004, 293). Clearly there is friction between persistent and emergent realms of Jamaica's gender system with the church in opposition to the influence that dancehall exerts on the public display of female bodies.

The Rastafarian movement seeks to liberate black people from white oppression; ironically, it also promotes male domination and female subordination (Lake 1994). As per observations, men are the designated spiritual leaders of the movement, the heads of households and the rulers of women. They are to "spread their seed" without regard to their marital status, while their wives must remain faithful. At the same time, however, men are to be sensitive to the needs of their wives and develop a close relationship with their children. A woman becomes a Rasta through her man. She should wear a long dress and cover her head. She should not speak in church or talk directly to God, and is subject to menstrual taboos when she is "unclean". One of the main aims of

Rastafarianism is to reassert the dominance of poor and working-class men, perhaps in response to a matrifocal upbringing. It also offers a new male identity, based on Haile Selassie, the black messiah, possibly as a substitute for the absent father. Barry Chevannes provides an overview of the development of these beliefs in his book *Rastafari: Roots and Ideology* (1994).

In general, for a significant number of Jamaicans, God, the creator and master of the elements, is generally a peripheral but benevolent figure who is respected and perhaps feared. Haile Selassie, the Rastafarian saviour, is regal, dignified and powerful, but he is also a kind, compassionate man of peace. Jesus is seen as a merciful, loving, forgiving friend and protector. The Holy Spirit is the force or power behind the ecstatic experiences of revivalists and Pentecostals. Revivalists interact with a number of male and female angels, who bring power and knowledge. Satan is a demonically male personage, particularly to Pentecostals, aided by apparently genderless "fallen angels". Many Jamaicans also believe in *duppies*: spirits of the dead, of either gender, generally malicious, but not always, who are claimed to visit people at night while they dream.

In the face of the assertions of patriarchal norms among Rastamen, Rastawomen are beginning to reassess the dynamics of their gender relationships within the movement. Tafari-Ama explains the ideological roots of this feminist movement, linking it to the historical paradigm of the Caribbean women's movement, which is "informed by the living metaphor of a rebel woman tradition in the person of Nanny the Ashanti Maroon queen" (1998, 90). Through this identification with a national heroine, Rastawomen are challenging the traditional patriarchal relations of Rastafari families, issuing a new "dawn [that] is hastened by the awakening consciousness of the 'sistren', the sometimes silent rebels" (ibid.). Tafari-Ama further acknowledges that the spiritual awakening that is conferred through participation in Rastafari has provided fodder for these shifts, as Rastawomen embrace their roles as queens and empresses in relation to the Rastaman as "king . . . ministering to his queen and offspring in domestic affairs" while simultaneously challenging manifestations of patriarchy in role divisions, menstrual taboos and male spiritual dominance (p. 92).

Rastafari is not unique in its religious manifestation of patriarchy. Christianity brought European morality to Jamaica where it became the bastion of middle-class respectability, centring on the sanctity of marriage, the nuclear family, the patriarchal role of the husband as provider and head of the family, and the wife as homemaker and mother. The working class was thereby excluded and developed Revival as an alternative. However, when a working-class woman gets married, she often joins a Christian church as a sign of her new status. These churches are always led by men, and about 45 per cent of their members are male. About half of all Revival churches, on the other hand, are led by women, and men made up only 37 per cent of a large congregation studied by William Wedenoja. A leading expert on Jamaican revivalism, Wedenoja (1989) notes that revivalists practise a popular form of healing known as *balm*, which is usually performed by an older woman referred to as a "Mother". Mother offers divinations, baths, herbs, candles, incense and prayers to cure spiritual afflictions. Healing is therefore associated with women, and the healing relationship is modelled on the mother-child relationship. In contrast, *obeah*, the practice of sorcery, is always practised by men, as is *science*, the use of magic for good fortune.

SUMMARY: RELATIVE STATUS OF MEN AND WOMEN IN THE RURAL BLACK JAMAICAN GENDER SYSTEM

In this chapter, I have presented the collective features configuring this contemporary gender system. Visualized as a "molecule" in the form of DNA, its backbone of intertwining masculinity and femininity encases the specific systemic components as indicated by the chapter's subheadings. These features are bonded by longevity-mutability and collectivity-uniqueness. As Tafari-Ama has observed, the longevity of male dominance in religious leadership, for instance, is undergoing shifts within the Rastafari movement as women consciously draw from regional feminist scholarship to re-imagine their place within Rastafari beyond domestic and sexual servants of men (1998).

I have also sought to avoid the pitfalls of homogenizing, flattening and portraying an ethnographic present and indicating variations from the black rural gender system, indicating across race/colour/class lines. In this vein I have pointed to emerging changes, especially in cultural definitions of femininity through a greater assertion of sexual agency by adolescent girls both in transactional sex and through dancehall culture. Given the nature of this collectivity and my initial suggestion of variation, what can we conclude about the relative status of women and men in this gender system?

First, women are better educated, have a higher rate of literacy and a greater life expectancy than men, but in every other respect there is inequality. Men are the official heads of households, the leaders in government, politics and churches, and the managers of businesses and industries. Men control the major institutions of society, including the economic and political systems and the media. Women, regardless of class, race or colour, are subordinate to men in almost every sphere of life. The main areas in which women have influence are within mother-centred homes, child rearing, education, churches, higglering, healing and hospitals.

Male dominance is particularly clear in relationships between the sexes, which have been characterized as adversarial and lacking in trust (Bailey 2004). Women are expected to cater to the needs of men. The double standard prevails, in that men but not women can have multiple relationships without sanction. Men also feel free to physically coerce women and are thought to be "soft" if they do not, but women are not supposed to strike men (Chevannes 2001). Women suffer a high rate of violence from men, including rape, with little recourse, in spite of domestic violence legislation.

Rural Jamaican society remains patriarchal, yet it is also representative of striking dichotomies, emblematic of intersecting, subversive gender systems. On the one hand, there persists the entrenchment of male dominance evident in limited economic, political and religious parity for women, the prevalence of heteropatriarchal norms, homophobia and heterosexism. Yet these ideologies do not remain unchallenged. Instead they have been discursively disrupted by the vibrancy of Jamaica's indigenous feminisms that have disseminated into popular discourse, generated men's movements and literally shaken up – to the rhythm of the dancehall street – colonial notions of racialized, classed, colour-coded, sexualized gender identities. Above all, rural Jamaica is not a space of complacency or disinterested apathy when it comes to gender, but a paradoxical space of struggle and dynamism, set against conservative ideologies with both dangerous and rewarding repercussions for the bodies that shatter them. Thus, having laid out the historical roots of the contemporary rural black Jamaican gender system in chapter 3, and discussed its components here, I now move onto a discussion in the next chapter of systemic ruptures and contestations amid reproduced inequality, viewed through the lives of individual Frankfielders. Viewing each chapter as a building block itself, I have constructed the outer strands of masculinity and femininity as well as the rungs of the gender "molecule", each feature of the gender system represented as rung embodying the characteristics of continuity-malleability and collectivity-uniqueness. Now, I ask readers to stretch the metaphor further, imagining individuals located on the rungs as individual genes would be located on the actual DNA molecule.

Chapter 5

Storying Gender through Personal Narratives

GENDER NEGOTIATIONS

IN THIS CHAPTER I build on the previous chapter's outline of the general features of the gender system lived by rural black and brown Jamaicans, by storying gender through personal narratives. Their narratives are personal threads in a cultural tapestry: gendered narratives are stories of "ordinary" people that are crucial in appreciating the wider systems of which they are a part and the new gender systems that they are in the process of producing. This chapter includes three interlocking goals. The first is to elucidate through the presentation of personal narratives of ordinary Frankfielders, Abu-Lughod's concerns about individual variation, highlighted in the introduction to the previous chapter. Abu-Lughod urges anthropologists to address the "contradictions, conflicts of interests, doubts, and arguments" – the stuff of everyday life that emerges as individuals *negotiate* meaning and behaviour in relation to the broader gendered systemic that they live within. I emphasize the term "negotiate" in the previous sentence to introduce my second goal. Here I wish to demonstrate, through personal narratives, the notion of "gender negotiations" that emerges from Mohammed's groundbreaking work, *Gender Negotiations among Indians in Trinidad 1917–1947* (2002). The third goal links to the methodological objective of this ethnography stated in the preface to this text and provides the rationale for including gendered narratives as part of an exploration of the black Jamaican gender system. This objective is to detail the process of feminist ethnography, demonstrating the use of a feminist ethnographic framework to understand the lived experiences of people and how they are shaped by cultural constructs of raced and classed notions of femininity and masculinity. Towards this end, I offer a discussion about the emergence and application of the personal narrative as a methodological tool for feminist ethnographic research tailored to address the anglophone Caribbean.

The idea of gender negotiations brings to light an additional set of processes through which we can observe how individuals come to define their gendered identities, and in turn, how these individual concepts help to maintain or, conversely, to reconfigure the outer strands of masculinity and femininity of the metaphorical gender molecule. I have already noted Abu-Lughod's view that people "do not live as robots, programmed according to 'cultural' rules or acting out social roles, but as people going through life wondering what they should do, making mistakes, being opinionated, vacillating, trying to make themselves look good, enduring tragic personal losses, enjoying others, and finding moments of laughter" (1993, 31). I have also pointed to Butler's insight that individuals *perform* their genders, both reproducing gender norms and "mocking" them as a form of rejection in the face of the conforming pressures of socialization and enculturation. Each of these frameworks contribute to our understanding of the contingencies of gender identity by focusing on the intrusion of daily living and self-presentation on conceptions of gendered selves. However, neither details the process of engagement with others that mould these identities into what we can call "cultural constructs". The idea of gender negotiations, however, does provide an analytical framework for understanding how gender norms, practices and ideologies are sustained and manipulated, and thus how individual lives both reflect and disturb a gender systemic.

Mohammed's research demonstrates how descendants of indentured East Indian migrants in Trinidad struggled to articulate meaningful identities by reconstituting gender norms and ideologies. The migrants drew from both cultural memory of their Indian homeland as well as the multiplicity of gender systems in colonial Trinidad, linked to the ethnically and culturally diverse population inhabiting the island. Similarly, in rural Jamaica, cultural formulations around gender that shape children's socialization and enculturation processes are not simply received and internalized in a linear fashion. Chevannes's work, while stressing the importance of children's informal observation and daily training, nonetheless assumes an overly direct and straightforward process of gender-role internalization. He states the following about his work in the Jamaican community of Grannitree:

> In this rural community, the gender socialization of children takes place for the most part informally, in the context of everyday life, when the culturally rooted behavioural norms and the values underlying them are acted out or expressed. Activities are coded with gendered values and these are quickly learned by children and reproduced among themselves. Preparation for gendered life begins fairly early, after the toddler stage when the child begins to show acquisition of cognitive awareness. (Chevannes 2001, 66–67)

My own observations support part of Chevannes's work in that daily, informal processes are indeed extensions of attempts by parents, older siblings and teachers to socialize children into dominant gender roles and identities, and that clearly to some extent gendered values are reproduced. However, keeping in mind the DNA metaphor, continuity or longevity in gendered practices and ideals is paired with mutability, training our ethnographic gaze to simultaneous transformations. My own observations suggest that children do not so readily absorb prescribed gender identities. In childhood, and increasingly in adolescence and adulthood, the process is uneven and not without varying degrees of reflection. I concur with Mohammed that gender identities and gender roles as an expression of identity are in large part the products of negotiations. Children are exposed to the wider debates, discrepancies and contradictions surrounding the societal critique of masculinity, emerging notions of femininity and tensions between the two. They internalize those tensions just as they may conform outwardly to parental instruction to avoid punishment. Yet the exposure of ambiguities about appropriate behaviour may ultimately find expression. Moreover, there is also tension in gender roles between identities defined as conceptions of self and the ultimate expression of those conceptions. While roles may be regarded as a component of a holistic conception of identity, for heuristic purposes I would like to distinguish between people's reflections about expectations and norms pertaining to gender and the manifestation of these expectations, or gender roles. Frankfield residents are deeply reflective, but the capacity or willingness to translate self-reflexive rejections of roles and expectations is limited by many factors. For example, young women may be fearful of reprisal from parents or a sexual partner, as well as ostracism or exclusion from the norms of respectability persistent in the community. In addition, they might also fear unknown repercussions. Economic necessity and the limited availability of employment opportunities – the pressures of gendered political economic arrangements – also drive gender-role designations. Because many poor black women in upper Clarendon parish continue to rely on men financially, their dependence places constraints on their willingness to experiment with new roles. It is important to peel away the dimension of gender identities that resides in self-conception from practice or behaviour. In this way we can imagine a kind of dialectic between the two, mediated by negotiations.

Gender identities, Mohammed demonstrates, are the product of negotiations between received ideals obtained through socialization and the contradictions with those ideals that persist in daily life. These clashes emerge in internal struggles when personal dreams are shattered; when public debates highlight differential community expectations; through domestic discussions, arguments and agreements; and through socialization processes in popular culture and multiple other venues that are central to a community's making of itself, and to individual lives that constitute the social. As Mohammed emphasizes, negotiations "are not about sitting at a table in a conference room confronting each other. They comprise the compromises, the arguments, the conflicts in the domestic sphere, or in the wider society, by legislation, media debates, or other organized or unorganized forms of female or male resistance . . . these are the ongoing processes at work between men and women in most societies everyday" (2002a, 14). Moreover, Mohammed states that negotiations occur at many levels, including between individual men and women, as well as between groups and institutions.

I would like to add two additional layers of negotiations. First, individuals negotiate with themselves, pitting their desires against realities, seeking ways to manipulate and transform those realities, arguing with themselves about their capabilities. This negotiation also occurs in many other self-reflexive ways. Second, individuals negotiate with groups. My example, from the introductory chapter, of Nurse Dunkley's public wedding toast for her nephew, chastising him to treat his wife with respect and equality and to confide in Jesus rather than drown his troubles in rum, indicate a negotiation between an individual and a collective – the wedding community – as does the quotation I shared of the prominent citizen at Frankfield's community council meeting, where he bemoaned the condition of male youth, stating that these young males were staying out late in the streets, not working hard, "smoking ganja and dancing to the music". This description was provided in order to sway the council with the weight of his observations. The former urges an individual, and, by their association as witnesses, the wedding guests to adhere to principles of gender equality and to resist conventional patterns of male dominance. The latter implores the community to think of ways to reshape young men, employing the nostalgia of the past as a model for the present and thus colluding, to some degree, in the demonization of the youth who may have legitimate cause for rebellion.

Through the methodology of the personal narrative, we see how individuals reflect on their gender roles both directly and indirectly, revealing where possible, their understanding of their own gender identities and roles arrived at through these multiple levels of negotiations. This brings me to the third goal of the chapter, reflected in its title, "Storying Gender through Personal Narratives". The personal narrative has emerged as an important feminist research methodology and ethnographic discursive device. It is with this in mind that I turn to the role of the personal narrative within feminist ethnography to elucidate methodological practices that help us to explore the relationship between individuals and the wider gender systems of which they are a part.

THE NEW FEMINIST ETHNOGRAPHY: PERSONAL NARRATIVES AND THE CRITIQUE OF ANTHROPOLOGY

What promise do personal narratives hold, both as a feminist research methodology and as an ethnographic product, for documenting the ways that gendered realties are part of the fabric of everyday lives, alongside the relationship between individual lives and the wider gender patterns that they are a part of? Over the last few decades, personal narratives have served a particular role for gender-based research in seeking to craft a participatory methodology. Through a collaborative process between researcher and researched, the collection and production of personal narratives seeks to disentangle anthropologists from the traditional self/other dyad that has conventionally characterized the relationship between data collector and subject, establishing the researcher as an authoritative expert, replete with the power to generalize about entire cultures and members of these cultural groups.

As I discussed at length in the opening chapter, this original relationship was created in the context of nineteenth-century colonialism, when many early anthropologists colluded with the Western colonial project. Since then, feminist anthropology has sought to render itself distinct from this history, such that "feminist anthropology projects can now be characterized by attempts to listen; to translate; to give women a voice; and to provide a forum for the documentation and presentation of the conflicting, contradictory and heterogeneous exploration of women cross-culturally" (Personal Narratives Group 1989, 263).

Joining these currents is masculinity studies, which has also been an important development in the study of gendered identities. The men's movement, men's studies and the study of masculinity have all been an outgrowth and response to the academic and activist interventions of global women's movements and gender studies. Proponents of Caribbean feminisms have always been oriented towards gender relations, combining this focus with an effort to integrate women into Caribbean history and to tell women's stories. As Patricia Ellis notes, men's movements have taken on two forms: "at one end are those groups whose focus is still on blaming women and on trying to turn back the clock, and on the other are those that are more concerned with understanding the factors that are responsible for and that perpetuate gender inequalities and discrimination" (2003, 152). For the latter group, these issues include domestic violence, the socialization of the genders and the growing gender gap in the educational system, with fewer boys attending university. These are combined with notions of fatherhood, manhood and men's roles in the family. In the 1980s Barry Chevannes, the prolific Jamaican anthropologist, launched Fatherhood Incorporated, an organization mainly for working-class men in Kingston, Jamaica, both as a response to increasingly negative media portrayals of men as "absentee and neglectful fathers" and as a way to work with men to gain a sense of pride in fatherhood and responsibility to society (Reddock 2004). Fatherhood groups also discuss sexuality, male/female relations, condom use and peer-counsellor training to encourage positive contributions of men to families (Ellis 2003, 153).

Another important contribution to masculinity studies was the now ubiquitously cited publication of Errol Miller's *The Marginalization of the Black Male* (1994), in which he examined the now widely disputed theory that Jamaican men are marginalized because of deviant behaviours generated through a mainly feminized school system that produces female academic success. Feminists responded critically, arguing that while the female students were indeed succeeding in school in greater numbers, males maintained dominant political and economic power. Spurred on by these debates, Janet Brown (formerly of the Caribbean Centre for Childhood Development), Chevannes and other scholars launched systematic, pan-Caribbean studies of masculinity and manhood as these concepts were understood and practised by a wide cross-section of men. One such study, entitled *Why Man Stay So: Tie the Heifer, Loose the Bull*,[1] argued that

> the gender debates of the 1980s and 1990s have left most Caribbean men confused and defensive at best, if not angry at presumption that do not seem to take account of their own feelings of role confusion and sometimes powerlessness in the face of overarching inequities resulting from historical realities, present economic constraints, education and class barriers, and political machinations. (Brown and Chevannes 1998, 3)

Men, they continued, resent being collectively labelled "irresponsible Caribbean men" and "absentee fathers". Their study emphasized men's contributions to family life, which they noted is greater than popularly understood, and includes domestic work such as washing and cooking and guidance for their school-age children. All of these behaviours extend beyond the narrow role of breadwinner and disciplinarian.

Interest in the construction of masculinity, the meaning of manhood, the socialization of boys and other related topics rapidly unfolded, generating insights into multiple, competing patriarchies existent throughout the Caribbean, including dominant White patriarchy, African/Creole patriarchy and East Indian patriarchy, as is the case in Trinidad (Mohammed 2004). Most recently, in 2003, the Centre for Gender and Development Studies, at UWI's St Augustine campus in Trinidad, organized the first regional conference on the theme of masculinity, leading to Rhoda Reddock's edited volume *Interrogating Caribbean Masculinities* (2004). The narratives included here are therefore both about men's and women's lives, reflecting current scholarly and popular interest in the meanings attributed both to masculinity and femininity, even though "gender" is still largely popularly interpreted as relating to all issues *feminine*. Interview questions probed the nature of partnering patterns, socialization of children, perceptions of fatherhood and motherhood and parenting behaviours as well as definitions of the "ideal man" and "ideal woman". As a result, the narratives comment on and speak to the storytellers' values and beliefs with respect to gender identity and meanings, underscoring their role in the gender debate as "organic intellectuals" (McClaurin 2001, 4). Organic intellectuals are those members of communities who are not formally trained academicians, but who are nonetheless engaged in active reflection and evaluation of the conditions of life, striving for amelioration. Some of the men I have talked with, who have at least one child they do not live with and thus technically and narrowly could be identified as "absentee fathers", reflect on this designation, their stories revealing that they have some degree of involvement and emotional stake in their children's lives.

One man, a local barber, told me that by his mid twenties he had five children, with three different baby-mothers. At the time he did not reside with any of them, but was struggling to make a living to provide economic support by establishing his own business. He claimed that he was turning himself around after years of a life of violence and fear living in downtown Kingston. He had initially gone to Town from Frankfield to seek opportunity, as do many rural youth, but found himself caught up in a rough crowd. He escaped from that life, he said, and returned to Frankfield, leaving behind a baby-mother and child. Once in Frankfield he became involved in a number of visiting relationships, and two of his girlfriends also became pregnant. Whenever he could, he tried to provide support to both of the women. The first remained with her mother in a neighbouring town, and the second he finally ended up living with – content and proud of himself for settling down. He can now be seen around the community, holding the hands of his small boys or accompanying them to and from school. His story, like so many others, reveals the shifting textures, struggles and achievements of individual lives, rendering stereotypical labels such as "absentee father" thin and limited in their explanatory power. These examples coexist alongside stories of women raising their children alone – whispering to me as we walk through town, "there's the father – he does NOTHING!" Examples of fathers who migrate seasonally, returning to their families when work ends, coexist alongside examples of fathers who remarry, begin new families and abandon their previous families in Jamaica. Individual lives are rarely mirror images of the dominant cultural ideal; they are more often complex blends of "fitting in", as people say, combined with both subtle opposition and outright rejection of these ideals. What emerges from these narratives is a cultural tapestry of gender in the everyday lives of rural Jamaican men and women, a tapestry that is simultaneously both flexible and rigid.

Finally, in addition to their capacity to unearth gender constructs and address anthropology's historical imbalances between researcher and researched, is the role that narratives play in producing a conversation between cultures. This conversation is produced first through the ethnographic process of collecting the stories and further developed once the stories are published and readers in faraway places can imagine and even empathize with other realities. As such, narratives achieve "cross-racial, cross-cultural, and cross-class communication" (Ndambuki and Robertson 2000), revealing insights into "the real relationships of men and women" (Sacks 1979, 122). In the first stage of crafting the narratives, I interviewed, analysed and drafted many of these stories with assistance from my students at Bridgewater State College, who travelled with me as research assistants, and Frankfielders themselves. For one summer in 2006, I employed two young women graduates of Edwin Allen Regional High School, who interviewed members of their community, shared with me the transcripts, returned with follow-up questions based on our discussions and presented final transcripts, which I then edited into stories. I also continue to work with a Frankfield resident, a graduate of UWI with a degree in history and a passion for Jamaican folklore, and Moses, the Rastaman of the Nanny Gravel story in chapter 2. The excerpts I include are a *bricolage* of interview transcripts, written statements by some informants themselves, analysis generated through group discussion and follow-up interviews. This process renders them true collaborations, from the initial interview to what appears here. Through feminist epistemological methodology, the narratives encapsulate "understanding, revealing and seeking to alleviate women's oppression, wherever it exists" (Cole and Phillips 1995, 4) – the very same political aims of the feminist movement. They also advance goals of the progressive men's movements to re-imagine masculinities based on gender equality. These intertwined objectives position everyday working-class women and men as valuable interpreters, creators of meaning, and generators of their own culture.

In addition to presenting and interpreting the narratives, I am also concerned with sharing some of the textual forms that personal narratives can take. As part of the anthropological struggle with authoritative stances and colonial collusion (Marcus and Fischer 1986) the 1980s spawned an engagement with various forms of writing known as "experimental ethnography" or the "new ethnography" in order to create "grounded ethnographies . . . that derive from particular encounters and impart a positions knowledge" (Ashkenazi and Markowitz 1999). As the "objective" persona of the ethnographer has been unveiled to reveal instead culturally positioned, emotional, opinionated human beings, anthropologists have sought to illustrate the complex interpersonal dynamics of field research through a multiplicity of forms. These include, among others, the publication of full interview transcripts; self-reflexive contemplations of the impact of one's subjectivity on cultural interpretation; "critical ethnographies" that challenge homogenous, generalized accounts of "a culture;" and even "pathologies of power" that draw on personal narratives to illustrate the ways in which systemic oppression is manifested in individual lives.

Today, many of these textual strategies, some of which I have sought to incorporate throughout this manuscript, have become normative ethnographic practice. In keeping with my own objective of elucidating the relationship between anthropological knowledge production processes and ethnographic outcomes, from formal interviews to the ubiquitous serendipitous encounters that permeate the ethnographic experience, the stories below exhibit some of this variety.

The narratives have achieved, in varying degrees, the liberatory processes outlined above. Most of the interviews generated conversations between cultures that led to "enhanced mutual understanding" (Ashkenazi and Markowitz 1999, 14), and they crossed race and/or class differences. I have worked with numerous research assistants, having travelled with small groups of students since 1995. These students have mainly been white, working-class American students and a handful of middle-class students, both male and female, as well as both working-class and elite Haitian female students. Most have been Catholic, and most are first generation college students. More recently I have worked with Jamaican research assistants from Frankfield, who, when they conducted interviews, noted that their interviews opened up discourses intra-culturally, producing empathetic understanding and generating insights into the actual relationships of men and women. When the two recent graduates of Edwin Allen Regional High School interviewed community members, they created cross-generational conversations as well on topics such as sexuality and partnering patterns not typically discussed openly between youth and adults. Among all participants, the interviews led to a sense of accomplishment and professionalism with the specific task, as well as a deeper contemplation about the need for community-wide discussions on troubling issues surrounding gender relationships. Towards this end, one particular conversation comes to mind that underscored the need many residents felt for greater openness about painful topics generally surrounded by silence, among them, domestic violence.

One afternoon of one summer, the first of the new millennium, I walked down to the river with "Miss Elsie", a washerwoman who cleaned other people's soiled clothes by transporting loads of laundry in a plastic tub that she carried on her head. We walked down a winding, steep hill to the riverside. Miss Elsie was barefooted and wore a torn, faded dress that I had seen on her many a day. A woman of limited means, she carried herself with a regal demeanour. Passing me on the roadside, she stopped, appearing rather surprised to see me and asserted: "You're here again? What brings you this time?" As is often the case in anthropological fieldwork, some of the most enriching interactions occur serendipitously. I replied, "I'm here again doing research, looking into the relationships between men and women." Miss Elsie nodded with a knowing look and beckoned me to come along with her. As we walked, she told me that she had grown up as one of thirteen children and had six herself, all of whom grown and living abroad in either Canada or the United States. She took care of five of her grandchildren and occasionally received remittances from her own children. They all lived in a small, two-bedroom home, where she had lived with her own children. I had often seen the children playing in the yard as I climbed the hill. They would be running and laughing, hanging laundry, or poking the dusty ground with sticks as a few mangy dogs and skinny chickens pecked about.

Miss Elsie told me she was a "Witness of Jehovah" and often read their magazine, entitled the *Watchtower*. Years ago, she been in a common-law marriage that had ended when her husband died, but it was not a happy union. I learned this as she put her head in her hands, pausing from scrubbing the skirt she was washing, and said, "Him beat me for every likkle ting [he beats me for every little thing]." And then, looking up at me, she asked me, "Do you know what we need in Frankfield?" "No, what?" I asked, waiting expectantly.

"What we need here in Frankfield is a *human rights organization*!" Miss Elsie pronounced each word carefully, nodding in ascent with her own statement. "What do you mean?" I asked, surprised first at her use of the term, and soon after, ashamed by the ethnocentric nature of this surprise. Miss Elsie went on to say, "Ooman [woman] beaten every day and there's no place to go" to get sanctuary. She told me she had read about human rights organizations from the *Watchtower*, and then, perhaps as evidence, she pulled out a worn, folded copy she had tucked into her dress. I quickly glanced at the article and was stuck immediately by its anti-human rights stance. The article was actually dismissing the international human rights movement as the imposition of "man's will against God's laws". So I said to her, "But this article disagrees with the human rights movement". Miss Elsie nodded and said almost dismissively,

"But we need them here! People need to talk about what's going on." I asked Miss Elsie if she had spoken to anyone about this, and she said she had not; this was the first time.

In recounting this episode, I recall my own ethnocentrism in not only my surprise that Miss Elsie would use the language of human rights to refer to the domestic abuse she had suffered and which she recognized was a wider problem, but that she would reject the interpretation of the Jehovah's Witness magazine and arrive at her own. Here is an example of a behind-the-scenes critique, personal reflection, and, until now, silent negotiation between an individual and her community, that would not have met the public eye without the ethnographic enterprise. If narratives have the capacity to stretch the horizons of those who collect them, then it is likely they will do the same to readers, challenging and undoing our easy assumptions and judgements about "the other" as "simple" or "backward". If the narratives are able to communicate to a non-Jamaican readership the complexity of daily realities, and perhaps even to a middle-class Jamaican audience the insights of the rural poor, then they have achieved an important final objective. Such an understanding would emphasize the significance of "ordinary" lives (as opposed to those characterized by fame, authority and socially sanctioned leadership), endowing the tellers of their stories both with a sense of the value of their own experiences and the insights they produce, and perhaps even disturbing readers' views of the meaning of "the ordinary".

INDIVIDUALS IN PERFORMANCE: INITIAL EXAMPLES

I begin with some examples that demonstrate my observations of individual expressions of gendered selves in performance, the modifications and adjustments of behaviours through various social arenas that demand of different gendered personas (Middleton 2002, 33). The intertwining concepts of self-reflection and negotiation assume a social interactionist view of the self that "targets the public and adaptive behavior of individuals operating in everyday contexts" (ibid.), underscoring the ongoing tension between features of the gender system that stress malleability and those that encourage continuity. In rural Jamaica the everyday contexts through which these poles are played out include such spaces as yards, homes, workplaces, schools, open markets, churches, shops, restaurants, bars and street corners. Each social space – even spaces within spaces, such as movement within the domestic realm from yard to bedroom – is governed by normative constraints where particular values place pressure on personal conduct, thereby enforcing conformity. In some instances, internal reflection on these structures of conformity is possible, but it does not always permit behavioural transformations, particularly when threats of violence are plausible outcomes.

During the Sunday service at the Methodist Church in Frankfield, I witness a benign expression of gender-role shifts: women sit quietly and expectantly on the benches. They adopt an appropriate demeanour in which to receive the commentary and reflection on the gospels delivered by the reverend in this conservative space where bodily restraint is expected. Over the past decade, reverends have been both men and women, generally from outside of Jamaica, including Haiti and Ireland, although more recently a Jamaican female reverend has lead the congregation. The leadership of women in the church is unusual in Jamaica, as I pointed out in the previous chapter. It is a realm of power reserved mainly for men. However, the same women who sit modestly in the pews as members of the congregation will become filled with stature and authority when they are invited to the altar to share a story or to preach as pastor. Women move comfortably from one set of gendered expectations to another, a practice which begins in childhood when they are called upon to recite a poem, sing some songs or read a passage from the Bible during children's week (a special time set aside to focus on children at church) or on other occasions such as school fundraisers where children perform in front of an audience, receiving folded bills from volunteers impressed by their presentation. Some girls are hesitant in performance while others, who are more practiced, burst with confidence as they stand in front of the church congregation; eventually most become comfortable passing through this invisible line from one presentation of self into another ((Middleton 2002, 35). However, their moment of leadership from the pew is circumscribed and does not spill over into other spaces.

Cultural spaces are symbolic of particular codes of behaviour, and again, conformity is enforced at risk of social ostracism and even violence, as is the case with men who would risk openly homosexual behaviour or women who might inappropriately assert a role of authoritative spiritual leadership from the bench. Still, opportunities for new, unrehearsed manifestations of gender also arise, as do daily acts of nonconformity, performed behind the scenes. Anthropologist Sumi Colligan (2000, 197) has noted that close attention should be paid to the words and actions of women at the margins for they can provide clues for strategies for grassroots initiatives that improve the quality of life for women. While structural inequalities produced by national and international processes may contribute to cultural, economic, and social paralysis, we must not disregard the role of human agents in generating cracks through which new possibilities emerge.

In *Gender Trouble: Feminism and the Subversion of Identity* (2006), Judith Butler reflects on her notion of gender performativity, stating that "there is no gender identity behind the expressions of gender . . . identity is performatively constituted by the very 'expressions' that are said to be its results" (25). In this conception, gender is an enactment, a series of practices and a script, rather than an essence or "essential self". In Butler's view, this is a potentially hopeful and liberatory analysis of gender because, while people do enact restrictive and oppressive gendered selves, they are also malleable and capable of transformation. Viewing gender as performance creates conditions of possibility for change as individuals push against and beyond restrictive norms through negotiations that reproduce social inequalities and gender oppression.

Deborah Kapchan contends that we must consider the "role of the myriad informal practices of everyday life, the resistances, the evasions, and the ways of getting by . . . We cannot assume that silence means consent. Indeed, the powerless are commonly expected to pay lip service to their oppressors" (1996, 230). In the same vein, African-American feminist writer bell hooks asserts that "women who are exploited and oppressed daily cannot afford to relinquish the belief that they exercise some measure of control, however relative, over their lives. They cannot afford to see themselves solely as 'victims' because their survival depends on continued exercise of whatever personal powers they possess" (cited in Colligan 2000, 202). These insights underscore that there is an intersection of factors that inform negotiations of gendered identity among both men and women in rural Jamaica. Among these factors are the following: the rigidity of the Jamaican gender system; the human potential for gender malleability; and the exercise of personal strengths, beliefs, circumstances and desires. There is an ongoing relationship between individual agency and structural conditions such that daily life opens the possibilities for varied expressions of individual variation around systemic requirements and normative ideals. Upon initial exposure, Jamaican gender codes appear inflexible, but they are not. If they were, the ubiquity of gender issues including public discontents and debates that pervades the society, from the popular press and ordinary conversations to academic and scholarly circles, would not exist. I refer readers back to the notion that I raised in chapter 1, that gender systems acquire new manifestations over time, transforming into new systems.

Ethnographic construction of personal narratives opens critical passageways into public and behind-the-scenes reflections on pressure to conform to heteropatriarchal norms. In asking people to share with me their self-reflections about their gendered selves, I have sought to understand not *whether* Frankfielders negotiate their way around gender prescriptions, but how and in what ways their lives simultaneously reflect obedience to the normative gender system. Gender tales from Frankfield reveal that everyday life is marked at once both by conscious reflections on gender ideologies and practices, as well as unexamined subscription to behaviour deemed appropriately male and/or female. It is my hope that the narratives and their analysis will contribute to the ongoing efforts of Caribbean scholars to document and understand these myriad informal practices of everyday life, "the resistances, the evasions, and the ways of getting by" to produce a deeper recognition of the pervasive contradictions within the gender system and how it intersects with other foundational features of rural Jamaican culture.

THE EVERYDAY LIVES OF ORGANIC INTELLECTUALS

I begin with selections from Nurse Dunkley's life. Because narrative is both a process and outcome, I will share with readers how I decided to work with Nurse to tell her story.

As I conveyed in chapter 1, I met Nurse Lynette Dunkley in June 1991, when I had just turned twenty-six, and I was still a graduate student. But it was many years later, in 2000, when I had returned for the fourth time to stay with her in her home, that I realized that perhaps others would find the stories of her life as inspiring and compelling as I. I also realized that, while I had learned a lot from Nurse about her life through our frequent informal conversations, I would learn still more with formal interviews. For me, there is always some slight awkwardness when a formal interview takes place, particularly when it introduces a new form of communication into an established relationship, but I found that once we got started, the interviews flowed much like conversation. I think this was in part because we both enjoy talking with one another so

Figure 5. Lynette M. Dunkley outside her Frankfield home. *Photo by Heidi Savery.*

much. In this respect, my assumption about the constructiveness of a formal interview versus informal conversation was not completely accurate; Nurse did not tell her story chronologically unless I asked her to try to identify dates, which I have done on occasion, to understand the sequence of events in her life. But for Nurse, particularly now, a linear flow is not significant. Instead, what is important are the stories of her relationships with people, the decisions she has made, a reflection of her values, and, increasingly, her appreciation for the people who care about her, expressed in the frequent utterance, "I am blessed." In addition, in recent years, Nurse and I have driven to outlying communities, including the Milk River baths in southern Clarendon. Here mineral springs collect into Greco-Roman modelled pools, and the waters are upheld for their healing qualities. Nurse used to come here frequently with her husband, and the place holds fond memories. As we drive, passing through small towns, Nurse tells tales of events and people; the landscape is storied and embodies memories of significant events in her life: a car breakdown in the rain when she was returning home late one night and a group of Rastamen coming and assisting her (a story told to me perhaps to express how she developed greater openness towards people she was initially suspicious of); a home where an old friend used to live; a place where she used to pick mangoes with her friends as a child or a place where she crossed the river on a donkey when its flow was high and strong.

There are many themes that run throughout Nurse's life that are significant. One is her strong commitment to her faith. She has many stories about her dreams, which include elements of faith, reflections of her life devoted to "my God", as she says. In the summer of 2006 she shared with me the following dream about her death and impending ascent to heaven, which she talks about frequently these days. We were sitting in her backyard on some turned-over plastic jugs atop pavement that she had just finished sweeping. I expressed admiration that she had just exerted herself so extensively. Nurse responded by saying that she didn't know how much longer she had to live, but she still had to try to maintain herself and her property. "When I'm gone," she said, "all this will be the responsibility of others." "What do you think will happen then?" I asked, in my own mind reflecting on who would continue living in her house, and what would happen to the property. But Nurse responded in her typical humour and laughingly said, "a funeral!" Then she continued, taking the conversation further in that direction, "Some people will cry, some will be a little sad, others will rejoice." "Rejoice?!" I exclaimed. "No!" "Well, yes," she went on, "some will. But I will be with Jesus." "Is that a place?" I asked. "Well," Nurse commented, "no one knows where heaven and hell are. But I believe I will be with my loved ones." "Do you feel sad?" I asked. "No," she said solidly. "No. No sadness. No fear. I will be with my loved ones." She then launched into a story.

> You know I had this dream about three years ago that I died. We saw the river Jordan. It was beautiful. On one side, we were all lined up, wearing white gowns. On the other were the angels. We all had to cross the river one by one. When it was my turn, I crossed and the water was up to here [*she motions to her calf*]. As I walked across the angels opened their arms wide, reaching toward the sky. [*Nurse opens her arms and bursts into song*] Halleluja! Halleluja! Halleluja!
>
> I am telling you this now, because I want that played at my funeral. I've told two people, you're the second. Now you know! When I was in England last year visiting my children [she refers to her nieces and nephews and her adopted son, all of whom she raised and now reside in London] we looked for it, but I wasn't sure about the name of the piece or who the composer was. I bought a tape but I'm not sure if this is what we heard. I knew you'd know.

After she finished her story I responded: "I'll bring the CD with me, next time I come, Nurse," I said. "And I'll make sure that it is played at your funeral." Nurse nodded and smiled, "Thank you, my dear." "Nurse," I ask, suddenly realizing that I want to recount this story among others, and noting that I haven't yet asked the standard anthropological protocol: "when I write about you, should I use your name?"

"Well of course!" she replies, surprised. "That way, I will live on. My story will live on. And someone may read it and say, 'I know her!'" So in July 2007, when I returned to Frankfield, I brought the CD. Nurse held it to her heart and went to play it immediately. She then asked me to read the CD insert with the words from the Bible about Christ's birth. As I read, she recited the lines by heart. She then took my hands and said, "My dear, you have no idea what you have done. There is nothing else you could have brought me that I would appreciate as much as this." Throughout the visit, I heard the sounds of "Hallelujah!" echoing from her room.

During an earlier visit in 2006, Nurse told me another story that includes a dream sequence, which I found significant because of the spiritual power the dream affords to her female ancestors as icons of strength, healing and family unity.

> I remember when I was a little girl, I think it was before I was in school, but I can't remember, you know. I remember the event, but not the exact time. You ask me when but I can't really remember. Anyway, see this toe? [*Nurse points to her second toe*] I got a nail in it, and my mother took me to the doctor. I got an injection; I still have the mark. I became paralysed. Did you know that? Yes. I couldn't feel a thing in my leg. It wasn't until I was in nursing later that I realized it was my synaptic nerve that the doctor had mistakenly injected.
>
> One night as I slept I dreamt that a lady came to me. She had a little bottle, like a cream jar, and it had some brown paste in it. She asked me if I can move my leg. I said I couldn't. She said try, so I tried but I couldn't. She took some of that brown paste and rubbed it on my leg. The next morning I told my mother about the dream. She said "don't say a thing", so I kept quiet. The next night and the night after that, she came again. On the third morning I woke up, and I had some feeling in my leg. After that, I took a stick from a coffee plant in our yard and used it like a cane, and slowly started to walk again.
>
> I asked my mother who that lady was, and she said that it was her own mother. You know, I never knew my grandmother, never saw pictures of her. In those days, people didn't take pictures too often, and people didn't have money for those things.

Nurse is a devout Methodist, but as the above story indicates, her beliefs are syncretic, and the notion that she received a benevolent visit from her grandmother's spirit is not contradictory to her worldview.

Another theme running through Nurse's life is her belief in hard work as a foundation for individual achievement and contribution to the community. Given her social standing as a well-travelled woman who owns a nicely maintained home and her emphasis on individual accomplishment, Nurse's appreciation of the value of all kinds of work to community life is remarkably socialist in nature. She frequently will declare the significance of the street sweeper, whose work maintains not only the town's aesthetics, but its health as well. It is not the menial nature of the work that Nurse examines, but its contribution to the standards of a well-maintained, shared space. As important is her sense of ongoing responsibility to the youth. She currently boards a young man headed for college and rents her flat to a young couple. Both fall under her watchful eye, as she chastises them about littering, schools them on proper manners and lectures them on finding a career path. Nurse is particularly troubled by the young woman, a nineteen-year-old who lives with a boyfriend. The woman was not particularly successful at school and is not directed. Nurse pushes this young woman to think about her future as an independent person, not as an appendage to her boyfriend, whom she waits for all day till his return in the evening when he comes home to a prepared meal. Nurse is vexed by this woman's overly traditional role. Although her own mother was married and bearing children at that age, she strongly believes that this generation of young women should be more career oriented. Nurse engages in daily negotiations with people within her sphere of influence so as to convey her values. These values, she asserts, are progressive, incorporating "longtime" standards of decency with new opportunities for women, opportunities that began in her own youth, as I will point out later when I explore her career as a nurse.

Among the qualities that endear Nurse to others is her sense of fun and the joys of life – for Nurse these include long telephone conversations with neighbours, adventure and travel, as well as family gatherings. Nurse used to take frequent trips to the Milk River baths. Nurse also loves to relax at home on her veranda, overlooking the town and the mountains beyond, capturing the breeze, and basking in the sweet scent of lilies and other potted plants she lovingly cares for. Indeed, in her retirement, after a life committed to others and with her sight gone in one eye, Nurse feels no shame in being served meals. She also leaves the daily household obligations to others, and receives gifts and assistance from her wide, extended family, whose career successes, in many cases, can be attributed directly to her: "I sent all my children to school, or helped them in any way I could," she frequently comments, using the term "children" to refer to all of the youth who were "raised up" in her household, including her own biological and adopted sons, her nieces, nephews, and children from the wider parish who continue to board with her.

Over the course of her adult life, she took over twenty children into her home, in part because of her proximity to the town and schools, in part because of her rural middle-class standing and the reliability of a steady income through her profession as a nurse and midwife, but also because of her love for children and her self-defined goal "to help my people". Her current ability to relax, rest and be served reflects her status in her family and community, her control over her own resources, and her ability to command the work of others towards her conception of the proper and desired role for an elderly woman of the rural middle class. As a widow, Nurse has executed significant independence – although not without the ongoing advice and economic support from her extended family as regards her financial affairs and the maintenance of her properties. At the age of eighty-two, Nurse was involved in making decisions about a new roof and retiling her floor, negotiating with contractors. She also wrote a letter to her parish representatives seeking their aid in cleaning up a pile of dirt and rocks left in front of her driveway following some construction work involving a burst water main. Interestingly, in writing such a letter, which she dictated to me, Nurse invoked the name of her late husband, who sat on the parish council ten years before, both to identify herself in relation to political power and to assert her ability to exercise her influence.

Yet Nurse's condition as a receiver of care from her family members is relatively recent and not as common as public officials would suggest. In fact, even after her retirement, Nurse returned to work as the nurse at Edwin Allen Regional High School, both for continued income and to serve her community. She continued to work there well into her 70s. As Nurse recounts, she was asked especially by the widely respected principal of the high school to serve as its nurse, and she felt unable to turn down the request. Joan Rawlins points out that, as women age, they are still expected to perform their familial roles, and this only changes if they become too ill to do so (2006, 65). Many elderly women continue to work for various reasons: their skills are needed, their personal situations render work an economic necessity, and/or they wish to serve their communities (p. 78). As a widow, Nurse continued to work for all three of these reasons. In Rawlins's reflections on widowhood, based on a series of case studies of women from August Town and Hope Gardens, she identifies a discourse of liberation set against a prevailing discourse of disorganization. This offers a perspective that mirrors Nurse's own views of her life subsequent to her husband's death. As Rawlins states: "In considering widowhood, a discourse was revealed that was found to be full of power; enabling the alternative lived experience of some widows to be effectively denied or suppressed" (p. 118). Rather than lives collapsing into chaos, many of the widows experienced new freedoms "to come and go as they please", and maintained a sense of themselves as sexual beings. While many felt lonely (mainly those who lived alone), they also responded that "they were perhaps not much worse off than they had been when their husbands were alive" (p. 121).

Widowhood produced ambivalent feelings, which Nurse appears to reflect. She frequently talks about her late husband and what a good and kind man he was, yet she also clearly has valued her independence and is solidly confident in the roles that her status as head of household confer: economic decision-making power, the issuing of directives to those who reside with her, and the assertion of her expectation to live a more relaxed life and be served.

Nurse can be full of mirth and playfulness, yet there is a profound seriousness that pervades her perception of herself and the familial position she occupies. Her stories reflect these many-faceted emotions, as she seeks to explain morally ambiguous behaviours and "superstitions" in light of her self-defined commitment to "her God". Through these explanations, she reassures herself that she is on solid ground, that her decisions to marry and later "to tief" (steal) one of her nieces from her sister-in-law, bringing the girl home to raise, were effectual and confirmed by "signs from above".

Born on 1 April 1925, "the day of fools" she says, Nurse devoted the years before her marriage to a nursing education and career, marrying only in her forties, which, as I have noted, is not uncommon for working-class Jamaican women, and Nurse was certainly poor before she married, by her own account. Her husband died after only ten years of marriage due to a diabetes-related illness. She now resides with her devoted niece and nephew, who run the household operations: all tasks related to the "cook shop", animals and garden. Only in the last year or so has her home been relatively quiet; like many Jamaican households, its composition has been in frequent flux. Yet she continues to host visitors, including my own family and regular crew of students. In the spring of 2007, Nurse took in a boarder, a young man attending Edwin Allen Regional High School, both as a form of extra income (although she does not state this upfront) and as a way to help others. "I do what I can to help my people", she says frequently. Nurse is indeed a generous and kind woman, as well as a shrewd businesswoman, managing her boarders and her three rental properties with both expectations (boarders must conform to household rules and obligations) and compassion. Nurse is flexible in receiving rent; for instance, she allows partial payments, "as long as they give something", she will say. But when months lapse without a payment, Nurse will go to court and retrieve an eviction notice. In one instance, I accompanied her to court in May Pen, where she obtained papers to serve a tenant who claimed not to have paid the rent because "duppies" occupied the house. "Can you imagine!" Nurse proclaimed. Indeed, when we then brought the papers to the man, he launched into his duppy story, leaving Nurse feeling both vindicated in her action and outraged that a good Christian woman's property could be so derided.

In our own unfolding relationship, I have felt many connections with Nurse and she with me. One such connection revolved around our shared loss, of my own father and her husband, both of whom died of diabetes-related causes. In 1998, Nurse met my parents, two years before my father passed away. Not only did she travel to the United States to attend my wedding and stay with my family for a month, but in later years, my mother, brothers, sister-in-law, and a nephew came to visit Frankfield, along with my husband and daughter, travelling far out of their own element to visit what had been "my stomping grounds" for so many years. Nurse and I now both cherish a photo of my mother and Nurse sitting together on her veranda. Across cultures, religions and an age gap of almost forty years, Nurse and I feel a deep bond, but only in part because of our losses. As anthropologist Renato Rosaldo (1989) has written, emotions serve to connect people, and the emotions of grief are among the most powerful. Yet we have also enjoyed companionship, and Nurse has mothered me in a faraway land, so I have come to connect Jamaica with her and think of her as extended kin. I would add to Rosaldo's observation that love is just as, if not more, powerful than grief, which is ultimately born out of love, and I know that Nurse too, with her unwavering faith in Jesus' love, would agree with me.

Nurse herself has said that although her married life was brief, she has not been alone for a number of reasons: she has always had the company of those she has welcomed into her household, a strong and respected place in her community. The main reason, however, is that she has Jesus in her heart. Nurse contends that her religious convictions have permitted much and she has enumerated the abilities religion has provided: "to stand on my own two feet"; "to rely on myself"; "to earn my own living"; "to tell my children, what I have is mine, now you go get yours!" Nurse has explained that her strong faith has not come blindly, but rather through a life of struggle, loss and questioning her belief in God. Given her outward manifestations of constant faith, I was surprised when I first learned that she had reflected on God's existence: "I would think that everyone questions sometimes," she said to me in one taped interview. "If you think, then you must question." In this short but pithy statement, Nurse revealed the depth of her self-reflexivity, her understanding of her own enculturation and the power she ascribed to herself as a thinking person.

Nurse and I sit down on her veranda, and I test the tape recorder. We are a bit tense as this recorder introduces a new formality to our conversations. I begin by asking Nurse to share with me one of the most important events of her life. As these two excerpts demonstrate, there is no story in the sense of a beginning, middle and end. Nurse recounts fragments and seemingly unrelated pieces of information. Time does not flow chronologically, and events become intertwined and even confused. I must prod her, asking her to explain how the pieces are connected. Throughout, she wants me to rewind the recorder so she can hear us. She leans forward, listening intently, laughing at her own voice and nodding along, agreeing with herself. The interviews take a long time because she discovers so much pleasure in hearing our conversation.

BECOMING A NURSE

Born in 1925, Lynette Heron was one of ten children living in the small house built by her father in the hilly agricultural community of Grantham, a community neighbouring Frankfield. Lynette knew from girlhood that she wanted to be a nurse. At about age nine, she moved to the parish of St Anne to be raised by her mother's sister, her auntie, who became a second mother to her. Lynette joined her older sister and brother, who already were being cared for by their aunt. This aunt was a teacher and did not have any children of her own. Nurse felt early on that she had a calling, and one evening she told me about it, as we sat on her veranda. Her story is not a linear tale about becoming a nurse; rather, it is interwoven with the challenges she faced with racism, family illness, decisions about family life, and the complications of travel in the 1950s and 1960s. Yet through all this is a tale of perseverance and commitment to the wellbeing of "my people", as Nurse says of the Jamaican populace.

Nurse Lynette Dunkley: It was always my desire from very early on in life that I wanted to become a nurse, and the opportunity came in about 1956 when Mr and Mrs Allen, the minister of parliament and that same Edwin Leopold Allen – that very same one –

that the high school is named after [in Frankfield]. They went abroad and organized a programme so girls from Jamaica could go abroad and be trained as nurses and in other fields. There was a cousin of mine who dressed well, and I thought she was a nurse when I was a child. She was a teacher. But I used to look at her. I used to think if I were a nurse I would have been better able to help. So I decided to pursue the course in nursing. I was about twenty-three. Once I passed my third-year Jamaica local exam (the exam to get into college), I taught as a probationer, a junior teacher, to earn some money. But I really didn't love that. I started taking the first-year teacher's exam, but I saw a friend of mine who used to be a supervisor and organizer of the Jamaica Social Welfare Programme. I saw an opportunity to do social work, so I left teaching and went into social work, which I liked very much. But then came the chance to go to England with this programme organized by the Allens. So I went.

I did three years of nursing school in London at Whittington Hospital. After another year I went to Gloucester to join the Royal Hospital. I was a state registered nurse. There I also took the Central Midwife exam, and I was successful, so I became a state registered midwife. Then they had this premature babies course because, being a midwife, it was important in case there were problems. I took that too and worked as a district midwife. From England, I signed a contract to go to Canada because I wanted to do public health. I couldn't do it there in England. Two of us coloureds took the exam with some white girls and we both had the midwife and General Nursing part 2, so we could practise on our own. The two white girls, only had part 1, but they were given the opportunity to do public health, but we coloured girls were not allowed to do that. We had to stay in the district. So that's when I decided to go to Canada. I felt there was discrimination.

But then my auntie became sick. I said, "I'm going home." My supervisor said to me, "But Nurse Heron, you can't go home." But I told her what was happening, and she said they'd pay the fare! So I told her I'd sort it out, whether I'd go by plane or ship. The next day I said, "Thank you very much. I appreciate it, but I will take my things home. If everything is alright I will leave my things, go home and come back." In those days a plane would land the same day a ship would land because planes weren't so regular, and the ship would save money. So I went to Southampton. I had some family in Wolverhampton. They all took me to Southampton to see me off. I took a carpet to Auntie to make her feel good because she always loved a carpet. It's that one there in the living room [*Nurse points to the carpet*].

When I got home, she was still in hospital. I stayed there with her 'till she could go back to work as a teacher. So I didn't go back to England. I stayed in Kingston working at a hospital. It was then that they wrote me from Canada, because I had stayed, they were going to sue me for breach of contract. Remember I was going to do Public Health in Canada after I left England. So I said to my auntie, "Let me go, and if I don't like it,

I'll come back." When I went there, they were very nice to me. I didn't realize then that I breached my visa, that I should have gone directly from England to Toronto. So I had to get a new passport and visa. I got a work visa, and I went straight into nursing. I was there for four years, then Auntie took sick again and I came.

My son was born a year before I went to England. My mother raised him till he was old enough to go to school. Then her auntie took him.

Diana Fox: Was that hard? Being away from your son for so many years?

LD: [*Nods*] Well, yes. But I knew he was in good hands. And I had to make my way. One thing I want you to include in telling my story is about what I said to the matron in England. I told her that when I am finished with my training, I am going back to Jamaica to serve my people, after which, I have done so, and I am very, very proud and happy about it!

MEETING HER HUSBAND

Lynette often speaks lovingly of her husband, so during one of our conversations, I asked her about how they met.

Diana Fox: Where did you meet your husband, Martin, Nurse?

Nurse Lynette Dunkley: Mmmm. I met him in St Ann. I was doing social work there and living with my auntie. My auntie couldn't have children, so I went to live with her. I loved her as a mother. Well, when I came back home, I was living with my mother, adopted daughter and my son. My son stayed in Jamaica when I went to England to learn nursing. I went because of Michael Manley. I applied for a scholarship, and I got it. After England, I went to Canada where I practised nursing. I loved it. Then I had a job offer in California, but I got word from home that my auntie was very ill, dying. So I came home right away.

DF: So when you came back to Jamaica, you didn't find nursing work right away?

LD: No, I was working as a social worker until I started to work as a RN and midwife at Spalding hospital.

DF: And this was where you met your husband?

LD: Yes. So one day my brother came by and he needed to take care of some papers – there were some land sales – he needed signatures.

DF: How did that connect you with your husband?

LD: Because my future husband was justice of the peace, and my brother needed to go to him. I begged my brother to go along. There was Martin. And then we began, one talking to the other, you know [*Nurse giggles, a young girl once again*]. His first wife had died in the hospital. I didn't even know her, you know. And when I saw Martin with my brother, I remembered I had seen him before. One day I was just going through the ward, and I saw him, and the principal of Edwin Allen Regional High School, then. He was there too. And seeing them, you know I went to greet them, and he showed me his wife, but she was far gone then. I said I would go back to see her, but I was sad. And I wasn't able to see her. Then, the next day when I went back, she was dead, unfortunately. When I met him later, with my brother, she had been dead for some time. We were dating for just a year before we married. He said, you know, my wife is dead, and the children are grown up, if you are interested, would you marry me? I told him I'd have to think about it. I was thinking about it for about three months, and then I got in touch with my old teacher. He was my guardian angel, my counsellor. So I told him; I let him know. He wrote me a letter counselling me. First thing on getting my letter, he knew what I wanted because I was always strong. I knew my own mind. He went to a concert and they sung a song, "I don't know about tomorrow, but I know who holds my hands." So he told me, be sure that the Lord is holding my hands and he will lead me into the unknown. It was really good counselling. I was scared to marry Martin, and that's exactly what I said to him. But Martin said, "Well, the children are grown up; you're not going to marry the children!" "You have the personality," he said, "to win these people" – my family – "over; you can talk to them, see how they feel about it." So that's what I did. But when Martin came back, I didn't tell him "yes" right away. I told him I was still thinking about it.

DF: Even though you knew?

LD: I kind of made up my mind, and said, well . . . because I always pray about these things. I had prayed. And one thing I asked God, beforehand, before I met him, if I'm going to marry someone, let us have the same initials. And he must be someone who would not prevent me taking care of my parents or my relatives. If he can't help me, just leave me alone; let me do what I want to do. First thing, I won't be a bother to him. I'm not going to use what he has to help them. I'll use from my own.

DF: What do you mean the same initials?

LD: I wanted to see some sign, to make sure he was the right person. I just don't know; it was like asking God for a sign. If that is the right person, let us have the same initials. Martin is ML, and I am LM. Lynette Miriam and Martin Luther Dunkley. His father was a teacher, so quite likely he was named after Martin Luther. I finally told him about two months after. He lived here, in Frankfield, so it was easier. He used to operate a truck; he had a citrus farm. I could always drive up the road to the hospital. It was much easier for me to go up to the hospital. He had this house before I met him. He rented it out to the Baptists, and then we moved in.

DF: He came from a family that had property? Was that important in your decision to marry him?

LD: Yes, rather than someone running from place to place. I wasn't accustomed to that kind of thing. It was stable. He was a very good man. Very good. People loved him.

DF: Were you in love with him when you married him?

LD: I think I grew to love him. He was very thoughtful, and he treated me as a lady. And my son and adopted daughter lived with us, and he treated them like his children.

In this excerpt Nurse's values are clear: she did not marry for romantic love but for stability. She grew to love her husband because of his kindness and dependability and also because he treated her like a *lady*. Given what I have discussed about the importance of *ladyhood* versus black womanhood, Nurse's choice of words to describe how she was treated are significant; she felt highly regarded, respected, endowed with the qualities of a lady. As well, she wanted a man who would not impede her ability to care for her parents – a responsibility typically taken on by grown daughters rather than sons, and she wanted someone to help her achieve her goals, but not to provide for her. She is not "looking money" and her husband is not "looking sex" – qualities I pointed out in chapter 4 are significant in the relationships of mistrust that characterize many male/female relationships in the rural black gender system. In fact, Nurse rejected the biological father of her son because "he was always playing around with other women, and I wouldn't stand for that". Rather than living a life of mistrust, she pursued independence, as many Jamaican women do, until she found a man who shared her desire for companionship, a unified household constituted by their respective family members, and a relationship of mutual respectability and trust – acknowledged and supported with the blessing of the community, as Nurse's counsel with her "guardian angel" underscores. It is clear too that Nurse's ultimate decision to marry was the product of a series of negotiations not only with her husband and his family, but also with herself, through the medium of "her God", as she sought to meet her own complex desires. Both Nurse and her descriptions of her husband seem to me to embody inherited values of masculinity and femininity as well as those shaped by feminist and cultural nationalist themes. Threads of masculinity and femininity from multiple gender systems are intertwined and superimposed on another in these individual lives, lives situated on the "gender molecule's" outer strands.

NURSE'S HOUSEHOLD OF CHILDREN

Diana Fox: How did you start taking in so many children?

Nurse Dunkley: Well, one day, it started first with my adopted daughter's [her niece's] sister. They have the same mother. So one day we went up to Unity, the town where I was born – my parents are buried there in the yard, where they live now [*Nurse says this with laughter, reminiscing, a twinkle in her eye*] and then we went and saw this nice little child, my other niece, and I say to my daughter, you know, you could keep her. And she say, "Yes Mommy, take her." And the mommy didn't want her to come. So, we said, we just take her. So we call out to the car, and the mother said, "That's a good pickney [child]!" She said, "You can't take her." I said to her mother: "She just spend a few days with me." And then she got in the car and close the door, and we drove away [*laughing heartily*].

DF: You mean, you took her, and her mother didn't want her to? And then she just stayed?

LD: Mmm hmm. By the next day we sent her to school.

DF: What did her mother say?

LD: Well, she cried you know, but she wasn't very well, you see. I wanted to kind of ease it, convince her . . . but she wouldn't agree if I didn't do that, take her, you know. So I took her and the next day she was at school, Frankfield Primary. I just got some material and things to the mother and she made her uniform, so she went without the first time. Then a boarder came and went to the high school. That's three children. Then one day, one of the girls' friends just come and visit them and she would stay . . . and till finally . . . I just don't know how she got into the house. She finally just lived here. She's from up by Lampard district. She used to live with a couple up the hill as a boarder, till finally she had to go back to her mother. But she just came here and she stay one night, two nights, three nights . . . home sweet home! Then two more . . . till there was a houseful.

DF: This is in the late 1970s?

LD: Mmm hmm. The next two, they were in the same age group and they were going to Kilsyth school in Grantham [a town neighbouring Frankfield]. So at age twelve, they come to Comprehensive [Edwin Allen Regional High School]. Now it was hard for them to travel all that way up from Grantham. So, I say, all right, spend your school days here and then you can go up home for the weekend. Those are my other nieces. So they came and they finally stayed. They stayed so that they could get help with their exams. They did well too. They had As and Bs. After that they went to college, then to university. Then some went to England to get their Master's degrees.

DF: So then there are six girls and your son. When does your adopted son come along?

LD: Well, he was born as part of triplets at home. One died at home and then they brought the two boys into hospital. He was tiny. Oh gosh, the whole capillary network . . . you could see everything. He was in an incubator. I was there as the midwife, but I was trained as a general trained nurse when I was in England. But at the hospital, they didn't even know that I was a general trained nurse. The other boy died, so just one was left. He was just so tiny. Once he could come out of the incubator I bathed him, and I put him in a crib, a little bassinet, and put him out in the sun. And everybody called him "Nurse Baby" [Nurse's baby].

DF: What happened to his mother?

LD: I think she's somewhere, but I don't know.

DF: She never came to claim him?

LD: I tell you, one day, I was on the maternity ward for about two years, and a lady came up, and said, "I come to see the children." I thought she was talking about those older children. So I said, "No, this is the maternity ward. Children's ward is at the top, so you can go up there." I didn't see or hear anything more about her until I got ready to adopt him. You know, they have to go and investigate the family before the adoption can go through, and they found the girl's mother – it was a teenager who had the triplets – and she, the girl's mother, said she shouldn't bring any more children into the house. She was a young woman, and she had already had so many. But she was honest. When she came to the hospital, she did ask for them. And the nurse sent her up to the children's ward. She couldn't care for him.

DF: Were there other children? Not that eight is a small number . . .

LD: Well, we had another one: Martin's goddaughter. She was also going to Comprehensive. So she came and joined us. And over the years, they come and go . . .

For those unfamiliar with the "shape shifting" qualities of Jamaican households, and the waning but still important ethic of community parenting, Nurse's story of the capture of her niece will appear shocking. However, Nurse feels she is not on any shaky moral ground with her action; rather, the sisters were able to grow up together and attend school regularly. Nurse's household composition, as unusual as it was to me, was not an anomaly. Moreover, Nurse did not ask her husband for permission to take in these children. She did indicate to me that they discussed it, but she had married a man who willingly accepted her self-stated desire to "help her people", as she would frequently state. Moreover, her standing in the community, although achieved in part

Figure 6: Lynette M. Dunkley accompanying the author on a field trip to Kingston

through her husband's status, was significantly enhanced through her own "good works". These were well known through her long-term membership in the Methodist Church, her participation in the Community Counsel, and, perhaps most of all, her work as a nurse and midwife. Nurse helped to elevate these children into the minority middle class in Frankfield, onto higher education and, for many, overseas migration. Later on, when she worked as the school nurse at Edwin Allen Regional High School, she kept a watchful eye on new generations of children who passed through her household. Nurse loved this job, although she was exhausted doing it, because she felt it kept her in tune with the community. Everyone waved to her, and smiled as she drove through town in her nurse's uniform and little white cap.

Woven through these stories from Nurse's life are threads of the theoretical frameworks under discussion – the DNA metaphor, gender socialization and gender negotiations – each interwoven and enriching our understanding of the decisions, social structures, beliefs, values, norms and political economic factors shaping her life. Lynette regards herself as a teacher of children even though teaching was not her chosen career path. Instead she is a teacher of received middle-class values about the importance of hard work in and of itself and also as a pathway towards upward mobility. Following a reflective religious life is also important, as is contributing to one's community. She has pursued these choices herself and seeks to emphasize their importance to those she resides with and the many children she has raised. The gender roles she has occupied have been drawn from available selections within the gender system of her youth. This system, however, is shifting under Jamaican independence and emerging cultural nationalism that enabled her to pursue her dream of becoming a nurse through overseas study and serving "her people". At all stages she negotiated her options and opportunities in order to achieve her ideals. Part of her conceptual vision of herself was as a poor rural girl, raised in a family participating in conventional households of shifting membership that enabled others (such as her auntie who desired motherhood) to attain their sought-after, gender-appropriate goals. Nurse herself therefore sought middle class, respectable status through marriage, a gender-appropriate career, motherhood and community service.

This next interview similarly demonstrates the nexus of negotiation, gender socialization and attributes of a malleable yet resistant gender system.

MARLENE FRANCIS (PET NAME: JOAN)

This interview with Marlene ("Joan") Francis was collected by her eldest daughter, a graduate of Edwin Allen Regional High School. She did an initial interview, and then brought the transcript to me so we could work together on follow-up questions. She then returned to Joan and presented me with these final notes. Joan gave me explicit consent to include her real name in this ethnography.

Family Life and Work

I have been married for sixteen years. I live with my husband and four children – three girls and a boy. I try to let my partner feel happy and comfortable by preparing his favourite meals and a nice and clean home environment for him. The challenge I face is a financial challenge in that sometimes my husband doesn't have a job, and I am a minimum wage earner and sometimes that cannot carry us through. He is a migrant farm worker in Canada. He comes home for Christmas for about three months. I work in a restaurant. I had other choices, yes, but I settled for the first one I got. I like my work very much because I can help myself, and I like working along with the customers, although sometimes I have difficulty with them. Sometimes they come in and order food and then they change their minds. In my community I work with the church in preparing food and beverages for some services, and when some people are going abroad they ask me to make grater cake and drops [coconut desserts] for them to carry.

I take care of my family by looking after their living environment, preparing their meals and sending the children to school, and going to church together. I also make pastries and preserves. My husband and I are head of the household, but sometimes it changes because my husband has to travel abroad, so during that time I stand as the head. I want to see that my children are brought up in the right and proper way, to see that they go to school clean and tidy and to ensure that they are properly fed. I decide who do the shopping and prepare the meals and how money is spent while my husband is away. I am the disciplinarian who do not like foolishness and want my children to be better persons. I learned a lot about raising children when I was growing up. I was grown up in an extended family, and I used to help with my smaller siblings. All my children have the same father except one that has a different father. I had the first child with a different man before I got married. The girls are quicker to help around the house than boys. Also, my son can be idle. Him love to play and watch TV. His sisters push him to do well because him lazy.

Religion

I attend the Full Truth Church of God and Deliverance Centre [a Pentecostal church]. I mainly go once per week, but sometimes more. It has a good effect on my life because by going to church and reading the bible it helps me to know more about God as a creator because He gave us life, and that we can have it more abundantly. As a mother, it guides me in rearing the children in a way that they can know that we serve a living and true God and that they can also serve him as their saviour. Going to church changed me into a better person the more I read the Bible. It changed my lifestyle, like my approach toward other persons and the way I dress . . . modest. After hearing the word, it teaches me the way, and I just see it fit to turn my life over to God, and so I started going to church. It teaches me that we are to be our brother's keeper and to love one another and live together as brothers and sisters in Christ.

Gender Ideals

In my view a man is twenty-five and up and fully mature. Because I don't look at any male under that age as a man; I see them as boys. A man should take up his responsibility in that he should take care of his family. A man should be hard-working. Well, I can say a woman is twenty-two and up, after they have passed their parents' responsibility. Because for me they won't be a woman until they pass the stage of parental responsibility. A woman must be hard-working, responsible and know how to get around the house, meaning they should know how to care for their children, as some women don't know how to go about doing this and the consequences are that the husband might stray, leave and end up not being properly cared for. I was grown in the manner that we can't have the man or woman approach until we have reached a certain stage in life. As you all know, the girls do the duties of the house by cleaning and tidying up the place, and the boys do the outside work by sweeping up the yard.

Joan's brief discussion indicates the presence of the twin pillars of mother-hood and religion in her life. Like Nurse, she sees herself as a teacher of chil-dren passing down the values she learned as a child and pursued later in life. Although not explicit, She indicates that at some point she swayed away from the path of her childhood, and the church helped her to get back on it. At some point, she chose to change her manner of dress and to conform to the ideals of modest femininity which she regards as God's wishes. She does not delve into her self-reflexive negotiation, but it is clear that at some point she had a dialogue with herself and took the necessary steps to become the wife of a migrant farm worker. This put her in the position, which so many women occupy, of a temporary household head. Importantly, when her husband is home, she identifies herself as joint head of household with him, not relin-quishing her matrifocal status obtained in his absence. It is likely, in my esti-mation, that this is the result of a negotiated understanding between herself and her husband, not a self-evident status. It is a status made possible by a gen-der system in flux that grants the possibility of women's co-headship with men.

MISS JONES (PSEUDONYM)

"Miss Jones" is a woman who reveals more of her internal reflections, allowing us to see her struggle over her relationship with an unfaithful partner, and the pride and obligation she feels as the result of taking a parenting course at the University of Technology to care for her boarders, in the absence of biological motherhood. She is raising her two female boarders to conform to the values of modest femininity, a longstanding value of the gender system. As well, she encourages academic and career success, a continuous value for black women who have sought to survive and make a living through wage work. It is also a relatively new value in the gender system because academic and career mobil-ity were largely impossible objectives for the majority of poor, rural, black women until this period. The interview was collected by Nurse's grandniece, also a graduate of Edwin Allen Regional High School. We followed a similar pattern as in the previous interview, but Miss Jones also added her own written testimony.

Partnering and Household

I have been in a visiting relationship for the last ten years. I try to be open, frank, loving, caring, being able to accept his opinion, and I also try to be here for him at all times. The challenges are him being unfaithful, not being able to communicate effectively, not being truthful. I try to get professional help and then act accordingly. He is in Manchester now. I am the head of my household, and I live with two female children who are boarders. My responsibilities are waking the children at a certain time so that they can reach school early, making sure that they eat breakfast and that their uniforms are pressed the night before. The students are cooperative and disciplined. I don't have to tell them not to watch television because they know that the books come first. Because I am the household head, I make the important decisions. From the beginning, when they first came to live with me, I had to let the girls know what I stand for. These are codes of dress, deportment, manners in public: say good morning, thank you. All these have to be taught and practised at home before the children can go out in public. In my household the girls divide the tasks equally. I learned how to care for them by doing a parenting course at the University of Technology.

Work

I am a teacher because of my love for children, and being a teacher can help me to pass on certain values to these children. I have always wanted to be a nurse, but because I was not good at mathematics, I had to resort to teaching. I enjoy what I am doing when I send fifty-five students for the CXC examination and fifty-three pass. It is more rewarding than an increase in salary. When students are able to grasp certain concepts then it makes you enjoy what you are doing. Also, my work helps the community. People will always come and ask me advice, and ask for recommendations and other things that are needed to be done. It's difficult when students are not willing to learn and being unable to grasp certain concepts. I need to be able to identify the students' areas of weakness, then I try to create an environment in which students will want to learn. Then I use a variety of teaching aids to help overcome these difficulties.

Religious Ideals

I am Moravian and go to church every other Sunday. My religion is important because I learn more about God and his greatness. From I was younger I have been involved with the Sunday school. It has shaped my behaviour a lot. Now that I am an adult, these values are still with me. I believe that God created man and when he saw that it was lonely he created woman, so that they can take care of each other and live loving.

Gender Ideals

Men should be the head of the household. A man should possess certain qualities: being loving, kind, truthful, honest, goal oriented. He should be able to communicate effectively. I am not sure if today's men know what they want in a woman. They are placing emphasis on the physical beauty and neglecting the inner beauty. Some men I know are involved with more than one woman. I asked a friend who is married why is he involved in another relationship? His reply was "lust". So I ask him, "Can you love two persons at the same time?" His response was "when a mother have seven children don't she love all of them?" Peer pressure is leading them to do the things that they should not do. Men are gravitating towards the physical aspect. Men and women are both God's creation; we are living creatures; we breathe, inhale and exhale; we are the same this way, but some work demands more masculinity than femininity.

In reflecting on Miss Jones's gender identity, her belief that men are the rightful heads of household appears to be linked to her biblical literalist views, such that her status as household head is by default, resulting from the absence of a male head. However, that she endows herself with this title, rather than leaving it blank, so to speak, is a reflexive compromise, that is, a negotiation between her church values and her civic reality. As a teacher, we also see her reflecting the expectations of both teachers and parents, which I discussed in the previous chapter, to "pass on certain values to these children", as she herself states.

SHAKIRA (PSEUDONYM)

In this interview with "Shakira", we see how a younger woman, not yet a mother, embraces a sense of her autonomy. She sets a course of self-determination, born out of her understanding of Jamaica's colonial history, a history which she views as unjust for black women. Shakira was interviewed by one of the Edwin Allen Regional High School students, and then added her own written testimony as well. I attempted, on two separate occasions, to share my write up that blended these two narratives together with her through the email address she gave me, but she never replied. I did not meet her again on subsequent visits, but I believe that what follows reflects her own sentiments.

Shakira is a single woman in her mid twenties. When these interviews took place, she had recently begun to live on her own in the small, studio-style flat connected to Nurse Dunkley's home, although she no longer resides there. The flat, one source of income for Nurse, along with two other properties she owns and leases, is connected to the main house through a carport. The carport is empty, since Nurse Dunkley no longer drives, and it is enclosed by the walls of the flat and Nurse's home. The front entrance is framed by an elaborate grate, looking out to the road, the town and the lush green hills beyond. The carport has always been a place of play for Nurse's grandchildren and neighbourhood children, as well as a space for household members to relax after a long day of hard work, while it grows dark. Shakira frequently joined in these quiet evenings, when the crickets' and cicadas' songs pervade the night, along with the bellow of an occasional cow. Shakira's narrative consists of a series of reflections on herself and on gender relationships, influenced by her relatively new status as a high school teacher, her new living arrangement away from her parents, and her views of men and women and their gender socialization, in addition to her historical analysis I mentioned above. She reveals how tasks were delegated in her natal household based on skill and experience rather than gender alone, indicating that negotiations around these qualities likely ensued.

Household

I lived with my mother and father before, but now I am living alone and have been doing so for the last eighteen months. When I lived with my parents both had a dual/equal authority in the home. Now that I live alone, I consider myself the head of my household. I decide what to buy, how to place the furniture, when to clean, how much energy to use, and just about all the other decisions. Because I am the only member of my household, I have to arrange my work in the best possible way that I can manage. When I lived with my parents the work was arranged according to who would best manage the job, the person with better and more experience for the task at hand.

Gender Ideology

I believe that men and women are different in the sense that in Jamaica they are brought up to hold different values. For instance, for a man promiscuity is acceptable. But for women it is damned. Also women are expected to be housewives and do the housework and rear children, however, for men this is a demeaning work. Women doing strong labour are seen as extraordinary and sometimes out of place. People I know live up to these ideals, not all the time but some of the times. Not all persons are brought up to respect these ideals and hold them true. Depending on the background and religious orientation of the individuals, his values and customs may differ from the general population. Also, our Jamaican culture is a potpourri of ethnic mixes. There is the East Indian, African, Asian, European and North American culture that assimilate every day. Mixing and shaking, blending and turning, coming together to create that one Jamaican culture. However, there are elements that are common to all Jamaicans: our language, food and music, also our sense of independence. Once a colony, we had to fight for our independence from Britain, and I think all Jamaicans hold that dear in some way or the other.

For me, the ideal man has an ambition and a goal in life. He has the knowledge of what is right and what is wrong, has a conscience and is grounded in his beliefs whether they differ from the general population or belong to a group. He seeks to maintain the status quo of the general society. The ideal man in my opinion is open to emotions and has an open mind to new ideas and varying cultural traits. The ideal man embraces his responsibilities and knows a line of demarcation when it comes to gender inequality.

The ideal woman also has an ambition and a goal in life. She has the knowledge of right from wrong, strives to be independent, has a grounded sense of self-esteem, beliefs, personal identity (she has to know who she is and what she wants). Therefore she will know how to approach her dreams and aspirations. For the woman who knows that life is not a level playing field, however, hard work and determination will pay off. The ideal woman is open to emotions and has an open-minded approach to change, culturally and in the general lifestyles of people.

Shakira's narrative reflects an awareness of gender inequalities and the qualities women need to be successful. She reveals some contradictions in her views, indicating the clash of coexisting values and norms around masculinity in particular, when she states that she wants a man who supports the status quo but also one who is open to change – "new ideas and varying cultural traits". At the same time, ideal women should have ambition, presumably career ambition, which indicates instability around the idea of a male breadwinner, currently part of the status quo. Being in her mid twenties and just starting out on her own, it is not surprising that her views are unfolding, not static, as the critique of gender socialization reminds us, but attentive to emerging gender system features.

MRS HIGGINS

I was outside Moses's "Poor Man Struggle" Rasta shop one day, when the conversation turned to rumours that there was a two-hundred-year-old woman living nearby. I was certainly curious, and comfortable enough to say "that's impossible. No human being has ever lived that long." A local woman, university educated, insisted this was the case and told me she would take me up to see her right then. Five of us jammed into her small car, and we made our way up the hilly potholed roads, where we stopped to pick up two more, squeezing on laps and barely breathing. I was excited to find out her real age and if I could learn anything about her life. When we got closer and pavement turned to dirt track, we drove as far as we could, parked the car and walked up to the house. The driver asked the woman who came to the door, "Does the old lady live here?" When we found out she did, Janine explained about my work, and we were told to wait out on the porch. Eventually we were invited in. Mrs Higgins was lying in bed, apparently not feeling overly well, but well enough to see us. She was in a small, dark room. Blind and weak, she nonetheless was excited when her daughter-in-law, the woman who invited us in, told her that she had some visitors from the United States who wanted to learn about her life. She spoke softly and mumbled, so it was difficult to understand her, but I did record some of her story. The first thing we cleared up was her age. Someone went to find her birth certificate; it was remarkable in itself that she had one, and I learned that she was 104 years old. Although it was hard to make out her words, after playing the tape of the interview over and over I managed to discern the information that follows.

I live a rough life. I work hard to raise the children dem. I don't know where my life go to. I had four sons and three daughters. One son is living here now, four children die. Sometimes the children come to visit. My life mash up, *mash up* wit me husband. [My life was very difficult with my husband.] He die and leave me wit de children. I have to raise the children and farm. I work hard like a man. Grow yams, coffee, cane. I couldn't find no place to work. Me went to the river to wash. The boys go to catch shrimps and cook it. My husband came from India – Coolie [East Indian] country. Him half Coolie. When me a pickney, my mother do everything. My father was a cow man. Him go with other women to make pickney. I am the first one from him – him no tek care of me. We used to go to Cave Valley to sell. The farm is still in the family. My son farm now. Him in his sixties. One daughter went to school. She finished and is a teacher.

Me father tek four, five women. Me a de first one from me daddy. Me father not married to me mother. Him take another woman. The wife no care about me or the other children dem. The old people, they're wicked. I looked after her children. Me father send me a school but he no keep me in the school. I learn a little something by myself.

Sometimes we went to Frankfield. I remember the court house. We just pass through, ride the donkey. We never realize like these pickney in these days [we are not as aware/ enlightened as children are today].

Sadness and bitterness are dominant themes in Mrs Higgins's life. Rejected by her father and his later wife, a man who cared more about his women than his daughter in her eyes, we are left to imagine a lonely child. Later left alone with her own children due to her husband's untimely death, she worked "like a man" in the fields to provide for the children she later lost and also did traditional working-class female jobs such as washing other people's clothes. At the same time, she managed to keep the farm in the family and she revealed a sense of pride in this accomplishment. Her son, in his seventies, wandered in during our visit on his way back from "the bush". Mrs Higgins seemed very aware that times are different today, reflected in her statement about the knowledge that children have as compared to her own youth. It may be tempting to see Mrs Higgins's life as a relic of a previous gender system's rigid adherence to a division of labour and racial/ethnic stratification (her husband was a "Coolie"). However, if we recall the Clarendon report issued by the Bureau of Women's Affairs, it is clear that there are women today whose lives are not that different from that of Mrs Higgins – women who are struggling to raise a houseful of children by taking out washing, subject to the abandonment of men, and victims of physical and psychological abuse. For these women, it is unclear if existent and emerging shifts in the rural black Jamaican gender system that I have discussed hold much promise since they are embedded within daily struggles with little opportunity to transform their life conditions. Here it is useful to think about the metaphorical quality of cultural DNA. Just as DNA can be regarded as a recipe or blueprint for genetic information, we can similarly reflect on the gender molecule as harbouring a kind of "long term storage of information" (Patricia Mohammed, personal communication, September 2008). Mrs Higgins's tale of her life would not be unrecognizable to many rural Jamaican women today.

MOSES

The narrative of Moses emerged from a blend of formal interviews and informal conversations that took place over a number of years. Moses was thrilled to have his story told, and on two occasions in the summer of 2006 he even

Figure 7: Moses visiting the author and her family in Kingston.

travelled by bus from Frankfield to the UWI campus, where I was residing, to pursue our interviews. One night, I found myself listening from late afternoon until nightfall to Moses's life story, as we sat on my front porch of the house in Nuffield Flats on UWI campus. I was in "friend" mode rather than anthropologist, so I took no notes, although I was struck by the richness of his tale, the "sufferation" that he says he has lived, and the assumptions and beliefs about gender roles embedded in his account of his life. Returning to Frankfield, he eagerly offered his time for an interview at his shop.

The next day, I wrote down as much as I could remember and then went back over the story with him for clarification. The narrative draws on poetic licence. I write in the first person, moving between English and phonetic patois. My follow-up questions were somewhat chronological, beginning with his parents' marriage and moving to his birth, childhood and adult life. However, as he retold his story, this time to a tape recorder and my notetaking, I interjected questions, as did Heidi, my long-time research assistant. I have edited out the questions, linking pieces together in a condensed story, which Moses then read and commented on. It was then edited accordingly so that this piece met his approval.

I was born Aaron Ferguson, May twelfth 1965. My mother had seventeen children, the first when she was sixteen. Six died in childbirth. The first five she had with a first baby-father from St Ann, but she lost two. When she met my father she brought three pickney into the marriage, two girls, one boy, and she had eleven more with my father. My father died in 2001. My mother was married fifty-four years. Eleven of us are still living; I have a sister in Kingston, but de rest dem in Canada and your country [America].

In the earlies my father, Joshua Ferguson, him went to England to work in a metal factory. But he had an accident: him cross road and hit by vehicle and break his ribs. When him get better, he came back with nothing! Just a loaf of bread, one can bully beef, one pound and a suitcase. After six years. [*Moses laughs heartily at the irony of it*] That's when he start to farm again; just him alone. When he come back, that's when I was born. He get up and work from six to six.

When me father in England, my mother was at home with my sisters. She always say she had to be father and mother. She have to maintain the father part; she have to govern the children when my father no around. She bring in money. She have to go to market, to May Pen, buy and sell, have to have something in between when the farm doesn't give enough. Sometime she barely mek [make] food money.

Me growing up as likkle boy me couldn't attend school so regular. Maybe two, three times a week. I have to stop to pick coffee on Thursday. Every Thursday and help with the animals, cows and goats and a donkey. Me father sold the goats when he need to pay for school fee, tax and bills. I alone work on the farm. My brothers, one went to Canada when he was seventeen or eighteen; another, my mother's second son, was grown by his granny, him not grow amongst we.

When I was fifteen years old I have to leave school. I see poverty all around. My mother sent me to Kingston to work for a Chinaman; I build aquarium for pet fish and learn to breed the fish. When I start, I make ninety-five dollars a week, and I have to give my mother seventy dollars a week to help me sisters. One sister went to the USA. It is I who work to send her to school. She was a nurse and went to further her education, but later, she didn't help me. All my other sisters went to school and finish high school. When I was eighteen, my son was born. I have a girlfriend, and she get pregnant. I use condom, but you know, sometimes you get carried away. When she told her parents she was pregnant they yell and shout "you pregnant!" and throw all her things out of the house. So it's all on me. Well, I grow my son out of my ninety-five dollars. I trade fruits from the farm in Kingston to buy baby feed to support the baby-mother. I'm a very skilful guy; I make some music; I do some painting, any likkle ting to make money. Later, she get married, and the stepfather, he take them to the USA when my son was ten. After three years, my son came back searching for me. Every year they come back searching for me, but they can't find, because I'm not in one place; I'm moving all around, and I have no contact with the baby-mother; in those days there were no cellular phone. The year before last they found me. This time she said, they're going to find me; she remembered that I was around here – this place. My son was twenty or twenty-one. He taller than me, bigger than me! I was so happy to see them. Last summer I wanted to go to his graduation, but I get the visa three weeks after the ceremony pass.

I also have a daughter. She was born when I was twenty-five, same way. She's fifteen now. She lives in Mandeville with her mother. And I grow her too, the same; I send her mother money every week. I see how my mother and father grow and struggle to help the child. When a youth grown by mother and father then he a govern [grown with discipline]; he have male and female gender, so have no problem with ooman [woman] or man. But a girl grown up with a father, no female energy; a boy grow up with just a mother, no male energy. Him have a problem moving amongst the ladies. This is one of the biggest problem in Jamaica with de youth dem. Dem not govern by male and female. Have no love.

Time in Kingston

I was seventeen years in Kingston. On the weekends, I come back to country Friday evening and work Saturday and Sunday on the farm, then go back to Kingston for Monday morning. After four years I got a raise to $160/week. My boss can leave, say, "Moses, take care of everything." When he went to foreign it's me alone in his house. He give me bed, TV, bicycle to ride to work. There are seven guys working, but me the best one. In the last year I got a raise to $300/week. But in 1997 there was a change of government, a new prime minister, and the owner, my boss, he sold the shop. He said, "I'm not staying here with this rule of government." So I came back to Frankfield. My father was getting older. He needed some more strength, energy around him. I thought better go to country straight back to the farm.

PRIEST

Priest's story is the outcome of one interview, which took place in his house, in a hot little room with the tape recorder running. Also present were archaeologist Ron Dalton and Heidi Savery, my travel companion and research assistant since 2004. I asked most of the questions about Priest's household growing up, his education, common-law arrangement and relationship with his children. Ron also contributed by asking questions about Priest's music, and the way Priest relates to his son and daughter. Priest showed us his picture albums of his extended family.

My name is Hopeton Kelvin. Most people know me as Kelvin. I am also called Priest because I spent six years in a Jerusalem schoolroom at the Prince Emmanuel Foundation in Bull Bay. I'm a Boboshanti priest. I was ordained a Rastafarian priest, so I'm called

Priest. I describe myself as love. So I try to live to the character of love. Have to have a balance, a spiritual and temporal balance.

I was born the sixth of February 1958; that's Bob Marley's birthday as well, so I always have a nice birthday. I get to celebrate with all the music and other tings going on. I was born in this house. I used to live here with my grandparents; my mother left when I was three to England, and my father left when I was two. But it never trouble me, because I didn't grow with dem. I went to Frankfield Primary, then I went to Edwin Allen for two years, then to Clarendon College for five years. I then went to an agricultural school for two years. I always wanted to do music, but the farming, learning about agriculture, was a way to make a living. I used to work with the Soil Conservation Department making ditches and waterways, levelling the ground, levelling the land for plants. I went to work in the head office in Kingston and worked there for one and a half years, and then I went to Trelawny to work for the soil extension service. But then I tell myself, I'm always Rasta. The calling just came. So I went to Bull Bay. The more you're in the "system" the more you can't really match up; there's an imbalance. So I stopped eating meat, drinking liquor.

It was glorious at Bull Bay. GLORIOUS. I was in a world where everybody thinking on the same level. Living in praises and righteousness, cleansing and purifying of self. At Bull Bay, men and women lived in separate quarters. Women were not allowed to be priests. It was a kind of traditional thinking. I never saw women smoking the chalice with men, but women can reason. The men reasoned together.

I never say me leaving; I think it was after my grandmother died and no one was here at this house. Everybody – brothers, sisters – in America or England. I was the only one. It was natural that I come home. My natural responsibility. After a while when I was home, I met my baby-mother, and she gave birth to our son Tafari – Taf is what everyone call him. Now it's just Taf, me and four guys from the football club living here. Baby-mother died three years ago of pneumonia. We were in a common-law situation. Her name was Mac. She was Mac and her friend was Miss Mac. Danny's baby-mother, who's in America now, she would say, "Hi Miss Mac, it's Mac!"

We had a business, a shop where I cooked and sold Ital food. But from hurricane Ivan, I stop the shop. I have a daughter too. She's about twenty now. Taf is thirteen. My daughter is at UWI studying mass communication. I raised her till she was four, but when my grandmother died, she went to live with her auntie. Her mother was teaching in the Bahamas. I always kept up financial support. With my son, Tafari, I try to make him know basically that nothing is greater than self; he has to build himself, more knowledge and principles of life. Keep himself tidy and clean, respect himself and fellow brethren and sistren. You try to enforce certain discipline and knowledge. You have to hope for the best and stick to principles. He needs to work more, to be more serious about his work. When him was younger, he let his dreadlocks out of his hat and some-times got into fights with other boys. Him wear the hat now though him growing more; most of the childish things out of him.

I believe in the truth rightness, oneness and community, the real oneness. I try to really practise it. To love, to build the character of truth, love, tolerance, patience. Very few times I beat Taf. Most of time me just talk to him generally – me don't really believe in that, in beating. I treat my daughter same way. When Taf get in trouble in school, gets in fights, I tell him stop the violence. I want him to be best of what he choose to be – well, I always tell me daughter she should come and help her people, get educated for self, but it no justice or love if it come to naught. She's very disciplined, getting lots of prizes. She's always excelling. She's living in Crooked River – not very far – so I do see her often. She went to Edwin Allen and lived here, then Clarendon College; now she's at UWI.

Taf was so close to his mother; she help get things ready, food, clothes, for school. So now I take on this; at times it's challenging to be mother and father. I have to play both roles. I tell Taf, must have woman traits in you because as men we try to kill the female out of us, but I think that it must be there, tenderness. But I don't think it's really that good to kill it; you're your mother's child so you must have it. When she lived in the house we basically share. Most times in the restaurant I used to do the cooking so we eat from same pot. She did some baking: pudding, grata, drops [coconut]. She do most of washing, hers and Tafari; she basically do the cleaning inside. Outside sweeping, I do that and the garden. We have bananas, plantain, ackee, breadfruit, orange . . .

I would like to find another woman. I'm not really mourning anymore, but I know it's hard for Taf. I'm looking for someone who's truthful, tolerant, patience, loving, car-ing, sharing and forgiving, kind. Well, it's hard to find someone like that. Woman have to take care of man, and man have to take care of woman. You see, most times men who don't care for their children would like to care but circumstances . . . but don't have that amount of cash, so run away. Real love not really there; sometimes the woman guess who's the father, there's doubt, not like a man and woman living together and having a thing going.

Taf love music. We went to contest one time and he did very good singing. Even in Frankfield he win prizes. From when I was growing up, musician was only thing I wanted to be. I always wrote the music from school time. I never think I want to be doctor or lawyer. There was that push to go to school . . . but now I'm making music.

The accounts of parenting philosophies provided by Moses and Priest reflect both the scholarly work that has been conducted on masculinity and fatherhood in the Caribbean pioneered by Brown, Chevannes and others lead by the Centre for Childhood Development at UWI (Fox 1999), as well as popular discourse on manhood that I have referred to throughout the book and again earlier in this chapter. Both are men who take their parenting responsibilities seriously, something that appears to be more common in observant Rastamen. Both also reflect on difficulties they've had with women; in both cases, since the death of Priest's baby-mother, neither man has been able to find a long-term mate. In part this may have to do with their prominent dreadlocks and the absence of Rastawomen in Frankfield. Working-class black women aspiring to "ladyhood" would not select a Rastaman, because he would not help them to achieve this goal, his values and identity reflective of strand of masculinity that rejects the longevity of the colonial notions of femininity that aspire to upward mobility and their admittedly nostalgic conception of African femininity that we saw in the idealized construction on Nanny in the previous chapter.

Interestingly, the following narrative, collected by one of the Edwin Allen Regional High School research assistants tells a story of a man who is highly family-oriented, who is not Rastafarian, and who experiences tensions with his common-law wife over material goods. His narrative expresses a traditional conceptualization of gender-role division in the household, unlike Moses and Priest, who both support the notion, radical in rural Jamaica, that men in fact possess and should value, attributes and skills that they define as feminine. It also should be noted, however, that these attributes and skills, including emotional sensitivity and domestic capabilities, are drawn from a traditional conception of gender roles and gender identity rather than a broader view that they may in fact exist outside of an association with any particular gender.

As I discussed in the previous chapter, in the late 1990s, Janet Brown, Barry Chevannes, Jaipaul L. Roopnarine and others associated with the Centre for Childhood Development at UWI Mona, argued that Caribbean fatherhood was misunderstood in part because it was under-researched, and that in fact, the stereotypical profile of Caribbean men across socio-economic strata as "absentee or irresponsible fathers, unfaithful partners, frequent perpetrators of domestic violence and marginalized by choice or circumstance from the mainstream of family life" has been overstated (Brown, Anderson and Chevannes 1993, 2). John's statements below reflect this viewpoint.

JOHN (PSEUDONYM)

Partnering, Household and Work

I am in a common-law marriage for sixteen years. I undergo a lot of pressure for money from my baby-mother. She does not satisfy with whatever I give her, but it's okay even though I'm pressured, I live with it because I love my family. I have one son and one daughter, both are mine and my baby-mother's. I am the head of the household and this has never changed. I am responsible for buying food, paying bills, clothing, school fees, their education, shelter, everything. I alone do not decide things in the family. We come together, and we are a family that live in harmony. But if there's anything to be done at home, whoever sees it first will do it. I think that men can do household chores. My children are in high school now, so they know what to do. But my daughter, I don't want her to get pregnant.

In my opinion, men should be hard-working, honest and a family man, someone who tek [takes] responsibility in the home and cares for his kids. For me, those are the characteristics of a good man. A woman should be loving, honest and kind, and understanding. We are both living up to these.

SUMMARY

These portraits of Frankfielders reveal many shared themes, in spite of the diversity of personalities, beliefs and life circumstances. They are people who are working to survive financially, striving for ideals rooted in religion, struggling to overcome hardship and betrayal. They are reflections of thoughtful people showing perhaps their best sides to the researchers. In addition to these portraits, my research assistants and myself conducted thirty other interviews. We asked men and women similar questions about partnering and work patterns, household roles, religious affiliation and morality, as well as gender ideals. These, like the stories above, reveal varying degrees of frustration with the complexity of family and community life, the challenges of finding partners who meet cultural and personal predilections, the demands of lives of economic hardship, and pride in oneself and one's children. Farmers struggle with the lack of markets for their products while juggling additional forms of income. Many men perform chores traditionally considered feminine work, standing outside of rigid definitions of masculinity with respect to shopping and cooking, cleaning and washing. They, however, simultaneously consider themselves heads of household, disciplining their children with spankings and beatings, confirming their statuses through the morality of the Bible. One man put it aptly, reflecting general community values, when he referred to the Bible as the "blueprint for mankind". Thus his baby-mother, in an interview in March 2007, can discuss shared household chores without challenging his view of his own position: "My husband will do the cooking and I will wash the dishes. In the mornings, he will prepare the breakfast while I prepare the children. There is no set way in which we do it." In this household, as in many others, although both husband and wife work outside the home, and men and women share their responsibilities within the home by divvying up chores in various ways that often overlap rigid divisions of labour, both men and women consider the father to be the head of the household.

Still, as I have argued, any so-called blueprint coexists with alternate views, even those who articulate the ideal. In closing this chapter, we should not forget the challenges to this system that are unfolding, the number of women living alone, and the growing number of fathers raising their children while participating in domestic affairs with a partner or on their own. As one single woman said, "The Bible says that the man should be the head of the family. But my contention is that you have some worthless men, and I don't think that these men can be the head of anything." Or another single woman who said reflectively, in response to a question about the difference between women and men, "Men tend to feel that the world is made for them and so they tend to abuse their role as men. Women develop this tame and submissive nature that gives her the feeling that the world is to survive in, not to really live in. Both need to change." These philosophical views and many others I have shared do not reflect an automatic acceptance of abstract gender norms, but a complex interweaving of daily contingencies set against hopeful possibilities and real limitations. Gender negotiations are thus integral features of the Jamaican cultural landscape, as these Frankfield architects demonstrate, through their engagement in its ongoing construction.

Chapter 6

A Metaphor Comes to Life

Service Learning, HIV/AIDS and Cross-Cultural Knowledge

SCHOLAR-ACTIVISM AND "GIVING BACK"

As an anthropologist, I have always been anxious that the conceptual understanding I have developed through fieldwork generates some kind of value for the community, in addition to the long-term emotional bonds with the community that the research has produced for me as well as my adopted Jamaican family. This chapter speaks to this concern, demonstrating how I have engaged with the community as a scholar-activist, pointing both to problems and solutions developed by professionals or individuals in the community and wider Clarendon parish. These problems are connected to the gender system and require an in-depth understanding of the system to be solved. The previous building blocks in the book – the description of the DNA metaphor, the general patterns that the metaphor affords regarding gender ideologies and roles, and the specific permutations of the gender system expressed and negotiated by individuals – are an important backdrop for policy makers involved in gender and community work, whose own interventions and programmes could benefit from it (Patricia Mohammed, personal communication, September 2008).

My specific aim is to provide this activist lens by discussing some applied anthropological projects that I organized over the last decade, projects that required both my students and Frankfield residents to examine their gendered assumptions. The projects created opportunities for negotiations across culture, race, class and gender, further wedging open existing cracks in the gender system and providing opportunities for reflection on gender identity, and, in some instances, transformations across those boundaries. Employing the personal narratives as well as reports of field notes, the chapter also displays the methodological diversity of the feminist ethnographic approach to knowledge construction. For example, my American white female students have written about how they were taken aback by Jamaican norms that conflate white, middle-class womanhood with notions of what it means to be "a proper lady". Their eyes opened when they were accused of not behaving as such. Some white male students initially perceived Frankfield's men as a homogenous category of territorial aggressors. A Haitian American student was confused by shifting characterizations of her as a "Natural Sister Queen" (due to her short hair twists) and, at the same time, a threat to local women. A beautiful Eritrean female student felt stifled by persistent scrutiny from the community, men and women alike, while simultaneously enjoying the attention her presence obtained. The students' stories included here flesh out the DNA metaphor by underscoring the contingent nature of gender in culture, metaphorically understood as DNA mutations – as gendered identities collided in unexpected ways. As I have discussed earlier, gender systems are informed by external cultural processes and the importations of new ideas, one of these being the exchange of cultural ideals through travel. Insights worked both ways as my students and some Frankfield residents they interacted with examined their assumptions about gender.

Throughout the course of my fieldwork I not only reflected on the wider usefulness of this fieldwork for policy makers, but on a more personalized conception of "giving back". I have long been repelled by the idea that "the field" is simply a place to obtain "data" to employ towards one's own career advancement. At the same time, many contemporary anthropologists have noted that the discipline is marred by a history of supposed do-gooders, whose notions of cultural change were couched in ideologies of progress, notions that ultimately proved either harmful or irrelevant to people's own interests as they sought to impose their values on others. What I realized in the process is that approaching the community with a lens towards activism and "giving back" offered me new ways to learn about gender. These ways underscore the gender system as a living system, a system unique but shared, under transformation but historically rooted, ultimately a metaphor that has come to life. In addition, while I was perhaps always hyper-aware of the ethical dilemmas attached to the process of planned culture change, various attempts to "give back" nonetheless belied my presumed sense of altruism, presenting unanticipated complications and outcomes. At the same time, these complications led me down new avenues of insight into gendered identity and meanings, and how individuals, who possess disparate notions of these, interact about them.

"GIVING BACK": A FIRST ATTEMPT

Quite by chance one afternoon, while reading the *Jamaica Gleaner* on Nurse Dunkley's lovely veranda, I learned about a community organization located in one of Kingston's roughest neighbourhoods, Mandela Terrace.[1] The paper had an article about the organization Children and Communities for Change, also known as "3Cs". This organization was lead by a social worker in Kingston named Cebert Hines, and it drew children, ages five to eighteen, into educational and social activities. Most of the children came from homes broken and impoverished, in part due to drug abuse, HIV infection and violence. Cebert had refashioned a building, with various grants, into a community centre that provided a retreat from the violence of the streets. It was a place where children could receive after school tutoring, African drumming lessons, and training in choreography and drama. The children worked with community centre leaders to develop skits and dances with positive messages about healthy lifestyles, family relationships and HIV/AIDS.

I immediately picked up the telephone and left a message on Cebert's voice mail saying I was an anthropologist working and living in Frankfield, Clarendon where I had been involved in "culturally appropriate HIV/AIDS education". These educational efforts drew on accepted and valued modes of communication to convey difficult and culturally challenging notions. Since HIV/AIDS involves frank discussions about sex and sexuality, topics that Jamaican parents and teachers are loath to discuss with children, the vehicle of delivery is central to the receptivity of the message. I hoped that Cebert would return my call, so I could invite the group to come to Frankfield to perform.

Cebert did call back, and his call initiated both a friendship and working relationship that has lead to a visit from student members of 3Cs to my home in Providence, Rhode Island and various additional collaborations.[2] The first such collaboration resulted in a visit from 3Cs to Frankfield where the group stayed overnight in some classrooms at the Edwin Allen Regional High School, were fed by Nurse's niece in her cookshop and performed over a two-day period in a number of venues. The reverend of the Methodist church, at the time a progressive, fun-loving and committed activist from Haiti named Roosevelt Papaloutte, offered to organize two church events for us. Dressed in their gorgeous African kente cloth clothes, and carrying their Jimbe drums, the children danced onto their various performance stages singing about the importance of trust in relationships, devastation of AIDS and need for community support, rather than the all-too-common rejection and isolation wrought by stigma and fear. The following is an excerpt from my field notes after the performance in the town square. It conveys both the excitement and frustrations of organizing such events as well as the impact of gender ideologies on the children of 3Cs.

FIELD NOTES: CHILDREN AND COMMUNITY FOR CHANGE (3CS) AND DJ PARTY IN FRANKFIELD TOWN SQUARE: 6/22/01

Organizing events that involve outside groups can be both frustrating and rewarding. On the day that the group CCC was to arrive and perform by 3:00 p.m. at the Edwin Allen Regional High School, they didn't come until 4:30 p.m. The driver had left late to pick up the group from their community centre in Kingston and had apparently run into a lot of traffic in Town due to an accident. As I waited, I got increasingly anxious and found it very difficult to just "go with the flow", as I always urged my students to do. The primary school had already been disappointed since the group had postponed its arrival until the afternoon, cancelling the morning performance. When the bus finally rolled in, my own students and I distributed the box lunches of fried chicken and rice and peas that we had packed earlier, and the children began to dress in their bright-coloured African kinte cloth costumes. The girls wore gold skirts and bright-coloured turbans, while the boys wore red, gold and black shirts and headbands.

Their arrival coincided with an event I had been hearing about since our arrival a few weeks earlier. It was a big soundsystem dance in the square, sponsored by the Guinness beer company. Huge speakers twenty feet high were being set up on one side of the square and a stage on another. I've never seen Frankfield that busy, but what we saw in the late afternoon was only a fraction of the crowd that would turn out later. In any event, we tried to make the best of the missed afternoon performance, and the Guinness folks permitted the children to use the stage for half an hour at 6:30. Although the full sobriety of their message was drowned out in the excited crowd, they did attract a large group around the stage: some people sat on rooftops, while others clustered together on sidewalks and in the streets, backing up traffic. People of all ages could be seen, from elderly grandparents to small children. As the lead singer of the group, a striking young woman with a powerful stage presence, sang about the devastation of children coming home to crack-addicted parents, I noticed out of the corner of my eye – not without irony – a boy, not much more than nine or ten, barefoot, wearing ragged pants and a too-big T-shirt, hanging out by the back of the stage drinking a Guinness.

After their performance, we all made our way back to Nurse's house, where the group piled in the van again. My students and I all crammed into Reverend Papalloute's car along with my friend Saheed Henry, a Rastafarian poet, and made our way slowly up the road to Nine Turns. This is a sleepy little town up the top of an extremely potholed, winding road above Frankfield. It was a much smaller venue, although the church, which probably held about one hundred persons, was packed. Papalloute, as he was affectionately known, gave a welcome to both groups and then invited me up to speak before the congregation. I stood up in front of the eager group – coming out to evening church events is a favourite community activity – and gave a description of the work that I had been doing with my students. I then introduced Cebert and his group. Cebert stood up. All such events are quite formal, involving elaborate introductions and thanks to all involved parties, explaining the mission of 3Cs. Smaller groups of the children then danced and sang five separate numbers, all with the message of positive self-image. Parents talked to their children; it was an island of unity, self-respect and the importance of protected sex. Everyone was taking the issue of HIV seriously. Then Saheed performed a poem from the heart, and everyone was thrilled. The poem was one of the hits of the evening, and the audience urged two or three repeats. Below is the poem that Saheed wrote and performed:

AIDS Is a Dangerous Disease

By Saheed Henry (printed with permission of the author)

AIDS is a dangerous disease
But it cannot be caught in the breeze

You can still get it with ease
If you don't yield to precautions like these:

"No Doc.
That's wrong and slack
You can't use the same needle to stick Mac.
Pull a new one from the pack
Is HIV you want the man to contract?"

Promiscuous behaviour
Always means danger
You must not just jump and have sex with a stranger.
Always stick to one faithful partner.

Using a condom is a method of protection
But that is not the best to the situation
The rubber can burst and cause a confusion.
You can be free from AIDS. There is one solution
That is to abstain from sexual action.

Big lie
what dem a try
Tell dem you nay bug
No samfy [tricks/cons]
Everyone can get the virus,
Not only a gay guy.

My students had also drawn up big posters depicting the impact of HIV with little cartoon-like drawings of the "bad" HIV virus and the innocent white blood cells fighting the virus. Cebert then instigated and led a productive discussion, after a few moments of quiet. He asked the congregants to reflect on what they had learned. Then the congregation asked a range of questions: Where did HIV/AIDS come from? What are the various modes of transmission? What kind of stigma seems to exist island wide? Should one get tested given lack of available medications? Why is there no cure? Does the mosquito carry HIV after having bitten an infected person, and can it transmit the virus? The evening was long. When people come to church for an event, they expect it to fill their night, be entertaining and be worth their while. Afterwards, the kids ate sticky brown rum cake on the lawn of the church, and we piled into cars and went down to Frankfield, where the town was "bumpin'".

By 10:00 p.m. when we went back out, there must have been one thousand people in town. The smell of jerk chicken and pork was in the air, cashew vendors were selling their wares and everyone was drinking Guinness. The soundsystem was getting everyone excited, although the crowd was amazingly peaceful and just having a good time. People danced in place, and those who were more involved clustered up close to the stage where some people were dancing.

Then there was a raffle, and suddenly all my excitement was deflated. The selector starting speaking to the crowd: "raise your hands in the air if you're a chi-chi man; raise your hands in the air if you're not" (lots of men raised their hands and waved them). Then he said "chi-chi man, get back" and asked the men to wave their hands in the air if they had a beautiful woman with a pretty "pum pum" . . . This began an evening of lyrics combining heterosexism, homophobia and objectification of women, as the participants, mesmerized by the beat, chimed in. I must admit that when this began, I felt a fearful chill run through me. I left the party and went back to the house, not without some despair. But then I began to think about how just hours before, at Nine Turns, a Pentecostal church congregation had hosted a radical message of inclusion, safe sex and the value of information.

In a recent email exchange with applied anthropologist Gerald Murray, who has worked in Haiti on reforestation projects, I discussed the emotional pitfalls that often permeate action anthropology; that is, efforts to bring about positive change, in conjunction with community actors. Murray replied in a helpful fashion, shedding light on my field note reflections about the dissonance between the local level work we do with communities and the persistence of societal problems:

> I encourage you to continue promoting an anti-nihilistic approach to applied anthropology. Some anthropologists have made their careers critiquing applied anthropology without offering any pragmatic solutions to human dilemmas. There is a growing literature on NGOs. I have in past weeks reviewed some manuscripts for *American Anthropologist* in which the authors dismiss all non-governmental attempts in a conspiratorial world-systems framework. Those who do what we have done are depicted as pawns of capitalism and colonialism or some such. Anthropology can do much better than hurling elegantly formulated spitballs from the sidelines against efforts to solve problems. (Murray, personal communication, 21 June 2007)

In spite of my initial response of despair, the dancehall scene in Frankfield profoundly underscored the need for community workshops, and not necessarily their futility. Moreover, the above description of the collaboration with 3Cs, the Edwin Allen Regional High School, and local businesses that supported the event highlights the approach that I have taken in seeking to apply ethnographic insights. Collaboration to produce personal narratives, as described in the last chapter, is a centrepiece of feminist ethnographic work, and collaboration with community actors to bring about change that they themselves are working on is a pivotal component of a liberatory anthropology. Power relationships are never erased, but through much of 3Cs' performance and discussion, I, the anthropologist, sat on the sidelines as a facilitator and indeed as a student, learning from community actors themselves.

I will now move on to explore in more detail some features of my work with the American college students who travelled with me to Jamaica to work on service learning projects, injecting applied anthropological approaches, both of which I define below. To reiterate the link between these projects and gender in rural Jamaica, the connections we built in communities opened channels for discussion about gender ideologies and practices, and enriched my own understanding of the nature of the rural gender system by bringing different cultural worlds together. One guiding tenet of anthropological research is that exposure to other worldviews shapes insight into one's own. When the insights revolve around gender issues, then the process encompasses the feminist epistemological project of self-reflexivity. In conjunction with community members, the programmes we introduced varied from summer school programmes for children held at the Methodist Church that involved reading groups and games, to working with teachers in the Primary School, to HIV/AIDS workshops. The remainder of this chapter examines them and the feminist epistemological insights they produced, beginning with the earliest one.

DOING SERVICE LEARNING IN FRANKFIELD

In May and June 2001, I travelled to Frankfield with a group of students to work on a number of service learning projects in the community.[3] Over the last decade, service learning has quickly become an institutional phenomenon in high schools, colleges and universities throughout the United States. As anthropologists begin to accommodate their fieldwork sites for students who will ostensibly provide some "service", I began to think more critically both about the goals I hoped to achieve in designing these courses and the impact on the community itself. I was also interested in examining how these undertakings differ from purely research oriented field experiences that students participate in with their professors. In addition, I was interested in learning how returning to a community as a leader of such a programme, instead of as a single researcher, affects community perceptions of me and, more broadly, anthropologists who engage in a similar process.

In communities such as Frankfield where voluntary labour is associated predominantly with the church, as part of a wider proselytizing mission, or even civic youth groups that are guided by Christian principles, it is especially important to think about how community members understand "service". Perceptions of my students' service and my role as an organizer were interpreted through Frankfielders' own cultural frames of reference, which have often clashed with the goals of the programme as it was conceived from an academic office at home.

I will begin by providing some descriptive analysis of the service learning ventures, identifying those aspects of organizing and implementing the service learning experience with the specific aim of provoking critical thinking about the assumptions underlying the idea of "service". As part of this discussion, I explore some of the gendered, self-reflexive insights students acquired about themselves and their own sociocultural backgrounds, emphasizing this crucial and integral component of service learning. It is important to emphasize that the sites themselves have not been regular hosts to foreign volunteers. Prior to "naming" the sites as service sites, Frankfielders did not conceive of them as such. While the majority of Frankfielders do not refer to institutions in their communities in this fashion, those whom we worked with most closely began to adopt this language. They would ask both me and my students questions such as, "How is the service going?" or "Do you find that there are many things that need to be done?" This is particularly interesting in light of Foucauldian discourse analysis, which emphasizes the impact of particular discourses on constructing perceptions of reality, meaning and identity. I am interested in thinking about how naming sites as arenas for service by overseas student volunteers shapes both the relationships between students and their hosts as well as Frankfielders' perceptions of their own institutions.

ESTABLISHING THE SERVICE LEARNING SITES

In establishing sites where students could volunteer on an annual basis, I had two initial criteria. First, I wanted students to work in situations where the need was locally defined. Second, I wanted to be able to return annually to the same institutions in order to establish a programme over time. I exchanged letters with the principals of the Frankfield Primary School and Edwin Allen Regional High School and also to one of the head nurses at the Frankfield health centre. I also spoke with Nurse Dunkley, who helped me to arrange housing for the students. On the first day of our arrival, we all gathered at Nurse Dunkley's home for a meal. She began with her usual lengthy, emotive prayer expressing appreciation that we had arrived safely and hope that our mission would be fulfilled. After eating, I took students on a walk through town, and they drew maps as we walked. This began their formal engagement with the community, as various townsfolk greeted them, noticed them and asked about what they were doing.

Early the next morning, students awoke with the families and began to learn about the morning household chores. After breakfast, we all met at a pre-arranged spot, and I walked with each of them to each site, where I introduced the students and confirmed the nature of our visit. Two students were assigned classrooms at the primary school, and told that they should rotate to new class-rooms every three days. At the health centre, I left one student with the nurses to discuss further what contributions she could make. One other student was dropped off at the principal's office of the high school. Each day we all met for lunch and then students returned to their sites until 3:00 p.m., when school let out. I spent the first part of my days doing a range of activities, including spending time at each site myself, conducting some interviews and re-estab-lishing contacts.

Students knew in advance that their service sites would also be part of their participant observation since the "learning" component of the service involved a cultural analysis of the values, norms and beliefs, as well as economic condi-tions and historical events shaping the practices they engaged in. I also required students to conduct interviews both in and out of their service sites. The application of anthropological research methods is part and parcel of the service learning experience; service learning extends classroom experience into the community and provides students with the opportunity to reflect on the relationship between anthropological knowledge and the methods designed to create it. The relationship between methods and knowledge is a theme I stress as a way of emphasizing the anthropological character of their service experiences. I also conducted organized "reflection sessions", sessions that are encouraged by service-learning theory. These occurred in the evenings, every two or three days, and provided students the opportunity to share their individual experiences. I used these talks to relate their anecdotal accounts to broader theoretical questions we had addressed in class. Moreover, I required students to develop specific research projects extending from their service sites, so that they could begin to view their service as a series of cross-cultural interactions. I encouraged my students not to assume differences or similarities in values and assumptions, but to engage in careful observations and thoughtful analysis prior to arriving at any conclusions.

One student, we'll call her Stacy, was majoring in early childhood education at home and wanted to learn about Jamaican approaches. She knew from her teaching internship in the United States that there was a high likelihood that there would be Jamaican children in her south-eastern Massachusetts classroom since this particular area is home to many Jamaican migrants. She therefore elected to assist a teacher in a primary school classroom. This young woman had long, blond hair, and the female students began immediately referring to her as "Barbie". They gathered round her as she walked to school, stood in the schoolyard and returned home, reaching to stroke her hair and hug her. "Barbie" found this sudden objectification of herself disturbing in part because she was unprepared for her physical attributes to become a focus, and she had never before been a minority. In this instance, though, her minority status conferred a sort of celebrity that provoked extreme discomfort and even guilt. At the same time, she had to work to establish herself as a person with interests and feelings beyond her looks, and through this process she began to empathize with the experience of racial discrimination. "Barbie" also began to wonder whether a male student with blond hair in her position would have been called "Ken", the Barbie doll's male companion. She suspected not, when one of the male students, who did in fact have blond hair, received the pet name of "Tattoo" because his arms and legs were covered with tattoos. While this student's hair was not the focus, still the focus was on a physical attribute. "Tattoo" also started to think about gender and race relations in the United States through a new lens, as his physical appearance became the marker of his identity, with assumptions about his behaviour and values linked to his tattoos (for example, he must be "rough" or a drug user). Race and gender thus became recognizably intertwined categories for these students, permitting them insight into the links among colour, race and gender in this particular setting.

Over the next few weeks, "Barbie" also began to think more deeply about education as shaped by culture and gender. She had developed a research project exploring Jamaican approaches to early childhood education, using the service site simultaneously as a field site. She supplemented her participant observation with interviews in which she tried to learn more about teacher training and broader cultural values about the relationships between education, socialization and religion. Her initial shock and dismay at the prominent role of religion in the classroom and the lack of individual attention each student received had lead her to an initial condemnation of the system and an elevation of the US school system, rather than an attempt to understand. Since this was also a service site and not simply a research site, her challenge was to find a way to be helpful to the teacher and the children, understand the educational values and beliefs operating in her assigned classroom, and analyse her ethnocentric reaction. This was not easy, and she took every opportunity to talk to her host teacher about reorganizing class time so that children could work in small groups, thereby providing attention to individual pupils. Since a different set of pedagogical values were operating, this never happened, and after three or four days, she gave up and simply asked the teacher what she could do to facilitate the learning goals for her students. She began to ask questions about the emphasis on group behaviour, the cultural value of conformity, and the impact of financial constraints and overcrowded classrooms on pedagogy. In the process, she also noted that most of the primary school teachers were female and began to reflect on this similar trend in the United States. This led to comparative questions about cross-cultural gender roles, including the association between women and nurturing behaviour and the extension of domestic roles into the workforce. She was learning through immersion in another cultural setting how what I have referred to as "folk biological essentialism" operates in multiple social settings, particularly – returning to the DNA metaphor – in the backbone of the gender system, in this case with respect to notions of femininity.

A second student, a Haitian-born woman, made the health centre her service site. This student wore her hair in a short Afro hairstyle, and the men in town gave her a variety of pet names. As she walked down the main road, people called out to her "Natural" or "African Queen". Although she did not just "blend in", as she had assumed she would (any newcomer into town is noted), she nonetheless had cultural connections that facilitated her immersion into community life. Among these were familiarity with local food and music and a memory of the natural landscape of the Caribbean from her childhood in Haiti. "African Queen" spent each weekday, from 8:00 a.m. until 3:00 p.m., in the health centre, forging close bonds with the nurses and helping to organize patients' records. She talked to patients in the waiting room prior to their appointments; gathered information on the reasons for their visits, which she presented to the nurses; and developed patient information questionnaires seeking information such as date of birth, reason for the visit and associated concerns with their condition. These were for the patients to fill out on their arrival to the clinic. The nurses said that these tasks were helpful because the nursing staff were often so overwhelmed with patients that they had to work extra long hours to organize records. The information sheet quickly oriented them to the patients' needs and was filed as part of the records.

This student arrived in Jamaica with an established interest in cross-cultural perspectives of the body and approaches to illness and healing, so she also collected data on the structure of Jamaican health care and how rural clinics fit into this countrywide system. She became especially interested in the high rates of teen pregnancy, and both nurses' and patients' views about the young women and their baby-fathers. She too had to monitor her biases; interestingly, these emerged from class differences, so it seemed. Though she was familiar with the patients' stories about multiple partners and early sexual experiences, she strongly disapproved of these behaviours as a result of having been brought up in a strict family that monitored her own actions closely. This led her to empathize with the nurses who conveyed to her their feelings of frustration in the limited ability to affect problems including unprotected sex, poor quality of birth control supplies, lack of resources in general, and conflicts with the church over birth control. At the time of her service, the health centre did not provide HIV testing, something that is now available to all (after first being made available to pregnant women). Yet "African Queen" underwent a significant transformation in her thinking during her period of service. Her initial response to condemn the young women as immoral and weak transformed into a feminist critique of the positions of powerlessness in which many young women find themselves – young women seduced by older men, and prone to believing promises of support and care in exchange for sexual services.

Another set of reflections students brought to our evening sessions involved

Figure 8: Bridgewater State College students and Frankfield children and youth attending educational workshops at the Methodist Church. Future research assistant Heidi Savery, second row on the left.

thinking about how they were perceived by community members. They were concerned with fundamental human interactions. Did people like them? Why didn't young women in the town speak to the male students? How should the female students respond to the barrage of sexually explicit calls they got from young men as they walked through town? These questions led to fruitful discussions about gender relations and cultural notions of femininity and mas- culinity. The female students were angered and made uncomfortable by the sexually explicit comments, and they said it took a lot of courage to walk through town on their own. Other women students were baffled when their attempts at friendly conversation with young men were returned with offers of sexual involvement. I urged them to pay attention to how young women in the town related to the men and note the differences. At home, accustomed to open friendships with their male peers, they hadn't thought that their personal interest signalled sexual interest as well.

I also encouraged the students to think about how people perceived them as a result of the kind of work they were doing in the community, and I suggested that they should inform the townsfolk that they were working in the schools or the health centre. Since they were living either with the Methodist minister or with one of two highly respected Christian families, as word got around the students found that this information had a dramatic affect on the treatment they received. The selection of families contributed to the already existing class distinctions they were afforded, placing them squarely at a higher level than most of the townsfolk. Yet the welcome response they received about their service work mitigated the distance that class distinction created. Thus they were provided an opportunity to learn first-hand how gender constructs intersected with class, prestige and occupation, but also how these can be flexible categories, informed by daily interactions and reciprocal shifting perceptions. In turn, the students' experiences were shaping my understanding of the gender system, underscoring the metaphorical relationship between the DNA molecule and a gender system as a vessel for the long-term storage of information, while also emphasizing its mutability as my students themselves exhibited flexibility in attitudes and behaviours.

ASSESSMENTS: INSIGHTS INTO CLASS AND RACE

Based on these discussions and my own conversations with community members, I identified two major responses to our presence as part of a service learning "team". First, the religious members of the community, especially the reverends and ministers whom we spoke with both at church services and on our initial map-tour of the town, regarded the trip through the lens of "ministering". Both the Methodist minister (who housed one of the students) and the minister at the Church of God told me directly that they thought I was conducting a form of ministering, and my students were part of my ministry. Others, especially teachers and nurses, regarded the project as an educational experience for both students and townsfolk. In a formal welcome ceremony at the primary school, students and teachers sang songs and introduced us to the community. Many teachers and representatives from local organizations (for example, fire and police departments, clinic, library, churches) encouraged my students not to be shy with townsfolk, but to interact with as many people as possible, because it wasn't often that Frankfielders had visitors "from foreign", who were not relatives, in their own community.

A second set of perceptions was expressed by those who worked with the students on a daily basis. They either saw, or encouraged us to see, our visit as a precursor to something larger, generally as a well-funded community development project. When I initially sought out the service sites, I was careful to state the limits of our time and the objective of the trip as an opportunity for students to participate usefully in the community and through their participation to learn something about another culture that also provided insights into their own. Nonetheless, I was often taken aside and encouraged to share how the knowledge we gained would be put to broader use for the community good. I was asked directly by clinic nurses, ministers and teachers if I was seeking funds for future trips, and I was encouraged to do so.

Moreover, the general hospitality extended to my students was often couched in the language of tourism development. At the welcome ceremony the students were told that Jamaica wanted to encourage people "from foreign" to visit, not just the tourist areas but the rural interior, where foreigners would experience the true Jamaica. If students encountered any hostility to their presence, they were urged to regard these as isolated incidents, rather than see them as typical of local attitudes. Instead, the students were told that they would find rural Jamaicans warm and friendly.

Another interesting situation occurred during the middle of the first week when I noticed that the students had developed their own impromptu service opportunities.[4] After they finished with their half-day commitment at their prearranged sites, students would spend their free time with various individuals they felt comfortable with, as they sought to create a niche for themselves. Soon, however, these interactions became couched in the language of "service". One of these activities, reading to schoolchildren in the town library after school, became a regular part of every student's day, as well as my own. It is this activity which led to a series of events that produced both self-reflexive insights for the students and an ethical dilemma regarding service-learning itself as a framework for cross-cultural relationships. I should hasten to add that this was not the only situation that simultaneously led to internal reflections and moral quandaries.

After her first day in a classroom, where she suddenly found herself the only adult present after the teacher left and did not return, one well-intentioned student walked to the town library with schoolchildren and began reading to a small group. More children stopped by, and, for the next two days, an everexpanding group of children surrounded her, urging her to read one story after another. As the group grew daily, we decided to transform this into a formal event. First, however, I discussed the plan with the librarian, members of our host families and others I knew. Many elderly Frankfielders and teachers told me that they thought the storytelling hour was a good idea since many parents no longer had time to tell their children stories or didn't have books at home. Others said that parents no longer saw the value in recounting folktales such as the "Anancy the Spider" stories that they grew up with; still others said that young parents no longer knew these stories and, much to their consternation, only the old people still knew them. While folktales are still told during Christmas time, Easter and other important community celebrations, and are even built into the school curriculum in student readers, they are no longer part of the everyday socializing of children by adults at home.[5] Many thought that the story hour might inspire parents to tell their children stories or at least children would be encouraged to ask parents and grandparents to tell them stories. Thus, after the school day for the remainder of our visit, my students and I met in front of the town library where we held hour-long after-school reading groups for the children. One of my students drew a big sign advertising the reading hour. Promptly, as students got out of school, large crowds of children made their way to the library. Between fifty and seventy-five children regularly came to the tiny, one-room library, which has since closed and moved to another location, to hear us read stories. Since the space was so small, the reading groups spilled outside where we hovered in groups on the roadside. Shopkeepers and passersby looked on.

The librarian was excited about the numbers and told us she was going to send a notice to the high school to see if a student would be interested in continuing the reading groups after we left. By the time we did leave, she had apparently located such a person. Also, the librarian informed the library committee, comprised of a group of prominent community ministers, teachers and the high school vice principal. Soon after, we were invited to speak at the high school and lead the weekly school devotions with prayers and stories. At that event we were introduced publicly as "friends of the library" and later invited to a library committee meeting itself, during which we were honoured, and I was encouraged to give donations towards the construction of a new library. Over years my students and I have organized book drives at home and have sent large shipments to the Frankfield library. The reading hours clearly contributed to the idea that the library was a major focus of my own interests in the town. At the library meeting, the book shipments were acknowledged in a formal "acceptance ceremony",[6] and I was encouraged in particular to continue to be a supportive friend and to encourage others to become friends as well.

After the first week, the librarian told us how much the children loved the library, but that many students didn't have any books at home, or, in many instances, children did not return borrowed books and kept them as their own. One of my students thought it would be a good idea to bring paper and crayons to the reading sessions so that students could draw or write short stories and "take something home with them" after the reading session. They became excited about giving something to the children so that they could remember the reading groups and the students. Thus, every day prior to the reading groups my students walked to town and purchased coloured construction paper and crayons. They began giving each child a piece of paper and a crayon at the end of each reading session. On the second day following the first distribution, a group of children ran out of their classrooms at the primary school to accompany my students to town for their purchase. The children asked to receive additional paper and crayons.

At the end of each reading session, children began to ask for paper and crayons for their brothers and sisters who they said were unable to come to the library because they were needed at home to work. My students, feeling badly, started to distribute additional supplies to these students. To their surprise, arguments broke out among the children, accusing one another of lying about their siblings or taking too much for themselves. Some children tried to arbitrate by telling my students that there were still some children present who hadn't received anything, while others had returned daily and now had at least three crayons. Further, my students found that after the reading hour ended, groups of children began to follow them, asking my students to send them gifts from home and give them money. Many of these children used their paper and crayons to make lists of toys, books and videotapes they wanted mailed to them. They were incredibly persistent. Even early in the morning, on their way to school, the children would appear at the door of the homes we stayed in and would call for the students from the roadside. In the evening, up until about eight o'clock, and sometimes later, the children called to my students as they sat inside eating or relaxing.[7]

My students were taken aback by this reaction. They were at once saddened when they recognized how precious a piece of paper was to the children, and they were upset that they were viewed as sources for material acquisition. They were most disturbed by their own assumption of a piece of paper as a small token. I too was upset that I had not considered the ramifications of the paper and crayon distribution. The librarian was apologetic; my students felt guilty that she was apologizing to them. The students and I discussed the matter. They began to question themselves and their role in the town. Up to this point they had regarded themselves as do-gooders. They expressed how uncomfortable they felt, not only passing out the paper and crayons while shopkeepers and others looked on (disapprovingly they started to think), but throughout the day, surrounded by schoolchildren who were asking for various things. In a reflection session, students explored how their academic knowledge of their relative wealth had suddenly become emotional, subjective knowledge.

Anthropologists George and Susan Gmelch have written of about these kinds of insights in their essay, "Lessons from the Field" (2000, 45–55). Since 1978, the Gmelches have brought students with them to Barbados to conduct participant-observation research (not as a component of service learning, however). They state the following:

> Many students arrive at a new awareness of wealth and materialism . . . The initial response of the students . . . to the poverty they perceive around them is to feel embarrassed and even guilty that they, like many Americans, have so much wealth. However, such feelings are short-lived for as the students get to know the families better they no longer see poverty . . . they discover that most people not only manage quite well on what they have but that they are reasonably content. (2000, 49)

My students did not draw quite the same conclusions. While they did feel initial embarrassment and guilt, they did not conclude that people were reasonably content. Instead they became increasingly aware of the lack of resources in the schools (many children could not afford pencils or sharpeners, so they worked with pencil stubs gnawed down to a point), the overcrowded classrooms, and the fact that many children came to school without an adequate breakfast and without lunch or money to buy lunch. They learned that the health centre didn't have an adequate supply of Band Aids, let alone other materials. These, among other observations, emphasized the wealth of their own backgrounds and the needs that they were unable to meet. The students also realized that these conditions did not apply to all; dramatic class differences surfaced as they began to notice that one reverend drove a Volvo, the owner of the bus company owned a huge, imposing house, and other residents regularly travelled overseas. These observations led them to think about the divisions of class in their own society and consider historically how current conditions in Frankfield were potentially linked to the effects of slavery, colonization, independence, and national development policies. I encouraged them to buy the local newspaper, and we began to spend some time each day reading the paper and clipping out articles from the *Jamaica Gleaner* on related subjects. They started to notice that the paper was filled with articles on economic development, the presence of large international development agencies in the urban and tourist areas and that many issues, including crime in the shantytowns and school violence were framed in terms of development, progress, modernization and other related concepts (Fox 1999).

In addition to the curiosity sparked by the feelings of injustice, the students felt another set of emotions connected to the service project itself. They felt angry at themselves that what they had thought was a positive, generous gesture had instead sparked a series of actions that reinforced the differences in wealth between the children, their families and the students. They became concerned that the initial aim of the after-school reading project had been corrupted. Parents, grandparents and teachers had been genuinely interested in the storytelling. The students realized that it was they who had wanted to inject a material component, and that for them it was the gift of paper and crayons that meant something substantial. Since they couldn't measure the effect of the story hour itself, they had wanted some concrete evidence of a contribution. Instead the process of storytelling was subverted.

ADDITIONAL REFLEXIVE INSIGHTS

The Gmelches also write about the development of a new kind of racial awareness in their students. He says,

> In Barbados my students become members of a racial minority for the first time in their lives. Everyone in the villages in which they live is black, while nearly all of my students have been white. They feel awkward and in some cases hold negative stereotypes. The students have never experienced racial prejudice themselves . . . A few students become hypersensitive to race during the early weeks of their stay. (2000, 51)

My white students experienced similar feelings. Although I had informed all of them that their understanding of race as a cultural category would change as they became, for the first time, either a racial minority or a member of the majority, they did not anticipate the emotional reactions they would have. Initially, two white male students responded with fear to the responses they thought they received. These students thought everyone was looking at them with hostility and anger; they didn't want to walk through town alone, much as the female students didn't want to walk alone because of attention to their sexuality. For the first two days, the female students were truly on the verge of hysterics. At our first reflection session, they voiced their worries. "African Queen", already so named, and the only black student on two trips, was angered by their assumptions of hostility, telling them their feelings were the result of ignorance. She told the group that, by contrast, this was her first time since her childhood in Haiti where she was a racial majority, and she felt a sense of exhilaration and freedom from race consciousness. The young men were at first defensive and then sobered by her comments: they had never thought about her experience in the United States.

After about a week the male students felt more at ease and were able to think more critically about their earlier reactions. The transition went quickly perhaps because the service project provided them with a structured environment where other challenges immediately surfaced, requiring them to relate to people about ideas and the setting at hand. By the time they returned to a formal discussion about race, the two male students had already interacted with people, on a number of different levels, and this required them to think beyond their stereotypes and fears. The Haitian-American student also experienced a transition. She learned also, after about a week, that her own cultural differences, and Frankfielders' views of her class, minimized the racial affinity she had initially felt. She stood apart from the Frankfielders as well as from the other students and wondered if her experience would have been different if she had travelled on her own, and hadn't been associated with the project and the white students.

Perhaps the most important kind of service that such trips can provide is to establish a foundation for cross-cultural exchanges and the creation of relationships. Students should not set off on any overseas service learning venture with expectations that far exceed their potential, nor should host communities be misled into thinking that these exchanges are the preliminary stage of a larger economic development project. Instead, both parties should be encouraged to think about the true nature of service as a reciprocal process, which has the potential to reach across the self/other divide, and begin a life-long quest for cross-cultural understanding. Ultimately, it seems that both the students and Frankfielders who engaged with them were able to generate a consciousness through the exchange of the ways in which their individual lives are connected to broader systemic patterns of gender, race, colour and class. However, they also realized their potential for some degree of individual malleability. For the remainder of the chapter, I discuss the HIV/AIDS educational workshops my students and I organized with residents of upper Clarendon. I follow this with some American student narratives. These narratives underscore the ways in which the anthropological experiences they participated in shaped their perceptions of gender as a culturally informed feature of identity. As the students negotiated their way through the complex matrix of cross-cultural gender/ class/race/colour relationships, their experiences helped me to internalize a fundamental insight of contemporary feminist theory, namely the fact that gender is wedded to the specific cultural landscape in which it exists.

CASE STUDY TWO: HIV/AIDS, STIGMA AND THE PUBLIC GOOD

Following the experiment in service learning, which I carried out for two years,[8] in 2000 I began to think about an alternative model of community service based on a participatory approach, as described in the opening section of this chapter. I thought of community in a broad sense, not only Frankfielders, but also people engaged with the issues around HIV/AIDS who were committed to ending stigma and discrimination as well as educating about prevention and treatment options. The Rasta poet Saheed, who is quoted at the top of the chapter, is an example of someone who lives in a nearby town and composes poetry that deals with similar themes. Others who lived in neighbouring villages, but who worked in Frankfield, also helped to organize workshops, including Miss Joan, the restaurant worker who shared her story in the last chapter. The venue was the Pentecostal church.

I write this segment now, conscious of a question posed by the renowned physician and anthropologist Dr Paul Farmer. As part of a discussion held on Cambridge community television on 20 October 2006, Farmer asked: "What is a public good for public health?" While I did not frame our workshops so succinctly around this question, the philosophy that undergirds it was nonetheless present. It is a question that challenges notions of "the public" *writ large* as the assumed target of public health policies and programmes. He also asked, "Who is the public?" and at what levels, be they individual, family, village or society, should attention about treatment and care be directed? When the appropriateness of a definition of "the public" as the largest unit of society is challenged, individuals and their suffering are necessarily brought into focus. The HIV/AIDS public is constituted by many clusters of individuals: those who are dying of AIDS; medical professionals working in rural health clinics to urban hospitals; members of the Government of Jamaica including the Ministries of Health and Education; non-governmental organizations and other non-profit groups such as the Jamaica AIDS Support for Life; teachers charged with conveying information to students as well as peer counsellors both in schools and in emerging non-governmental organization programmes; family members of persons living with HIV/AIDS (PLWHA); and community members, some of whom contribute to suffering through their discriminatory acts including neglect, ostracism and violence. These members of the Jamaican public are situated within a broader public constituted by regimes of international lending practices around "public health".

Dr Paul Farmer has written and spoken extensively on this topic with the objective of disrupting low expectations about the possibilities of curbing infectious diseases, stemming from medical treatments attached to international lending practices. The production of unaffordable anti-retrovirals (ARVs) for treatment of HIV/AIDS in poor countries, for instance, is an exercise of power that increases risk of diseases and inhibits their control. Farmer refers to "the nature and distribution of extreme suffering" as "structural violence": a form of human rights violations that are "symptoms of deeper pathologies of power and are linked intimately to the social conditions that so often determine who will suffer abuse and who will be shielded from harm" (2005, xiii). Infectious disease is clearly distributed unevenly through the effects of this form of discrimination (Sen 2005, xiii). Today, 75 per cent of PLWHA in Jamaica do not have access to ARVs. This predicament combined with Jamaica's severe homophobia presents a significant challenge for AIDS activists on the island such as Jamaica AIDS Support for Life, and concerned international organizations such as Human Rights Watch. Both have condemned this rampant homophobia, which enshrines heterosexism and male dominance, thereby confirming that this virulent hatred is a form of structural violence that permeates Jamaican society.

In 2005, an article appeared in the *New York Times*, reporting on the violent murder of HIV/AIDS activist Steve Harvey, shot to death in a rural part of Jamaica in 2005. It stated that "the country will never defeat its AIDS epidemic – and the government will continue to attract criticism from human rights organizations – unless it takes strong steps to combat homophobia both among police, and in society as a whole" (*New York Times*, 13 December 2005). Similarly, a 2004 Human Rights Watch Report states, "On June 9, 2004 Brian Williamson, Jamaica's leading gay rights activist was murdered in his home, his body mutilated by multiple knife wounds" ("Hated to Death").

Tragically, such accounts of brutality against known or supposed gay persons are not uncommon on the island. Because the Jamaican government and societal leaders have not sought to combat Jamaica's deeply entrenched, pervasive homophobia, it persists as a form of structural violence. These feelings are epitomized by popular songs that contain phrases such as "batty man fi dead" and "man on man fi dead" (both equate to "gay men should be killed"). These songs are played openly on the radio and in community settings, such as the dance I described at the opening of this chapter. This feature of Jamaica's gender system is fueling the HIV/AIDS epidemic[9] as it burgeons amid a climate of hatred that is undergirded by religious fundamentalism. In response, fear of stigma and discrimination flourish, even though it is becoming increasingly well known in Jamaica that the virus is spread mainly through heterosexual intercourse[10], and women are experiencing increasing rates of infection. Homophobic cruelty and carnage interact with a mix of other factors, including poverty. This contributes to an ambiance rife for the spread of HIV/AIDS, as it discourages at-risk individuals from seeking the testing and information necessary to curb proliferation of the virus. Heterosexual normativity and male dominance are reinforced, contributing to an anti-homosexual climate. In addition, segments of the Jamaican population, including health care providers, also express suspicion of human rights as a discourse that privileges deviants, rather than those in desperate need of fair treatment. In this view, those desiring human rights are constituted as a collectivity of predators, pedophiles, murderers, gang bangers and homosexuals who are perceived to be seeking, and slowly attaining through human rights discourse, unwarranted protections by a government swayed by international donors and the most dangerously radical features of US society.

The view of Amnesty International that the expression of sexuality (including bisexuality, homosexuality, cross-dressing, transvestitism and transgenderism) is a human right is largely dismissed as grounds for the moral failure of society. There is not much support for the idea that persons, regardless of sexuality, have "the right to be free from violence and harassment . . . to have consenting sexual relationships with others without losing life, liberty or liveli-hood, or to be recognized as equal citizens and to be treated with the respect that is due all people" (Baird 2004, 8). For instance, as articulated frequently in letters to the editor of the *Jamaica Gleaner* or the *Jamaica Observer*, Jamaican society suffers from a degenerative attack on its Christian principles, threat-ened largely by "outside" supporters of homosexual rights. A specific example of this is a letter to the editor from 20 February 2008 stating the following: "I wish to commend Jamaican church leaders for not caving in to outside pres-sure from homosexual groups intent on corrupting Jamaica" ("Church Rebuke of Gays Commended", *Jamaica Gleaner*). The loss of livelihood is a fear I have heard expressed frequently in Frankfield, as I have pursued conversations about people's biases. For many who operate their own businesses, however small, there is the anxiety that if they provided services or sold goods to people who were deemed possible homosexuals, then they themselves would lose business. For people barely scraping by, for whom the sale of a hat or a dress determines whether there will be dinner on the table, this fear has real consequences.

Yet beliefs about sexual practices do change, suggesting cracks in the hege-mony of Jamaica's binary sex/gender system. This offers some hope, in the long term, for a shift in attitudes about homosexuality. Even against the paucity of information about sexuality, what constitutes accepted sexual prac-tice is slowly shifting in Jamaica. This is influenced both by dancehall culture as well as the mobility of the Jamaican population, which, as part of the Caribbean region, harbours one of the highest migration rates in the world. Sexual practices and ideas move across cultures, and they are reproduced and newly interpreted in local settings. This process of combining both outside and local elements is apparent; for example, in the re-appropriation of the practice of fellatio, which, long shunned among Jamaicans and considered the domain of prostitutes, now pulses through the lyrics of dancehall: "the exhortation that Baby Cham in his song 'Boom' that his woman has to . . . perform fellatio, shows the creeping tolerance . . . for the practice . . . as Baby Cham documents his own extreme ecstasy and the fact that his 'yeye dem tun ova' [eyes roll back] when him gyal a clean" (Hope 2006, 51–52). However, the recent flap over dancehall artist Lisa Hype's leaked photo of her performing the act has reinforced the conservative aspects of the gender system with respect to female sexual behaviour.[11] And while male artistes have not embraced cunnilingus in their lyrics, the female artiste Tanya Stephens has. Hope (2006, 51) notes that

> because men are on the receiving end, nowhere in dancehall discourse has there
> been any treatise by a male artiste that encourages or supports cunnilingus, as
> opposed to Tanya Stephens's song "Yuh Nuh Ready fi Dis Yet" which lyrically
> berated the self-praising man for his lack of sexual prowess and his inability to
> truly satisfy women. Her chorus, "yuh nuh ready fi dis yet, bwoy" (You are not
> ready for this, boy) rescripted the notion of male (sexual) superiority that is an
> important element of the sexual narratives of male dancehall artistes.

I thought that perhaps I could hold workshops that carefully examined
Jamaican sexual practices with Frankfielders in ways that might begin to open
up a dialogue outside of the health centre, exploring how these practices have
a bearing on the way HIV/AIDS is understood and experienced locally. Maybe
as an outsider as a researcher but also as an insider, having spent a great deal
of time in the community, I would have licence to talk about sexuality openly
in ways that many parents and teachers felt they could not. I also hoped that
the reflection the workshops might provoke or encourage a cross-cultural
discussion between my own teams of students and members of the community. I wondered if it would be possible to focus on the dangers of subverting
open discussion of human sexual diversity and the antipathy towards homosexuality.

In recent years there have been some slow-to-come but important achievements with respect to preventing and treating the HIV/AIDS virus. I hoped to
build on these, while simultaneously addressing the ongoing challenges. Merle
Mindonca of the Guyana Human Rights Association has outlined the achievements and challenges (for the entire Caribbean region, but he outline clearly
relevant to Jamaica's situation) in the following way:

> The good news from the Caribbean response to HIV/AIDS includes:
>
> - widespread information on prevention
> - increased availability of treatment drugs
> - an expanding range of care
> - treatment and support programmes
> - signs that the incidence of new infections may be slowing
> - inclusion of HIV prevention awareness in schools curricula
> - developing workplace guidelines and policies
> - growing civic involvement

The bad news is that

- information about AIDS is not translating into protective behaviour
- 75 per cent of HIV positives are still unable to access treatment
- donor procedures are complex and lengthy
- governments resist legal reform on MSM [men who have sex with men] and CSW [commercial sex workers]
- the virus is spreading fastest among girls and young women
- PLWHA continue to be marginalized
- high levels of stigma and discrimination undermine scientific strategies
- monitoring and evaluation programmes are virtually non-existent. (Mindonca 2007, 2)

In 2004 Jamaica received its first installment of a four-year, $23-million grant from the Global Fund, a combined public and private organization that works to fund projects helping to eliminate AIDS, malaria and tuberculosis (http://www.theglobalfund.org), to make ARVs available in the public sector to PLWHA, and $15 million from the International Bank for Reconstruction and Development. However, over 70 per cent of Jamaicans living with AIDS still cannot afford them (Ministry of Health 2005). These funds have been directed, according to Jamaica's National AIDS Policy, towards

> the implementation of HIV/AIDS/STI [sexually transmitted infection] behavioural surveillance; management of opportunistic infections; and training in the treatment of antiretroviral (ARV). The prevention of mother to child transmission programme has grown from its pilot phase to a countrywide undertaking requiring universal Voluntary Counselling and Testing (VCT) for all pregnant women with access to ARV and infant formula. (Ministry of Health 2005, 9)

Concurring with Mindonca's assessment, the Ministry of Health (ibid.) also notes that gaps remain in (1) human rights matters; (2) an integrated multisectoral approach; (3) prevention, care, treatment and support; and (4) monitoring, surveillance and evaluation.

IS DIALOGUE POSSIBLE? HIV/AIDS WORKSHOPS

In response to one hundred questionnaires my students and I distributed to primary school and high school students in Frankfield as well as to townsfolk, we learned that, in 2001, there were still great gaps in understanding about transmission of HIV. This fact was in spite of available information. We found that in some rural communities people were still unclear about how HIV is transmitted, particularly elderly people and primary schoolchildren. The people who were most well informed were high school students at the Edwin Allen Regional High School, where they learned about HIV/AIDS both in health and biology classes. Also, unsurprisingly, there was the pervasive view that HIV positive persons were of a low moral standing. The association of low morality with infection is a common worldwide belief that has permeated the history of infectious diseases. Therefore, with the help and instigation of many community members, some of whom were challenging Jamaican homophobia, heterosexism and economic inequality, we organized a series of HIV/AIDS workshops in Frankfield and surrounds over a three-year period from 2001 to 2004. Our workshops involved my own presentations, and skits and posters my students put together, as well as some kind of performance, either by local poets, members of the congregations themselves, schoolchildren, and, on one occasion, 3Cs. Our "public" included everyone present and their wider connections to their families and other groups in their towns. The goal was simply to provoke dialogue and disabuse people of misinformation. Our topics included human sexual diversity as a human right, the problems of stigma often directed towards PLWHA and the effects of gender inequality on teenage girls. These girls, who seek economic support from older men, are thereby unable to negotiate condom use. Beliefs such as mosquitoes transmit HIV or virgins cure men of HIV continued to be mentioned over the three-year period. Also prevalent was condemnation of not just the men who had affairs with high-school age girls but of the girls themselves. We introduced a wider critique of economic instability to replace the common view that girls sought out older men so that they could purchase clothing or pay for fancy hair styles. Instead, as Mindonca (2007, 7) reports: "Poverty is a key non-medical factor increasing transmission rates among younger women. Data collection from focus groups show the spread of the virus among younger females is due in part to predatory behaviour of older men. School girls are vulnerable to men buying their books, providing free bus rides to school and gifts in return for sex."

The workshops mainly took place in churches and in school classrooms. Both of these venues, it seemed to me, were the perfect places to meet to discuss the nature of the HIV/AIDS epidemic in Jamaica because these are spaces where male dominance and heterosexism are enshrined, both in institutional hierarchies and in morality teachings shot through with heterosexism. Schools bring church morality into their folds through daily prayer; posters with religious slogans hung across classroom walls, such as "Cleanliness is next to Godliness" (HIV infection implies "dirty" behaviour and hence distance from God); and classroom instruction in which fundamentalist Christian principles about monogamy, normative heterosexuality, creationism, and the like are cherished, while alternative modes of thought and behaviour are regarded as immoral choices. Moreover, the ambivalence that religious and academic institutions express about stigma and discrimination contributes to a climate of fear that prevents people from seeking testing and care.

In the workshops' public settings, we could broach some dimensions of stigma and discrimination, including the alienation of PLWHA and appropriate community responses. Other topics included the economic realities that generated patterns of multiple partnering such as the "Sugar Daddy" syndrome of young girls with older men. People expressed compassion and dismay around neglect of people dying from AIDS, and asked some specific questions in the open forum about some sexual practices and HIV transmission such as kissing when one has an open sore. Attempts to discuss homosexuality, however, were met with silence. Perhaps if we had returned to the same setting and built personal relationships with people, we could have addressed these topics, but it was naïve of me to think there would be an open discussion. The fear of ostracism is simply too high. This does not mean that people were unwilling to speak on an individual basis. At the end of the workshop, my students and I were approached by people who wanted to continue the conversation and explore our understanding of human rights, ideas regarding gender inequality as well as beliefs about homosexuality. People also wanted to build on the open discussion of sexual practices, speaking more intimately about oral sex, for instance, and methods of HIV prevention.

I completed the workshops, feeling that any discussion was valuable, but also coming away with a deeper awareness of the challenges faced by the staff of the Frankfield health centre. They see first hand, on a regular basis, the conflicting influences of their counselling and church influences. Common scenarios recounted to me are cases of young women coming to them seeking information about the female condom or how to encourage their male partners to use condoms (and to obtain them for free from the health centre). These women would also wish to learn about various forms of birth control. The nurses would counsel them privately and in group therapy sessions, and then, at some subsequent visit, they would learn that these same young women had recently gone to church and been saved. In the process of attending church, they would be discouraged from using condoms or asserting themselves in relationships with male partners. There was clear frustration on the part of these nurses, who were very religious women themselves. Yet these women had somehow found a way to develop a belief system that did not exclude condom use and actively rejected gender inequities in a way that I thought might provide an opening of dialogue between the nurses and the clergy. At the close of each workshop I would speak with the pastor or reverend present, encouraging a dialogue with the nurses at the health centre. Yet, in my most recent visit in 2007, such a dialogue had not emerged.

Still, the combination of deep Christian religious belief and support for AIDS prevention strategies that both embrace condom use and acknowledge the reality of multiple partnerships is worth discussing. Each day, activities at the health centre begin with devotions that are deeply felt and emotionally expressed. I recall the first time I witnessed this expressive prayer: prayer for the women to be courageous in the face of illnesses, unexpected or unwanted pregnancies, abandonment by male partners, domestic abuse and other indignities. I was both surprised and uplifted. The women sat on benches as a nurse stood in front of them speaking quietly at first with eyes closed. Most of the patients closed their eyes too and listened, initially silent and still. As the intensity of the prayer increased, the nurse's voice began to quiver, rise and fall. Patients nodded, fists clenching, tears rolling down many of their cheeks.

I watched and listened in amazement at this version of biblical literalism that did not oppose women's empowerment and agency, but instead promoted HIV prevention strategies by urging both condom use and encouraging "one faithful partner". This all occurred in a setting where women worked with other women to gain control over their sexual lives. Moreover, the nurses understood that treatment options for HIV/AIDS were limited. The one tool to allow people to live with AIDS, a combination of chemotherapy with ARVs, remains unavailable to the vast majority of Jamaicans. Nonetheless, they adopted a strategy of prevention and care that was not hopeless. At the Frankfield health centre, nurses are increasingly worried about the growing numbers of HIV-infected persons, prevailing stigma and lack of access to the treatment toolkit. They therefore take the path that is available to them: actively counselling HIV-prevention to bring about behaviour change, and, finally, in 2007, offering free HIV testing.

TREATMENT OPTIONS IN CLARENDON

In 1991, when I first came to Frankfield, there was no testing available and no ARV treatment. In 2000, funded by a US Agency for International Development project, counsellors called "contact investigators" or "motivation officers" were trained to reach out to PLWHA, educate the local populace about HIV/AIDS and encourage safe sex practices. Then, when George W. Bush assumed office, following his first legislative act to cancel US funding to overseas programmes where family planning (read: abortion and birth control) occurred, Frankfield's clinic lost its support for this programme. In 2002, the Jamaican government assumed funding, and mildly expanded services by providing free testing for pregnant women. Frankfield's motivation officer, a woman affectionately known as "Condom Lady", pursues her work alone, visiting people in their homes throughout Frankfield's districts. She treks into the hillsides to remote hamlets by day, and at night frequents rum shops where mainly men are found. Her teaching tools include dildos and a sense of humour: "You have to learn to relate to the men," she says, combining this approach with the urgent seriousness of her message, compelling men to demonstrate their skill in donning a condom on the "models". Condom Lady occupies a unique and important place in Frankfield's gender dynamics, crossing boundaries by talking openly about male sexual behaviour with men in a public setting. Through her "props", which men actually handle in front of other men, she is also demystifying the sacredness of the phallus. She introduces the male organ into the realm of the eminently practical (the avoidance of disease) through an unspoken but clearly homoerotic process. Ultimately, Condom Lady may unexpectedly aid in the painfully slow breakdown of heterosexism within a small locale.

Yet ultimately, for PLWHA in Clarendon, these efforts are barely adequate when AIDS remains a death sentence. About ten miles from Frankfield, in Chapelton, there is a STD clinic within the Chapelton Community Hospital, initiated in 1994. It is an office adjacent to a waiting room where patients congregate for all sorts of reasons. Individuals seeking counselling have privacy within the office, but everyone there will know who goes into the office. When I visited the clinic in 2001, numbers of known HIV/AIDS cases were identified with coloured thumb tacks stuck into a hand-drawn map of the parish and its towns. At the May Pen Hospital in the parish capital, other efforts at prevention and treatment are ongoing. Also in 2001 I met with Nurse Daubon, who runs the clinic, in order to gain her views about stigma, prevention and care options for residents of upper Clarendon. I began by asking her about her responsibilities.

Nurse Daubon: My job is to see patients with STDs and STIs and their partners. Contacts are elicited, counselling, testing, treatment. We have community outreach and education in the schools, churches, any organized group. We are collecting statistical data to learn trends. We often have STI and HIV training together, but it depends on the special needs of the group. Some may focus only on HIV/AIDS. Heterosexual contact is the main mode of transmission. In Clarendon, the highest areas of infection are in May Pen. It has the most clubs and drugs, but there is not much IV drug use. We Jamaicans don't like needles. Only 1.11 per cent transmission occurs through IV drug use. The main mode of transmission is sexual and mother to child. We focus on counselling, diet. The only people who receive drugs free are pregnant mothers. 7.7 per cent use crack cocaine.

Diana Fox: How do you see stigma attached to HIV positive people?

ND: We ask people not to disclose their status except to a significant other. Once it is out, they are not accepted by the community. Stigma comes from fear that HIV transmits through touching. In educational sessions people may say they know it can't be passed through touching, but they fear, nevertheless that it can, and that medical science hasn't yet discovered that it can be passed on this way.

DF: I've noticed when my students and I talk in classrooms, and just to people on the street that they ask us a lot about the origins of HIV/AIDS. People seem very concerned about this. What do you say to people at the clinic?

ND: In our training, we deemphasize it. Some think monkeys had sex with humans in Africa. People think that promiscuity is the cause and once that stops, the danger decreases.

DF: What are your problems and challenges?

ND: We need visual aids – pamphlets, posters, videos. The government says that there is no money for visual aids. We also need pre-test and post-test counselling. The contact persons in the rural areas are overwhelmed because they only can seek HIV positive people. People can't find the fare to visit the doctor. There is also burnout. Clarendon has only three contact investigators: one for northern Clarendon, one for central and one for southern Clarendon. And most parishes only have one or two contact persons. The urban areas – Kingston, Montego Bay, St Catherine – have more. But you see, education is not the top priority now. Now it's contacting infected persons. Mothers need information about HIV and pregnancy. We try to reach the rural communities for outreach at night. Sometimes it's in collaboration with the Jamaican Information Service. We go into areas together for training.

Later I learned that the health workers throughout the parish are guided in their philosophy about prevention and care, given the lack of access to afford-able treatment from Clarendon's medical officer of health, whose office is in May Pen Hospital. In a subsequent interview, Dr Copeland shared her under-standing of the public good for public health, under the current conditions.

Two undergraduate students accompanied me to this interview, mainly to listen and observe. Here, Dr Copeland explained to me the "whole person approach" to PLWHA, what she termed "empowerment and empathy".

Dr Copeland: We're now at the point that without the perspective of the behavioral sciences, our interventions will not be successful. We are adopting the "whole person approach". Our goal is first to combat stigma and develop community support for those suffering from HIV infection or full-blown AIDS. Second we are looking at developing aromatherapy and herbology. This combined with a diet that a doctor in San Francisco, USA developed. It is a high protein diet with vitamins for people who don't have access to ARVs. Third, we need to build on what we have – existing mechanisms for caring for the person. Modern medicine is born out of local, indigenous systems. The hundreds of years of such practices must be good for something. Fourth, health care providers must empower others to do outreach. There is a big difference between sympathy and empathy. They must be empathetic – people like Florence Nightingale and Mother Theresa brought more than just technique to people. Even HIV positive persons might be recruited. We need to fight burn-out among health care providers. We can't wait for inexpensive ARVs. We must build off of what we have. The parishes are given a lot of autonomy because local patterns exist and therefore approaches must be developed for each area. What works in Chapelton may not work in Frankfield or May Pen. In fact, as I'm talking with you now, I'm thinking that we must find ways to empower the young.

Diana Fox: Can you elaborate on how you use aromatherapy?

DC: We don't do anything strange or exotic. But the oils used in aromatherapy can help with some of the skin lesions – they can combat moulds and fungi that develop with AIDS.

DF: What kind of help do you need in implementing this whole person approach?

DC: We need a lot of things. We need a television and VCR to help communicate the message. We need posters – visual aids. We need condoms and multi-vitamins.

DF: Can you tell me how HIV/AIDS programmes fit into the structure of the public health care system?

DC: First we have family health. This includes maternal – prenatal, delivery at home or in the hospital and postnatal care. It also includes child health. After birth, there is a six–week check up with the first immunization, and we follow the child throughout to be sure it is fully immunized. We now have 80 per cent full immunization. We need to reach the nineties. Now we are polio and measles free. Then there is dental health, which is also part of the public health system. HIV/AIDS/STD/STI is another branch. When we developed a targetted approach, the concept of the contact investigator developed. There is contact training – every infected person may have sexual contacts – maybe ten, maybe more. We try to acquire the names of the contacts – since one third of contacts are likely to be infected. But we can't always find them. We also have health promotion and education. We need to widen the scope so that each programme can benefit. But back to the contact investigators. They are very important. They have helped to contain rates of infection. Numbers of syphilis cases are down. The investigators help promote knowledge, attitudes and practices. They organize groups promoting abstinence. At UWI there is a centre started by a professor for offering care and support for such patients where they receive education, treatment, testing and screening. We are aiming at universal testing of pregnant mothers, so we can learn the rate of infection per hundred thousand. We have also done comparisons with other countries. In Trinidad, there is carnival which brings increases in risky behaviour. In Haiti there is a low level of health care, and in Cuba the government very early decided to provide treatment to high-risk groups and to isolate persons infected.

In order to change behaviour, we have to change communication. The contact investigator uses a one on one approach to encourage condom care and education – how to put it on and remove it and storage.

DF: What is the approach toward educating children?

DC: For children, abstinence is the first message. We wanted to use a collaborative effort between the Ministries of Health and Education. But the Ministry of Education rejected this because our approach was too explicit. We defined many things in an open way. While abstinence for young children is encouraged, we wanted to provide practical advice. For adolescents we discuss treatment, sexuality, an explanation of hormones, emotional instability. We have a pilot for youth project that involves youth ages ten to nineteen from high schools in May Pen. The centre is here at May Pen Hospital. We look at everything that defines the whole person: emotional, social, sexual, spiritual aspect of their lives that make up the whole. We want to create a youth friendly centre. They will be able to access information from the Internet and counsellors will be available. There will be pregnancy testing also.

DF: How did the programme get started?

DC: A Peace Corps worker started it. She had the idea and it is funded by USAID [US Agency for International Development] and the Government of Jamaica. She thought of the youth friendly approach – she is non-judgemental, a good listener and has empathy. Youth are helping to design the programme. For the past two years, youth have summer camp training and will help staff the centre. They will do the painting and design the centre. Our major concern is how to reach children out of school. Some go to youth clubs and churches, but many are falling through the cracks.

The many challenges that Jamaica faces in overcoming its AIDS crisis, as Dr Copeland explains, are being taken up by youth. Throughout the country there are UNICEF-supported parish AIDS committees that seek to implement national AIDS strategies on a local level. These committees have established youth arms which work to reduce the rate of HIV transmission among youth "by providing them with information aimed at enhancing their sexual decision-making and promoting increased access to services and counselling" (Goodman n.d.). The emphasis here is on prevention and counselling rather than treatment, because, once again, affordable ARVs are lacking.

According to Dr Copeland, in 2005, *JIS News* noted that AIDS cases had doubled in Clarendon in 2004, bringing the reported number in the parish to seven hundred, and representing a 105.48 per cent increase over the seventy-three cases reported in 2003. Dr Copeland, who was interviewed for the article, stated that new cases were discovered through the Voluntary Counselling and Testing Programme, implemented in June, 2003, in which testing is provided for pregnant mothers and persons who visit the STIs clinic. She also said that the kinds of efforts cited above in my interview with her would intensify, including "targeting special groups such as commercial sex workers, employees in the hospitality and transport sectors, as well as continuing to educate adolescents in and out of school". She stated that eight thousand persons were reached during 2004 through clinics, counselling sessions and contact investigators.

AMERICAN STUDENTS, GENDER INEQUALITY AND HIV/AIDS WORKSHOPS

In this final, concluding section I offer some excerpts from Bridgewater State College students, which I solicited around issues such as gender inequality and HIV/AIDS. In the first, a young white woman named Danielle reflects on a workshop held with a youth group in Frankfield. Although in her early twenties, Danielle had been recently married to a Haitian-American man and had a two-year-old daughter, both of whom remained in the United States. She introduces her essay by stating: "I will explore issues from the perspective of a woman, student, and future anthropologist." She incorporates excerpts from a formal interview she conducted with a young woman from Frankfield regarding that particular woman's beliefs about gender relations as well as her knowledge of HIV/AIDS. She also discusses her "personal struggle with 'screens' of ethnocentricity, particularly concerning women's issues" within Jamaican culture.

DANIELLE'S REFLECTIONS

Quite often the discussion of the AIDS epidemic leads to cultural biases and assumptions. The notion of "the other" seems to be a practical means of displacing our fear and escaping our own cultural flaws. The HIV/AIDS epidemic is unique because it deals with not only a deadly virus but also unveils sexual practices and taboos, thereby creating a multifaceted disease, one that incorporates the culture's economy, gender roles, religion and medical practices.

In the first week of our stay we held a discussion group at the local youth group's meeting. Dr Fox left the four of us alone while we presented various topics about HIV/AIDS. We learned quickly how awkward and difficult this topic can be, especially in front of a group of adolescent girls and boys. When we began our discussion there was a lot of giggling and whispering. What was surprising was that even the adult leader became nervous and joked around. Apparently this is not a subject spoken about publicly.

We did, however, catch their attention when one boy asked, "But there is a cure, isn't there? Magic Johnson contracted HIV and he is ok." I explained to them that Magic Johnson is a millionaire, and the drug does not cure you, it simply stops HIV from progressing to AIDS. I also told them that these drugs cost about two hundred US dollars a week, and that the drugs are almost completely unavailable to Jamaicans for economic reasons. It was at this point that they began to truly listen to us, and they began to ask honest and difficult questions. Many of the girls grew quite nervous, their body language speaking their fear. One girl timidly asked, "Miss, does the sperm look, smell, or taste any different if the man has HIV?" We answered all the questions as openly and honestly as possible, and we had some of the young women follow us out of the building to ask us more questions when we were done.

Figure 9: Danielle and Moses outside his shop, "Poor Man Struggle"

Another major observation was distrust between the sexes. Surprisingly, the majority of suspicion was directed towards the young girls. The boys were uneasy because they said, "The girls can be having sex with you one minute then go around the corner and have sex with many older men, you just never know." Again this brings us back to the complexity of power relations.

Upon leaving the youth group I felt that they were taking precautions and that using condoms was an understood part of their sexual practices. But then I thought to myself, are they telling the truth? How does an anthropologist ever know if the interviewees are being honest? Especially concerning the topic of HIV, no one wants to admit one has been irresponsible or taken part in "high-risk" behaviour, although many of us have. I also asked myself, how honest should I be?

I had many young girls ask me about using condoms with my husband, and how did I have a baby if I was using condoms. All this after we had spoken about using condoms no matter what the situation. At the time I felt the best way to answer them appropriately was to tell them it was a personal decision that a couple makes, and that my husband and I had both been tested for HIV. Of course that does not protect either of us from infidelity, and quite frankly this realization made me do some self-reflection in order to answer these young girls as honestly as I could.

FORMAL INTERVIEW WITH "KARINA" (A PSEUDONYM) CONCERNING HIV/AIDS AND GENDER ROLES

Karina is a seventeen-year-old girl from a middle-class family in Frankfield. She appeared comfortable and self-assured as she sat across from me at Nurse Dunkley's dining room table. I briefly explained why our group was visiting and what our objectives were. I also mentioned to her that girls in her age group are in the highest risk category for contracting HIV/AIDS. Upon mention that any information she provided would be very valuable to our research project and education she engaged in conversation quite freely.

I asked her if young boys and girls were educated about HIV/AIDS in her local high school and, if so, to what level. Her response was insightful: she said that they were not well educated and that young people did not take the "guidance education" seriously. In fact she said that her friends constantly joked around in class, and very little sex education was accomplished. I joked with her and told her that this happens in America as well. If you mix the sexes at such a premature age, they giggle and feel self-conscious around their peers. But, I mentioned, this is no joking matter; the subject of AIDS is a serious one.

Karina's level of education on the matter was moderate. So we went over the handout we had prepared for our workshops, and I explained how HIV can be transmitted, how to protect oneself, and the difference between HIV and AIDS. She was very responsive and quickly absorbed the material. However, I was surprised she did not have a better background, which lead to some personal questions and conversation.

I asked whether young girls and boys in her age group used condoms on a regular basis. Her response was intriguing. She explained that she always uses condoms and others her age do as well. Boys in high school use condoms more out of fear of pregnancy than HIV/AIDS. The gender role of the young girls is quite different. Young girls she explained, have more power over boys their own age. She said that girls are more educated and mature. Therefore the pressure to use or not to use condoms rarely exists. The girls usually insist the young boys protect themselves. The current issues lie within the dynamic of older men seeking sexual intercourse with younger girls.

Karina, however, said that she did not date older men. She said that, although they usually have a partner, they sleep around with other women, many times girls around her age. Many of her friends have older lovers; she said it seems they enjoy the attention and the material gifts one receives from older men. Karina mentioned the common saying: "School boy money ends on Friday. Older men money never ends." There is a certain status when a young girl has an older man; he buys her things and gives her money. Very often these relationships are kept hidden from parents and other siblings.

I asked her whether the pressure to not use a condom is different when having relations with an older man. Her reply was quite worrisome. It seems the younger girls are easily persuaded not to use protection and, in these relationships, the power dynamic shifts back to the older men. Many of these girls, Karina stated, are tricked into thinking that they have a future with an older man. Usually the relationship consists of sexual intercourse and possibly sharing a child. This of course puts young women in great danger of contracting HIV/AIDS.

In conclusion, the interview with Karina proved to be an insightful window into the complex gender roles of young women in Frankfield. Since this was the only formal interview I conducted, it is difficult to determine if her perceptions are a cultural norm or simply based on personal experience. Therefore I do not feel it appropriate to make general assumptions in regards to the dynamics of sexual relationships. However, she did feel if the sex education classes were separated by sex, HIV/AIDS education would have more of an impact. Young people would feel more comfortable asking intimate questions, thereby learning the material and applying it to their own lives. This is a crucial factor in determining how not only to educate but also how actually get this particular age group to protect themselves from HIV.

THOUGHTS AND PERCEPTIONS ON GENDER AS A FEMALE UNDERGRADUATE IN JAMAICAN CULTURE

This brings me to some of my own personal challenges, and "lessons learned in the field", especially regarding gender. As an undergraduate in cultural anthropology I often find myself questioning the social "screens" that are ingrained in me. It seems as though these screens remain hidden to us, unless they are exposed through contact with other cultural traditions. This trip to Jamaica affirmed that there are many lessons one learns out in the field that cannot be acquired in a classroom.

Dr Fox had informed us it is highly discouraged that a "respectable" woman should go out, unescorted by a man, after dark. This took some getting used to because, after all, we were in Jamaica. I remember lying in my bed during the evenings, hearing the reggae music and voices drifting through the mountains and longing to join in the night life. It was quite the lesson in gender relationships knowing that I couldn't leave the home without risk to my reputation. It also spoke volumes about the differences in which American women anthropologists must adjust to gender roles in other cultures.

It was fascinating to me because it was one of the first times I felt so obviously restricted because of my gender. I found this fascinating and was actually quite grateful Dr Fox had set these guidelines because the attention we did get from men became quite exhausting. Simply walking through town was an experience all in itself. Walking around after nightfall sent out the message that you were "available".

In contrast to the above and Danielle's reflections, another student named Andrew, who travelled to Frankfield in 1999, offers a series of comments drawn from his field note "jottings". Themes of conformity, peer pressure and alienation run through Andrew's account. As a young white male experiencing minority status for the first time, Andrew frequently referred to the "aggressive behaviour" of young men in Frankfield, noting pressures of conformity and empathizing with hypothetical outsiders. Given Andrew's age (he was in his twenties), he was seeking his own identity and challenging various forms of authority in his own life. Andrew addressed these themes, weighing them against childhood and adolescent alienation. He starts by reflecting on what he learned about sexually transmitted diseases at Frankfield Primary School where he performed some service learning activities by helping teachers in a grade five classroom.

ANDREW'S FIELD NOTES

Through my research at the primary school I learned that students are exposed to information on STIs and general health as early as their first year; however, sex and hence contraception issues are only talked around and alluded to in relation to the content of the STI dialogue. In addition, children are disciplined under strong power relationships at school. This, coupled with a secretive community dynamic and public scrutiny within the classroom setting, hinders the flow of exchange between teachers and students in matters of such stigma. I found that the social singularity and isolation of STI sufferers permeates the classroom from the community and affects dialogue with children as young as the fourth grade. Abstinence is strongly encouraged of all grades of students despite common reports of six-year-olds engaging in sexual behaviour. There are poor programmes in place for sexually abused children, and the school is powerless to help abused children due to lack of training and the legal requirement that only parents can request treatment when it is recommended. Social stigma may reduce the number of abused children who receive treatment and may result in the movement of an abused child away from the community similar to the displacement of known AIDS victims.

Adults hold conservative ideas of marriage and partnering. It seems that parents often do not know the actual sexual behaviours or experiences of their children. Yet adults display common patterns of multiple partners even while it remains a social norm to be hidden and lied about; this further complicates the directions in which children are pulled as they assemble their own understandings of acceptable behaviour and struggle to explain conflicting values within moral and actual culture. Children, especially girls, report that, at the discovery of sexual activity in their children, some parents respond with harshness in order to scare the child from such activity, leading to less dialogue than parents who discuss sexual behaviour and condoms.

I experienced and observed what seemed to be aggressive male culture which includes both disproportionate power between sexes and male initiated codes of conduct around women. For myself, in attempting to build rapport with young men my age, it seemed that those who expressed voluntary exclusion from street culture in male society results in rejection, which may be most sorely felt in small communities. There is a seeming absence of a safe atmosphere where uninhibited dialogue can offer support for those youth who are on the periphery of dominant male culture or risky sexual practices. Prestige and respect are awarded to those who subscribe to aggressive male cultural behaviours. This influences youngsters as they adopt their own personality traits. It appears that multiple partner patterns in youth are reinforced by sexually aggressive popular icons and artists, while multiple partner patterns among adults seem to serve the male population. Multiple partner patterns in which the father does not support a mother and child, or when a mother and child become dependant on an irresponsible father, further widens the gap in gender equality and experience. As well, strong community identity in the town leads to intimate networks and familiarities among residents; this works with a particular community angle common around the island involving community crime control under which assailants and thieves are themselves attacked by town residents before being turned over to the authorities. Such strong group identity may create a thick atmosphere of stigma and isolation in cases where an individual is singled out.

With respect to AIDS in Frankfield, these local dynamics seem to produce an atmosphere of secrecy and uninformed assumptions of the AIDS presence which clouds the local awareness. The same is true of dialogue surrounding sexual behaviours and values; however, here we have a local language of abstinence, for instance, that does not adequately fit the experiences of youth because it does not reflect the actual set of conditions acting on youth today. Slang such as "gunshot" referring to gonorrhoea are absent from the posters on STIs present in the clinic and schools. I did not see any AIDS posters. So it seems contradictory that teachers, guidance counsellors, and other community leaders I spoke with seemed eager for an aggressive AIDS campaign, but seem to lack the initial promotion of the topic. It also seems that teachers and other leaders who express a conservative morality must eventually enter into negotiations with aggressive street and male cultures. If the ideal and actual experiences of youth become further removed from each other, sustaining affective dialogue will become more difficult. I can imagine community discussions in which different groups are charged with the promotion of discourse and the creation of points of discourse in which children, youth and adults may exercise and expand upon the AIDS and sex language they are learning. Many children right through the sixth grade level know only the basics of AIDS information that do not often exceed having heard of it, knowing it is a disease, knowing that it will kill you and that you catch it somehow from others. Support and funding will be needed to continue the flow of knowledge into local communities so that they can become empowered, autonomous and prepared to make informed decisions about wellbeing and cultural direction.

HEIDI'S REFLECTIONS

This reflection comes more than fours years after my first ethnographic encounter. The experience is truly a turning point for an anthropologist, as it becomes clear that no amount of classroom knowledge could have you entirely prepared. You must think on your feet with no notes to reference, and there is no cramming for this exam. All your preconceived notions, expectations and imagined scenarios play out differently. Of course, you have no control of the actors but one, and your part is being assigned to you as you go.

Until this opportunity presented itself, I was ignorant of Caribbean culture beyond tourism's stereotypic portrayals and some limited historical context. The other students I was travelling with had taken Diana's "Caribbean" course at the college. I recall being intimidated by my assumption that they would have the advantage of cultural familiarity.

Of course, this was a mentored experience with several informational sessions, regular discussion that often included cooperative approaches to the project itself. There is also a certain element of comfort that comes with being on the back end of a research project. Relationships and contacts have already been established, and I felt as though, at the very least, I could fall back on these.

As a research team of all young women, we found ourselves negotiating our own identities, often against essentialist notions of womanhood. We took cues from surrounding social relations and, at the very least, attempted to not "stick out" too much. Unfortunately, in order to do this I often held back the honesty that I was expecting from individuals in the community. Perhaps I should not have been so disappointed when one of my interviewees falsified his information. The following paragraphs are excerpted from a conference paper presented a few months after the encounter.

A young man, who I will call Wayne, introduced himself to me as I was conducting an interview with a local shoemaker for a community profile. As a musician and a soldier, he represented an alternative to shop ownership and farming which were more common employments. He also had strong opinions about the Jamaican people that took me by surprise. It was his opinion that a black man would do anything to keep another down. He chose to stay in the company of whites because he was more educated and respected than the majority of his fellow Jamaicans. As he went on, I had a difficult time listening without interjecting an opinion. I could only attempt to direct the questioning to an understanding of these ideas. Wayne claimed that he was not racist, but this was his experience.

I have since returned with Diana twice and once recently to begin my first independent project. Jamaica, my "first field", has become the focus of my own research. I periodically reflect on my initial introduction both nostalgically and as an important entry point into Jamaican culture, which has profoundly influenced me personally and professionally. I recall exchanges and interactions I had during this stay when encountering similar scenes. As my understanding of Jamaican culture and society continues to grow, my perspective on that sacred anthropological right of passage also grows. I recognize the process to be a means to an end, not the end itself. I believe that being a part of an initiative that actually engaged anthropology, resulting in strong community connections, helped to locate my own place within the discipline.

Finding one's location, whether within a discipline as Heidi says above, or more broadly, within a wider cultural system, is part of the challenge and process of becoming an enculturated person, a process all human beings are faced with. In rural Jamaica, a central strand of personhood within the cultural matrix is gender, and that strand is itself constituted by multiple, intersecting "building blocks" – components of the gender system. Moreover, the island's trajectory of transformation, including the slow undoing of the traditional colour/class/gender social hierarchy, has long been underway. The construction of the system itself embodied features of its demise in the rebellions that characterized slavery times. Today transformations are ongoing and evidenced at multiple levels, from perceptions of the past influencing contemporary choices to the struggles against new and old obstacles: HIV/AIDS, the debt cycle, and tenacious ideologies of male dominance reflected in both pervasive opposition to homosexuality and the reproduction of Jamaican patriarchal structures. When we conceive of gender as part of culture, as a metaphor for DNA in biological life, we can underscore simultaneously both individual expressions of gender, as well as their connectedness to something larger. We can develop a subtle understanding that acknowledges the contradictions of a system that people both cherish and wish to change. The footprint of the past remains in its reprint; it is interwoven with the hopeful possibility to become something else. This is knowledge that activists can harness towards liberatory visions of programmes for change.

Figure 10: Heidi Savery with children at the community centre for Children and Communities for Change (3Cs) in Mandela Terrace

Figure 11: The author with three Frankfield Primary School students

Chapter 7

Reflections on the
Culture-Gender Spiral

IN THIS FINAL CHAPTER I offer some concluding thoughts on how the DNA metaphor, as a conceptual tool that models the interweaving of gender and culture, contributes to the burgeoning literature on gender. I reflect on two questions: (1) How does the DNA metaphor help us to envision the ways in which gender, far from being an accessory to human life, is built into the very fabric of human culture? (2) How can the ethnographic example of rural Jamaica provide insight into wider human cultural patterns pertaining to gender? My objective has been to follow the longstanding tradition in anthropology of employing metaphors to describe and explain sociocultural systems, remaining mindful of the pitfalls of reifying those metaphors by emphasizing the fluid nature of systems themselves. By arguing that gender is to culture as DNA is to biological life I affirm the centrality of gender in human culture, assuming the risks of using a *biological* metaphor when discussing gender as a *cultural* idea. It is crucial to emphasize that while the image of the DNA molecule provides influential insights into our notion of gender systems, the fact that DNA is reproduced biologically should not imply that gender is reproduced the same way. I have underscored that gender and its interplay with race, colour, class and the human body itself is the outcome of human ideas, alongside the power to assert those ideas and control the access to and distribution of resources. These are all notions that feminist scholars have emphasized; however, the DNA molecule as a metaphor for gender systems integrates existing scholarship for me in a new way that I hope proves valuable to readers. When we tease out the various components of gender, we unravel its sym-

bolic/ideational, material and historical attributes. We see how ideas and practices surrounding gender interact with the human body, and notice that the
human body itself is imprinted with cultural, social, political and economic
realities. This is apparent, as I noted in chapter 2, with Henriques's early work
on the various race/colour categories during Jamaica's plantocracy, a plethora
of terms were devised to categorize various interracial mixtures: "The offspring
of a white man and a black woman is a mulatto; the mulatto and the black
produce a samba", and so on (Henriques 1953, 46; cited in Ulysse 2007, 28).
As Ulysse points out, in this "pigmentocracy or shade-ism as the contemporary
referent is named, not all the mixtures were equally colored. Greater value was
ascribed to whiteness because it is property that has both symbolic and material privileges that last over time. In other words, the lower one's black blood
quantum, the higher one's social position among the black and colored populations" (ibid., 28–29). Some aspects of intersectional identity, in this case the
low symbolic and material value attributed to blackness, "last over time"; however, change is also inevitable. Disruptions punctuate the continuities (ibid.)
from historic Maroon resistance up to and including contemporary dancehall.
This produces changing gender systems, systems that are always moving,
reshaping and *in process*. Just as feminist anthropologist Lila Abu-Lughod has
written against the idea of culture as fixed and bounded, so too we must see
gender systems as mutable.

The metaphor of the DNA molecule creates a visual aid for comprehending
a sense of time depth amid change, because DNA captures the longevity of the
origins of life itself. As such, the image of the double helix is a particularly useful heuristic to convey the simultaneity of change and persistence with respect
to gender. Gender systems have origins in the beginnings of human social life.
The work of anthropological colleagues in the subfields of feminist archaeology
and biological anthropology bears this out. For over two decades now, evidence
has been amassed to demonstrate that gender exists in the archaeological
record, although not as the androcentric, "man-the-hunter" thesis[1] has imagined it to be. Adrienne Zhilman (1983, 76) argued that "using an interpretive
framework constructed with detailed knowledge of primate behavior, especially
that of our closest living relatives, the chimpanzees, and of the behavior of
gathering and hunting peoples . . . specific female-male differences detectable
in the fossil record, offer clues to the behavior and sex roles of our ancestors
who lived millions of years ago and left no other historical record than their
own bones and teeth and footprints".

These scholars have re-examined women's and men's roles influencing early human evolution, unequivocally condemning the idea that "biology is destiny". Their research affirms that our earliest human ancestors assigned meaning and roles to biological sex, so we can say with confidence that some conception of the contemporary notion of "gender" is endemic to human social, cultural, political and economic life. In her article "Gender, Space, and Food in Prehistory", for instance, Hastorf (1991, 133) writes about how gender is visible in the archaeological record through the organization of space: "Gender is created out of more general relations within the family through division of labor, differential access to goods, social negotiation, production and reproduction. All are created from cultural ideas and cultural symbols that are seen in the use and placement of material items in space within the residential house."

The social relationships of gender mapped out spatially have also long been exhibited by differential control over resources even before the advent of *homo sapiens* (ibid., 134). As Zhilman further contends, in the Pliocene period (between approximately 2.6 and 5.3 million years ago) when, in southern Africa, *Australopithecus* was present, the first tools used by hominids were likely to have been invented by gathering females. While males were successfully hunting small game "*without* tools, females were using a tool kit to obtain (as in fishing for termites) and to prepare (as in smashing hard-shelled fruits) gathered foods" (Zhilman 1978, cited in McGrew 1983, 62, emphasis added).

The model of the double-helix that I have conceived as a "gender molecule", when applied to rural Jamaica, helps us to generalize about some features of human gendered behaviour that reach back into our distant past as a species: biological differences have provided a template for human cultural ideas about behaviour. Yet it also reminds us of the cultural specificity of particular configurations of gendered thought and action as we trace, through the case study example, the ways in which specific features of any given gender system are patterned. The general attributes of a gender system that I have employed by drawing from Mohammed and Barriteau – social roles assigned to men and women, cultural definition of masculinity and femininity, sexual division of labour, roles surrounding marriage and kinship, relations of power in gender ideologies and material conditions – are patterned in pairs of longevity and mutability, as well as collectivity and uniqueness. Through this model, it is clear that the human body persists, modified symbolically over time as layers of meaning are devised – by colour and class, for instance – and interwoven with these features of the gender system. With the movement of human populations, through choice, contingency or force, as in the transatlantic slave trade that brought African populations to Jamaica, these layers of meaning are carried with people. In varying degrees, they are interwoven with pre-existing gender systems to create new levels of the spiral. Cultural DNA is a backward and forward reaching system as well as a moment in time. It is an allegorical gender molecule that permits a holistic analysis of our human gendered selves.

Notes

PREFACE

1. Philosopher Martha Nussbaum (1999) states that "the denaturalizing of gender was present in Plato".
2. The term "cultural DNA" was first used by Richard Dawkins in his book *The Selfish Gene* (1976), although quite differently from its application in this book. As well, a quick Google search of the term indicates that the phrase has been widely adopted and applied across the disciplines as a marketing concept, a legal concept, even as a fashion concept. Interestingly, I had no knowledge of these prior uses when I thought of the concept, and it was two of my colleagues at Bridgewater State College, Ellen Ingmanson and Curtiss Hoffman, who pointed out Dawkins's apparent coinage of the term.
3. For an example, see Hamurambi's code. This was the first set of written laws providing the foundation for the legal system in the Middle East, ancient Israel and other area cultures. "Of the 270 laws engraved on an upright stone pillar, approximately 100 of them dealt with the problems of keeping women in line, assignment ownership and responsibility for them, and defining the boundaries of their sexuality" (Ward and Edelstein 2005, 37).

CHAPTER ONE

1. "Kathy" is a pseudonym. Many of the names contained herein are real, especially for Frankfield residents, and used not only with permission but with explicit directives to do so. For those from whom I could not attain permission, I use a pseudonym to protect their identities.
2. See Harding 1991.
3. "Foreign" refers to the United States, Canada, Europe, and places that are obviously starkly distinct from Jamaica, as opposed to other Caribbean islands. A person can be "from foreign" or "a foreign".

4.   According to the Clarendon branch of the Social Development Council of Jamaica, the population in 2002 would be approximately 3,544, based on the national population of rate of 0.5 per cent to 0.6 per cent per annum (2007).

5.   "Fictive kin" is the anthropological term for the integration of the anthropologist into a kin network in the course of doing fieldwork. As Rhoda Reddock, former chair of the Centre for Gender and Development Studies at the University of the West Indies, St Augustine, Trinidad, pointed out to me at a presentation of my work in Jamaica, this term is an "etic", or outside category, that does not reflect the actual emotions that these relationships encompass or the responsibilities and expectations that they produce. I gratefully acknowledge that this is indeed the case from my own perspective as well: Nurse Dunkley and her family are much more than "fictive" relatives as they have become intertwined in my own life and the lives of my family members.

6.   According to Frederic Cassidy (1962, 2–3), "Jamaica Talk . . . exists in two main forms, which may be imagined as lying at opposite ends of a scale, with every sort of variation between, but with each variant inclining in some degree toward the right or left. At one end is the type of Jamaica Talk that aims toward the London 'standard' or educated model, and, in many Jamaicans' usage, reaches it extremely well . . . At the other end of the scale is the inherited talk of peasant and labourer, largely unaffected by education and its standards . . . Moving toward the middle from the educated end, one finds an increasing inclusion of local elements – of Jamaican rhythm and intonation, words that the Londoner would have no reason or need to know, of turns of phrase that have grown up in the island-what may be called 'Jamaicanisms'." Throughout this text, I have attempted to capture the dynamics of individual variations of Jamaica talk, referred to as "patois", which, as readers will see, can include elements both of the "London standard" and the "inherited talk" of peasants and labourers.

7.   In her essay, entitled "Negotiating Identity and Black Feminist Politics in Caribbean Research", Karla Slocum explains how, as a student travelling to Grenada with other students, her experience as a black woman was different from the experiences of white students, where many of the white students were exposed to open hostility. Slocum recounts how she was often mistaken for a native, and when she revealed she was American, people expressed curiosity towards her rather than hostility. By contrast, Faye V. Harrison and A. Lynne Bolles, two black women anthropologists, had different experiences in Jamaica, where "people they encountered in the field were suspicious of their work and drew a clear distinction between the anthropologist as North American researcher and themselves as West Indian working-class people" (Slocum 2001, 140). Harrison says of her own research: "While the majority

of Oceanview people saw in me a middle-class 'brown' woman, some presumed and insisted that the 'American doctor doing research' was socially – if not genealogically – 'white' " (quoted ibid.).

8. Rastafari is a social movement, a religion and a revitalization movement that began in the 1930s. It centres around the worship of the former emperor of Ethiopia, Haile Selassie I (coronated in 1930), who defeated Mussolini's invading army in 1936. His achievement reverberated profoundly in Jamaica among impoverished and rebellious young men in Kingston's inner cities. Through the influence of charismatic leaders, and drawing on the Marcus Garvey's ideology of black economic self-sufficiency and African repatriation, the movement developed, emphasizing Africa as the fatherland and the source of emotional inspiration and black pride. Reggae music is the tool or the "weapon" used to communicate the messages of Rasta. Specific information on the development and lifestyle of Rastafari can be found in Barry Chevannes's *Rastafari: Roots and Ideology* (1994).

CHAPTER TWO

1. Maroon communities founded by former slaves date back to 1655, with the English conquest of Jamaica from the Spanish. The Spanish freed their slaves and many took to the hills or joined the Spanish in fighting the British. Under British colonialism, newly escaped slaves joined the already formed communities (Bayer 1993, 11–12).

2. Obeah refers to magical practices, originally both for good and evil, introduced into the Caribbean through African slaves. Under British rule, the practice was banned but survived underground, becoming primarily a form of sorcery. See Gmelch and Gmelch (1997, 145–47).

3. Higglers are open-air marketers, primarily working-class Jamaican women of African descent, who buy from wholesalers and farmers. Increasingly, as I will note in chapter 3, men are seen selling dry goods, and they have long been present in markets as fishmongers and butchers.

4. "Visiting relationships" are characterized as those in which a couple lives in separate homes; they are often the precursors of common-law and conjugal relationships and may be quite committed or not. Visiting male partners are expected to contribute to the care of children, who may be the product of these relationships, and even to household expenses. Whether they do or not is highly variable depending on the individual and the relationship.

5. This is not necessarily the case for other Caribbean islands where Taino and the other indigenous people, the Caribs, have managed to survive into the present. In

such cases, the strands of masculinity and femininity of their gender systems must be taken into account in understanding their impact on emergent gender systems.

6. It is worth noting that the notion of a "pure white race" is in fact purely ideological and not rooted in biological or genetic fact. Novelist James Michener has alluded to the irony of this assumption in the following fictional passage about the colonization of Alaska, in which Native Alaskans were treated with horrific brutality, justified through racist ideologies akin to those found in other parts of the world, including Africa and the Caribbean. Here, a fictional, would-be lobbyist named Marvin Hoxey spews out an ideology of race that is a historically accurate representation of the attitudes of the time, which is useful in understanding the inconsistent and fallacious standard of racial purity that the white planter class in Jamaica employed to measure itself against all others whom it ranked beneath: "Whenever Hoxey lobbied against legislation for Alaska he repeated the pejorative phrase *half breed*, spitting it out as if the offspring of a hard-working white prospector and a capable Eskimo woman had to be congenitally inferior to someone purebred like himself, with his Scots-English-Irish-German-Scandinavian-Central Asian heritage" (Michener 1988, 499).

7. Indentured servants also arrived from China; while Kempadoo (2004) does not discuss how Chinese women were constituted through racialized sexualities, they likely would have been subjected to a similar kind of Orientalizing as Indian women.

8. Cecily Jones notes, writing about Barbados, a country also built on a plutocracy, that "the differentiation of white female identities by social class meant that some white women were always whiter than others. The claims of poor white women to whiteness and its attendant privileges could therefore never be entirely secure, but always had to be negotiated" (2003, 215).

9. Gender relationships are central to the tourist industry in the nature of employment and the rise of the sex tourist trade; moreover, in the last decade there is increasing evidence to demonstrate links between tourism and HIV/AIDS in Jamaica. An article in the *Jamaica Gleaner* entitled "Study Shows Alarming Tourist Practice" discussed this particular issue (29 November 2008). This topic will be considered in chapter 5.

CHAPTER THREE

1. At the time, I was finishing a Fulbright scholarship at UWI Mona, at the Centre for Gender and Development Studies.

2. "Earlies" is a term referring to the early days.

3. "Loose community" is a term that Jean Besson has also applied to communities of Rastas (1998, 144).

4. The Akan are an ethnic group from present-day Ghana, where many Jamaican slaves originated (Stewart 2005, 23).

5. According to Hart (2002, 13), these papers, now housed in the British Museum, were donated by C.E. Long, a relative of the planter-historian Edward Long.

6. This war, which lasted a decade, from 1729 to 1739, was launched by the British to eradicate the Windward Maroon settlements to clear the area for extensive development of sugar estates. It ended in treaties signed by Cudjoe on 1 March 1739 and by Quaco on 23 June 1730, and established lands for the Maroons in Cockpit country (Hart 2002, 118–19).

7. The story is, of course, more complicated: this repositioning of blackness is part of a wider national transformation, as I will show later on, inspired by a revival of African pride and a form of black nationalist politics promoted by former prime minister P.J. Patterson, in what Deborah A. Thomas calls "modern blackness" (2002). This story of black male pride on a national level intersects with the local tale of descent from Nanny, which itself also exists at the level of national consciousness. Thus we see uniqueness paired with the collectivity, an emergent system born out of the longevity of the past written in cultural memory.

8. Moses uses the term "grandfather" to refer to the wisdom associated with age, including him in his kinship network as one who shares a common belief system.

9. I have come across only one sexual reference to Nanny, in an image on a blog by a Toronto-based artist who posts his own sketches: http://chriscann.blogspot.com/2006_11_01_archive.html. Here she is depicted as a young, modern woman wearing pants with a sweater tied around her waist, with long sweeping hair and prominent breasts, wielding a blood-stained knife. While an unusual rendering of a sexualized Nanny, it nonetheless depicts her mythical and powerful qualities.

10. I should emphasize that this is a general portrayal. There are certainly non-Rasta members of the community who respect Rastas for their consciousness-raising practices in Jamaican society and for the much-loved roots-reggae music or "culture". Many people refer to Rastafari as the "peaceful Rastaman".

11. From the song "Mama Africa" by reggae artist Peter Tosh.

CHAPTER FOUR

1. Anthropologists studying alternative gender identities, including the "two-spirits" of Native North America or the hijras of India, for example, indicate that while

third, fourth and even fifth gender categories exist (see Davies 2007), these are formulated cross-culturally, in relation to cultural definitions of femininity and masculinity.

2. An earlier version of this discussion appeared in Wedenoja and Fox (2004).

3. Frankfield houses one public health centre as well as two private doctor's offices. Each week is organized into clinics that address the different needs of the community, including one for pregnant women, one for mental health, one for community wellness and so on.

4. As Mervyn Morris (1999, 4) points out, Jamaican poet Louise Bennett has "poked fun at inconsistencies in the colonial attitude to language. In one of her *Miss Lou's Views* she reports: "My Aunty Roachy she dat it bwile her temper and really bex her fi tru any time she hear anybody a style we Jamaican dialec as 'corruption of the English language'. For if dat be de case, den dem shoulda call English Language corruption of Norman French an Latin and all dem tarra language what dem she dat English is derived from. Oonoo hear de wud? 'Derived.' English is a derivation but Jamaica Dialec is corruption! What an unfairity!"

5. "Punany" is one of many words in patois for the vagina.

CHAPTER FIVE

1. This is a saying, found in many anglophone Caribbean societies, which refers to the control of women versus the relative freedom of men.

CHAPTER SIX

1. Readers may recall that this neighbourhood gained notoriety during the trial of the 2002 Washington sniper attacks; the Jamaican youth who accompanied the Sniper was in fact, from this neighbourhood.

2. For example, after Hurricane Ivan wreaked its destruction in Kingston in September 2004, members of the Bridgewater State College community responded with generosity to my request for school supplies for the children of 3Cs.

3. A portion of this section is drawn from my 2002 article, "Service Learning and Self-Reflexivity in Rural Jamaica".

4. Beginning at about four after the reading groups ended, students had free time. This free time turned into additional service sites, as students met people and found ways to participate in their activities. For example, one student helped as a prep-cook in a family restaurant. There the student learned how to use a machete to cut

cane, pluck a chicken and cook over outdoor fires. Another regularly helped a new acquaintance with household and farm-related chores: feeding pigs and chickens, sweeping the yard and tending to fruit trees. A third spent her afternoons providing child care for some children whose mother worked until late in the evening. Typically, at ages seven and five, these particular children prepared their own suppers and amused themselves throughout the afternoon. The student devised games, helped them cook supper and read to them.

5.   Various explanations were proffered: (1) both parents worked or there was only one parent present and there was no longer time for storytelling; (2) the recent introduction of televisions and VCRs over the past decade and the construction of phone lines in the past five years has dramatically changed how people spend their time; (3) there is a general "decay" in youth values, increase of teen pregnancy, loss of community parenting and influx of American popular culture, all diminishing the value of and time for folktales.

6.   The ceremony consisted of each library board member making a brief speech, following prayers led by a minister and a deaconess. The speeches were gracious words of thanks; I realized for the first time that this group saw me as a friend of the library above all else, in spite of my return visits to the community over the years during which time I have been involved in many community events beyond the library.

7.   There are no glass windows on the building where the students stayed, but instead only shutters. When people come to visit, they stand outside the gate and call the name of the person they wish to see. Children began calling regularly, and when my students came out, they asked for gifts. Three or four times, some of the children brought gifts themselves. One child brought my student a glass from his home, wrapped in newspaper. Other children brought fruit or vegetables from their gardens, regarding the gift giving as an exchange.

8.   Components of this segment are drawn from my article, "New Directions in Rural Jamaican Ethnography: Embarking upon the Grim Reality of HIV/AIDS in an Agricultural Community" (2001), as well as Fox and Perkins (2005).

9.   The Jamaica AIDS Support for Life (JASL), a non-profit organization with three branches in Kingston, Montego Bay and Ocho Rios, is on the forefront of public education in Jamaica, asserting the following: "Recognizing the importance of education in the fight against HIV and AIDS, JASL has been engaged in a structured progamme of education, advocacy and research around issues pertaining to HIV and AIDS. As part of its efforts, workshops are conducted at schools, churches, business places and communities, clubs. We also engage the general public through the mass media on relevant HIV and AIDS issue and where possible through community initiatives" (http://www.jamaicaaidssupport.com).

10. According to 2006 AIDS data, "among all reported AIDS cases on whom data about sexual practices are available (76% of cases), heterosexual heterosexual practice is reported by more than 90% of persons . . . Among reported male AIDS cases on whom data about sexual practices are available (55% of cases), homosexual or bisexual activity is reported by 14% of men" (Ministry of Health 2006, 2).

11. For a report of the policing of sexual behaviour as regards Lisa Hype, see the article of 30 December 2009 by Krista Henry in the *Jamaica Star* entitled "Despite Being Fired by Empire . . . Lisa Hype still says 'Gaza' ".

CHAPTER SEVEN

1. The "man-the-hunter" thesis, based on an obsession with hunting as the most significant behaviour driving human evolution, hypothesized that early human social behaviour was based on a model in which males provided meat, the central feature of the early hominid diet, through the invention of stone tools and hunting weapons, as well as requiring complex communication skills. The confluence of these developments lead to increased brain size indicating that males played a critical economic role, protected females and their young and controlled mating. Essentially, males were the active agents of human evolution while females occupied passive reproductive patterns of behaviour: "In this view of things, females fade into a strictly reproductive and passive role – a pattern of behaviour inconsistent with that of other primates or of modern gathering and hunting peoples. In fact, the obsession with hunting has long prevented anthropologists from taking a good look at the probable role of women in shaping human adaptation" (Zhilman 1983, 75–76).

References

Abu-Lughod, Lila. 1993. *Writing Women's Worlds: Bedouin Stories*. Berkeley and Los Angeles: University of California Press.

Alleyne, Dillon. 2000. Employment, Growth and Reforms in Jamaica. Economic Commission for Latin America and the Caribbean. http://www.eclac.org/publicaciones/xml/2/4582/lcl1356i.pdf.

Anderson, Benedict. 1983. *Imagined Communities: Reflections on the Origins and Spread of Nationalism*. New York: Verso.

Anzaldua, Gloria. 2004. Speaking in Tongues: A Letter to Third World Women Writers. In *Women Writing Resistance: Essays on Latin America and the Caribbean*, ed. Jennifer Browdy de Hernandez, 79–90. Cambridge, MA: South End Press.

Ashkenazi, Michael, and Fran Markowitz. 1999. Sexuality and Prevarication in the Praxis of Anthropology. In *Sex, Sexuality and the Anthropologist*, ed. Fran Markowitz and Michael Ashkenazi, 123–42. Urbana: University of Illinois Press.

Austin-Broos, Diane J. 1987. Pentecostals and Rastafarians: Cultural, Political, and Gender Relations of Two Religious Movements. *Social and Economic Studies* 36 (4): 1–39.

———. 1997. *Jamaica Genesis: Religion and the Politics of Moral Order*. Chicago: University of Chicago Press.

Bailey, Barbara. 2004. Gender and Education in Jamaica: Who is Achieving and by Whose Standard? *Prospects* 34 (1): 53–69.

Baird, Vanessa. 2004. *The No-Nonsense Guide to Sexual Diversity*. New York: Verso.

Bakare-Yusuf, Bibi. 2006. Fabricating Identities: Survival and the Imagination in Jamaican Dancehall Culture. *Fashion Theory* 10 (3): 1–24.

Baker, Christopher. 2000. *The Lonely Planet: Jamaica*. London: Lonely Planet.

Barriteau, Eudine. 1998. Theorizing Gender Systems and the Project of Modernity in the Twentieth-Century Caribbean. *Feminist Review* 59 (1): 186–210.

———. 2003. *Confronting Power, Theorizing Gender: Interdisciplinary Perspectives in the Caribbean*. Kingston: University of the West Indies Press.

Barrow, Christine. 1998a. *Caribbean Portraits: Essays on Gender Ideologies and Identities*. Kingston: Ian Randle.

———. 1998b. *Family in the Caribbean: Themes and Perspectives*. Princeton: Markus Wiener.

Bayer, Marcel. 1993. *Jamaica: A Guide to the People, Politics, and Culture*. London: Monthly, Review Press.

Beckles, Hilary. 1998. Historicizing Slavery in West Indian Feminisms. *Feminist Review*, Rethinking Caribbean Difference, no. 59 (Summer): 34–56.

———. 2004. Black Masculinity in Caribbean Slavery. In *Interrogating Caribbean Masculinities: Theoretical and Empirical Analyses*, ed. Rhoda E. Reddock, 225–43. Kingston: University of the West Indies Press.

Behar, Ruth. 1993. *Translated Woman: Crossing the Border with Esperanza's Story*. Boston: Beacon Press.

Besson, Jean. 1998. Changing Perceptions of Gender in the Caribbean Region: The Case of the Jamaican Peasantry. In *Caribbean Portraits: Essays on Gender Ideologies*, ed. Christine Barrow, 133–55. Kingston: Ian Randle.

Brody, E.B. 1974. Psychocultural Aspects of Contraceptive Behavior in Jamaica. *Journal of Nervous and Mental Disease* 159 (2): 108–19.

Brody, E.M. 1981. "Woman in the Middle" and Family to Help Older People. *Gerontologist* 2 (5): 471–80.

Brown, Janet, Paula Anderson and Barry Chevannes. 1993. *Report on the Contribution of Caribbean Men to the Family: A Jamaican Pilot Study*. Kingston: School of Continuing Studies, Caribbean Child Development Centre, University of the West Indies.

Brown, Janet, and Barry Chevannes. 1998. *Why Man Stay So: Tie the Heifer, Loose the Bull*. Findings of the Gender Socialization Project in the Caribbean. Kingston: University of the West Indies.

Brown, Kimberly. N.d. Nanny of the Maroons: History, Memory, and Imagery. Gilder Lehrman Center for the Study of Slavery, Resistance, and Abolition, Yale University. http://www.yale.edu/glc/nanny.htm.

Brown-Glaude, Winnifred. 2006. Size Matters: Figuring Gender in the (Black) Jamaican Nation. *Meridians: Feminism, Race, Transnationalism* 7 (1): 38–68.

Brumfield, Elizabeth M. 2003. It's a Material World: History, Artifacts and Anthropology. *Annual Review of Anthropology* 32: 205–23.

Bryceson, Deborah Fahy, ed. 1995. *Women Wielding the Hoe: Lessons from Rural Africa for Feminist Theory and Development Practice*. Oxford: Berg.

Bush, Barbara. 1990. *Slave Women in Caribbean Society, 1690–1838*. Kingston: Ian Randle.

Butler, Judith. 2006. *Gender Trouble: Feminism and the Subversion of Identity*. New York: Routledge Classics.

Cassidy, Frederic. 1962. *Jamaica Talk: Three Hundred Years of the English Language in Jamaica*. London: Institute of Jamaica and Macmillan.

Castello, June Ann. 2004. Shake That 'Booty' in Jesus' Name: The Possibilities of a Liberation Theology of the Body for the Body of Christ in Jamaica. In *Gender in the 21st Century: Caribbean Perspectives, Visions and Possibilities*, ed. Barbara Bailey and Elsa Leo-Rhynie, 281–300. Kingston: Ian Randle.

Chamberlain, Mary. 1995. Gender and Memory: Oral History and Women's History. In *Engendering History: Caribbean Women in Historical Perspective*, ed. Verene Sheperd, Bridget Brereton and Barbara Bailey, 94–110. London: James Currey.

Chevannes, Barry, ed. 1994. *Rastafari: Roots and Ideology*. Syracuse, NY: Syracuse University Press.

———, ed. 1995. *Rastafari and Other African-Caribbean Worldviews*. London: Macmillan.

———. 2001. *Learning to Be a Man Culture, Socialization and Gender Identity in Five Caribbean Communities*. Kingston: University of the West Indies Press.

Clarke, Edith. 1957. *My Mother Who Fathered Me: A Study of the Families in Three Selected Communities of Jamaica*. London: George Allen and Unwin.

Clifford, James, and George Marcus. 1986. *Writing with Culture: The Poetics and Politics of Ethnography*. Berkeley and Los Angeles: University of California Press.

Cole, Johnetta. Foreword. 2001. In *Black Feminist Anthropology: Theory, Praxis, Politics and Poetics*, ed. Irma McClaurin, ix–xi. New Brunswick, NJ: Rutgers University Press.

Cole, Sally, and Lynn Phillips, eds. 1995. *Ethnographic Feminisms: Essays in Anthropology*. Ottawa: Carleton University Press.

Colligan, Sumi. 2000. "To Develop Our Listening Capacity, To Be Sure that We Hear Everything": Sorting Out Voices on Women's Rights in Morocco. In *The Challenges of Women's Activism and Human Rights in Africa*, ed. Diana Fox and Naima Hasci, 186–213. Lewiston, NY: Mellen Press.

Connerton, Paul. 1989. *How Societies Remember*. Cambridge: Cambridge University Press.

Cooper, Carolyn. 1995. *Noises in the Blood: Orality, Gender, and the "Vulgar Body" of Jamaica Popular Culture*. Durham, NC: Duke University Press.

Davies, Sharyn Graham. 2007. *Challenging Gender Norms: Five Genders Among Bugis in Indonesia*. Belmont, CA: Thompson Wadsworth.

Dawkins, Richard. 1976. *The Selfish Gene*. Oxford: Oxford University Press.

De Beauvoir, Simone. 1989. *The Second Sex*. New York: Alfred A. Knopf.

Douglass, Lisa. 1992. *The Power of Sentiment: Love, Hierarchy and the Jamaican Family Elite*. Boulder, CO: Westview Press.

Ellis, Patricia. 2003. *Women, Gender and Development in the Caribbean: Reflections and Projections*. Kingston: Ian Randle.

Farmer, Paul. 2005. *Pathologies of Power: Health, Human Rights, and the New War on the Poor*. Berkeley and Los Angeles: University of California Press.

Fox, Diana. 1999. Masculinity and Fatherhood Re-examined: An Ethnographic Account of the Contradictions of Manhood in a Rural Jamaican Town. In *Men and Masculinities* 2 (1): 66–86.

———. 2001. Aids In Jamaica: The Grim Reality of HIV/AIDs in Rural Jamaica. *Bridgewater Review* 20 (1). http://www.bridgew.edu/Review/archives/2001/June/jamaica.htm

———. 2002. Service Learning and Self-Reflexivity in Rural Jamaica. *Practicing Anthropology* 24 (2): 2–7.

Ferguson, James. 1999. *The Story of the Caribbean People*. Kingston: Ian Randle.

Fox, Diana, and Althea Perkins. 2005. What Is to Be Done about Sexual Diversity in Jamaica? University of the West Indies HIV/AIDS Response Programme, University of the West Indies HARP Annual Conference in Barbados, 15 April.

Geertz, Clifford. 1973. *The Interpretation of Cultures*. New York: Basic Books.

Genetic Science Learning Centre, University of Utah. 2010. DNA to Protein. http://learn .genetics.utah.edu/content/begin/dna/.

Gledhill, John. 2000. *Power and Its Disguises: Anthropological Perspectives on Politics*. 2nd ed. London: Pluto.

Gmelch, George, and Susan Gmelch. 1997. *The Parish Behind God's Back: The Changing Culture of Rural Barbados*. Long Grove, IL: Waveland Press.

———. 2000. Lessons from the Field. In *Conformity and Conflict: Readings in Cultural Anthropology*, ed. James Spradley and David. W. McCurdy, 45–55. Boston: Allyn and Bacon.

Goodman, David. Youth Challenge Myth, Stigma and HIV in Rural Jamaica. Unicef.http://www.unicef.org/jamaica/violence_2071.htm.

Hansen, Karen T. 1986. Household Work as a Man's Job: Sex and Gender in Domestic Service in Zambia. *Anthropology Today* 2 (3): 18–23.

Harding, Sandra. 1991. *Whose Science? Whose Knowledge? Thinking from Women's Lives*. Ithaca, NY: Cornell University Press.

Hart, Richard. 2002. *Slaves Who Abolished Slavery: Blacks in Rebellion*. Kingston: University of the West Indies Press.

Hastorf, Christine A. 1991. Gender, Space, and Food in Prehistory. In *Engendering Archaeology: Women and Prehistory*, ed. Joan M. Gerot and Margaret W. Conkey, 132–62. Cambridge, MA: Blackwell.

Hawkesworth, Mary. 2006. *Feminist Inquiry: From Political Conviction to Methodological Innovation*. New Brunswick, NJ: Rutgers University Press.

Henriques, Fernando. West Indian Family Organization. 1949. *American Journal of Sociology* 55 (1): 30–37.

———. 1953. *Family and Colour in Jamaica*. London: Eyre and Spottiswoode.

Herskovits, Melville J., and Frances S. Herskovits. 1936. *Suriname Folk-Lore*. New York: Columbia University Press.

———. 1947. *Trinidad Village*. New York: Alfred A. Knopf.

Hope, Donna P. 2006. *Inna Di Dancehall*. Kingston: University of the West Indies Press.

Human Rights Watch. 2004. Hated to Death: Homophobia, Violence and Jamaica's HIV/AIDS Epidemic. 16 (6B).

Jamaica Almanack. 1811–40. Jamaica National Archives, Spanish Town, Jamaica.

Jones, Cecily. 2003. Contesting the Boundaries of Gender, Race, and Sexuality in Barbadian Plantation Society. *Women's History Review* 12 (2): 195–232.

Justus, Joyce Bennett. 1981. Women's Role in West Indian Society. In *The Black Woman Cross-Culturally*, ed. Filomina C. Steady, 431–50. Cambridge, MA: Schenkman Publishing.

Kapchan, Deborah. 1996. *Gender on the Market: Moroccan Women and the Revoicing of Tradition*. Philadelphia: University of Pennsylvania Press.

Kempadoo, Kamala. 2004. *Sexing the Caribbean: Gender, Race and Sexual Labour*. London: Routledge.

Kincaid, Jamaica. 1988. *A Small Place*. New York: Farrar, Straus and Giroux.

Lake, O. 1994. The Many Voices of Rastafarian Women: Sexual Subordination in the Midst of Liberation. *New West Indian Guide* 68 (3 and 4): 235–57.

Leeming, David, and Jake Page. 1999. *Myths, Legends and Folktales of America: An Anthology*. Oxford and New York: Oxford University Press.

Leo-Rhynie, Elsa, Barbara Bailey and Christine Barrow, eds. 1997. *Gender: A Caribbean Multidisciplinary Perspective*. Kingston: Ian Randle.

Mair, Lucille M. 1995. *The Rebel Woman in the British West Indies during Slavery*. Kingston: University of the West Indies Press.

Malinowski, Bronislaw. 1922. *Argonauts of the Western Pacific: An Account of Native Enterprise and Adventure in the Archipelagoes of Melanesian New Guinea*. London: Routledge.

Marcus, George E., and Michael M.J. Fischer. 1986. *Anthropology as Cultural Critique*. Chicago: University of Chicago Press.

Matthews, Basil. 1953. *Crisis of the West Indian Family*. Port of Spain, Trinidad: Extra-Mural Department, University of the West Indies.

McClaurin, Irma. 2001. Introduction: Forging a Theory, Politics, Praxis, and Poetics of Black Feminist Anthropology. In *Black Feminist Anthropology: Theory, Politics, Praxis, and Poetics*, ed. Irma McClaurin, 1–24. New Brunswick, NJ: Rutgers University Press.

McGrew, W.C. 1983. The Female Chimpanzee as Evolutionary Prototype. In *Woman the Gatherer*, ed. Frances Dahlberg, 35–74. New Haven: Yale University Press.

McKay, L. 1993. Women's Contribution to Tourism in Negril, Jamaica. In *Women and Change in the Caribbean*, ed. J. Momsen, 278–86. Bloomington: Indiana University Press.

Michener, James. 1988. *Alaska*. New York: Random House.

Middleton, DeWight R. 2002. *Exotics and Erotics: Human Cultural and Sexual Diversity.* Long Grove, Illinois: Waveland Press.

Miller, Erroll. 1991. *Men at Risk.* Kingston: Jamaica Publishing House.

———. 1994. *Marginalization of the Black Male.* Kingston: University of the West Indies Press.

Mindonca, Merle. 2007. Twenty-five Years of Community Action against HIV/AIDS in the Caribbean. Paper presented at the IV Latin American and Caribbean Forum on HIV/AIDS and STIs.

Ministry of Health. Jamaica. 2005. National HIV/AIDS Policy: Jamaica. Kingston: Global Fund Jamaica and Government of Jamaica. http://www.ilo.org/public/english/protection/trav/aids/laws/jamai ca1.pdf.

———. 2006. National HIV/STI Control Programme: Facts and Figures, HIV/AIDS Epidemic Update. http://nacjamaica.com/images/content/aids_datajan_dec06final_07-08-30.pdf.

Mohammed, Patricia. 1998. Toward Indigenous Feminist Theorizing in the Caribbean. *Feminist Review* 59 (Summer): 6–33.

———. 2002a. *Gender Negotiations Among Indians in Trinidad 1917–1947.* New York: Palgrave.

———, ed. 2002b. *Gendered Realities: An Anthology of Essays on Caribbean Feminist Thought.* Kingston: University of the West Indies Press.

———. 2004. Unmasking Masculinity and Deconstructing Patriarchy: Problems and Possibilities within Feminist Epistemology. In *Interrogating Caribbean Masculinities: Theoretical and Empirical Analyses*, ed. Rhoda Reddock, 38–67. Kingston: University of the West Indies Press.

Mohammed, Patricia, and Catherine Shepherd, eds. 1999. *Gender in Caribbean Development.* Kingston: Canoe Press.

Mohanty, Chandra T. 1991. Under Western Eyes: Feminist Scholarship and Colonial Discourses. In *Third World Women and the Politics of Feminism*, ed. Chandra Talpade Mohanty, Ann Russo, and Lourdes Torres, 51–80. Indianapolis: Indiana University Press.

———. 2003. *Feminism Without Borders: Decolonizing Theory, Practicing Solidarity.* Durham, NC: Duke University Press.

Montoya, Rosario, Lessie Jo Frazier and Janise Hurtig. 2002. *Gender's Place: Feminist Anthropologies of Latin America.* New York: Palgrave Macmillan.

Moore, Henrietta, and Todd Sanders, eds. 2006. *Anthropology in Theory: Issues in Epistemology.* Malden, MA; Oxford UK, Victoria, Australia: Blackwell Publishing.

Moore, Jerry D. 2004. *Visions of Culture: An Introduction to Anthropological Theories and Theorists.* Walnut Creek, CA: AltaMira Press.

Morris, Mervyn. 1999. *Is English We Speaking and Other Essays*. Kingston: Ian Randle.

National Human Genome Research Institute. 2009. Deoxyribonucleic Acid (DNA). http://www.genome.gov/25520880.

Ndambuki, Berida, and Claire Robertson. 2000. *We Only Come Here to Struggle: Stories from Berida's Life*. Bloomington, IN: University of Indiana Press.

Nussbaum, Martha. 1999. The Professor of Parody. *New Republic*, February.

Nzegwu, Nkiru. 2002. Questions of Agency: Development, Donors, and Women of the South. *Jenda: A Journal of Culture and African Women's Studies* 2 (1). http://jendajournal.com/vol2.1/nzegwu.html.

Ortner, Sherry. 1996. *Making Gender: The Politics and Erotics of Culture*. Boston: Beacon Press.

Personal Narratives Group. 1989. *Interpreting Women's Lives: Feminist Theory and Personal Narratives*. Bloomington: Indiana University Press.

Planning Institute of Jamaica/Statistical Institute of Jamaica (PIOJ/STATIN). 1999. *Jamaica Survey of Living Conditions 1998*. Kingston: PIOJ/STATIN.

Prior, Marsha. 2009. Matrifocality, Power, and Gender Relations in Jamaica. In *Gender in Cross-Cultural Perspective*, 5th ed., ed. Caroline B. Brettell and Carolyn F. Sargent, 377–84. Upper Saddle River, NJ: Pearson/Prentice Hall.

Rawlins, Joan. 2006. *Midlife and Older Women: Family Life Work and Health in Jamaica*. Kingston: University of the West Indies Press.

Reddock, Rhoda E. 2004. Interrogating Caribbean Masculinities: An Introduction. In *Interrogating Caribbean Masculinities: Theoretical and Empirical Analyses*, ed. Rhoda E. Reddock, xiii–xxxiv. Kingston: University of the West Indies Press.

Roberts, George W., and S. Sinclair. 1978. *Women in Jamaica: Patterns of Reproduction and Family*. Millwood, NY: KTO Press.

Robinson, Tiffany, Trevor Thompson, and Brendan Bain. Sexual Risk-Taking Behavior and HIV Knowledge of Kingston Street Boys. In *HIV/AIDS and Children in the English Speaking Caribbean*, ed. Barbara A. Dicks, 127–48. Binghampton, NY: Haworth Press.

Rogozinski, Jan. 1999. *A Brief History of the Caribbean: From the Arawak and Carib to the Present*. New York: Plume.

Rosaldo, Renato. 1989. *Culture and Truth: The Remaking of Social Analysis*. 1st ed. Boston: Beacon Press.

Ruddock, L.C., and Sonia Robinson-Glanville. 1996. *New Civics for Young Jamaicans*. Kingston: Carlong.

Sacks, Karen. 1979. *Sisters and Wives: The Past and Future of Sexual Equality*. Westport, CT: Greenwood Press.

Sen, Amartya. 2005. Foreword. In *Pathologies of Power: Health, Human Rights, and the New War on the Poor*, Paul Farmer, xi–xviii. Berkeley and Los Angeles: University of California Press.

Senior, Olive. 1991. *Working Miracles: Women's Lives in the English-Speaking Caribbean.* Bloomington: Indiana University Press.

Sharpe, Jenny. 2003. *Ghosts of Slavery: A Literary Archeology of Black Women's Lives.* Minneapolis: University of Minnesota Press.

Shepherd, Verene, Bridget Brereton and Barbara Bailey. 1995. *Engendering History: Caribbean Women in Historical Perspective.* London: James Currey.

Sir Arthur Lewis Institute of Social and Economic Studies. 2009. Jamaica Census 1991. http://salises.mona.uwi.edu/databank/jamaica%20Census/1991/survey0/index. html.

Slocum, Karla. 2001. Negotiating Identity and Black Feminist Politics in Caribbean Research. In *Black Feminist Anthropology: Theory, Politics, Praxis and Poetics*, ed. Irma McClaurin, 126–49. New Brunswick, NJ: Rutgers University Press.

Sobo, Elisa J. 1993. *One Blood: The Jamaican Body.* New York: State University of New York Press.

Social Development Council of Jamaica. 2007. Draft Profile of Frankfield (Etrick Hall and Andrew Hill) Clarendon. Received via email (November 2007).

Simey, Thomas. 1946. *Welfare and Planning in the West Indies.* Oxford: Clarendon Press.

Smith, Raymond T. 1960. The Family in the Caribbean. In *Caribbean Studies: A Symposium*, 2nd ed., ed. Vera Rubin, 67–79. Seattle: University of Washington Press.

Stanley, Liz, and Sue Wise. 1993. *Breaking Out Again: Feminist Ontology and Epistemology.* 2nd ed. London: Routledge.

Stewart, Dianne. 2005. *Three Eyes for the Journey: African Dimensions of the Jamaican Religious Experience.* Oxford: Oxford University Press.

Stolzoff, Norman C. 2000. *Wake the Town and Tell the People: Dancehall Culture in Jamaica.* Durham: Duke University Press.

Tafari-Ama, Imani M. 1998. Rastawoman as Rebel: Case Studies in Jamaica. In *Chanting Down Babylon: The Rastafari Reader*, ed. Nathaniel Samuel Murrell, William D. Spencer and Adrian Anthony McFarlane, 89–106. Philadelphia: Temple University Press.

Taylor, S.A.G. 1976. *A Short History of Clarendon.* Kingston: Ministry of Education Publications Branch.

Thomas, Deborah A. 2002. Modern Blackness: "What We Are and What We Hope to Be". *Small Axe* 6 (2): 25–48.

Ulysse, Gina A. 2007. *Downtown Ladies: Informal Commercial Importers, A Haitian Anthropologist, and Self-Making in Jamaica.* Chicago: University of Chicago Press. 2007.

Van Maanen, J. 1995. An End to Innocence: The Ethnography of Ethnography. In *Representation in Ethnography*, ed. J. Van Maanen, 1–35. Thousand Oaks, CA: Sage.

Ward, Martha, and Monica Edelstein. 2005. *A World Full of Women.* 4th ed. Boston: Pearson Education.

Wedenoja, William. 1989. Mothering and the Practice of "Balm" in Jamaica. In *Women as Healers: Cross-cultural Perspectives*, ed. C.S. McClaini, 76–97. New Brunswick, NJ: Rutgers University Press.

Wedenoja, William, and Diana Fox. Jamaica. 2004. In *Encyclopedia of Sex and Gender: Men and Women in the World's Cultures*, vol. 1, ed. Carol R. Ember and Melvin Ember, 561–71. New York: Kluwer Academic/Plenum.

Wolf, Eric R. 2002. Facing Power: Old Insights, New Questions. In *The Anthroplogy of Politics: A Reader in Ethnography, Theory, and Critique*, ed. Joan Vincent, 222–33. Malden, MA: Blackwell. World Bank. 2007. Jamaica Country Brief. http://web.worldbank.org/WBSITE/EXTERNAL/COUNTRIES/LACEXT/JAMAICA EXTN/0,,menuPK:338345~pagePK:141132~piPK:141107~theSitePK:338335, 00.html

Wylie, Alison. 1991. Gender Theory and the Archaeological Record: Why Is There No Archaeology of Gender? In *Engendering Archaeology: Women and Prehistory*, ed. Joan M. Gerot and Margaret W. Conkey, 31–55. Blackwell Press.

Index

Abu-Lughod, Lila, 85, 123, 124
Africa, as idealized past, 75, 78, 79
African diaspora
  black feminist anthropology, 24,
    220n7
  and Rastafari folk gender system, 30,
    79
Afro-Caribbean family structures, 21–23
after-school reading project, 185–89,
  224n4
agency
  and perceptions of self, 102
  sexual agency of teenage girls, 121
  and structural conditions, 136–37
"AIDS Is a Dangerous Disease" (Henry),
  174–75
alternative gender identities, 223n1
  and dancehall culture, 89, 95–102
Amnesty International, 193–94
Anancy stories, 29, 186
Anderson, Benedict, 73–74, 82
Andrew (field notes), 209–11
anthropology
  action anthropology, and societal
    problems, 176
  applied anthropological projects,
    170–72
  colonial anthropology, 25
  critiques of systems analysis, 83–88
  fieldwork, and empathetic understand-
    ing, 4–7

generalizations, problem with, 85
historical moment of crisis, 18–20
personal narratives, 84–85, 86–87,
  123–24
relationship between knowledge and
  methods, 179–80
researcher positionality, 5–7
Anzaldua, Gloria
  "Speaking in Tongues: A Letter to
    Third World Women Writers",
    84–85
archival data, 28
aromatherapy, 202
Austin-Broos, Diane, 119

Baby Cham, 194
Bakare-Yusuf, Bibi, 97–98, 101
balm, as form of healing, 121
banana industry, 56–57, 58
Barriteau, Eudine, xiii, 28, 86, 88
Barrow, Christine, *Family in the
  Caribbean*, 21
Beckles, Hilary, 32–33, 47, 51, 52,
  53–54
Besson, Jean, 32, 68
biological essentialism, xvii, 89
black feminist anthropology, and
  African diaspora, 24, 220n7
blackness
  negative associations with, 37–38
  as principle of social change, 76

237

Fox, Diana
  feminist ethnographic methodology,
    24–26
  HIV/AIDS research, 24–25
  as student researcher, 1–17
Francis, Marlene (Joan), 153–55
Frankfield, 19
  Children and Communities for
    Change (3Cs), 173–76
  community market, 114–15
  Cow Pen, 61–62
  cultural history of, 28
  DJ party, 173, 176
  Emancipation Day celebrations, 34
  employment levels, 40–41, 42, 62
  family structures, 41–42
  first visit to, 7–17
  HIV-infected persons in, 199
  homeless people, and beggars, 39–40
  male youth, and community morality,
    44–45, 74, 75
  middle-class associations with Nanny,
    74–75
  as not "Town", 14
  origins of, 60–64
  parish of Clarendon, 35–38
  physical description of, 8, 61–62
  population, 8, 64
  racialized class conflict in, 74–77
  railroad expansion, 57–58
  Rastafarian imagined history of,
    64–67
  service learning, 177–78
  socio-economic profile, 38–46

gang activity, and male youth, 45, 106
ganja, 45
Garvey, Marcus, 34
gender, intersecting influences on, xvi,
  13–14, 191

gender ideals
  Marlene (Joan) Francis interview,
    154–55
  "Miss Jones" interview, 156
  Shakira, interview with, 158–59
gender identity
  agents of socialization, 103
  alternative identities, 88–89, 223n1
  centrality of in Jamaican culture,
    13–14
  and dancehall culture, 102–3
  and gender negotiations, 134–37
  gender norms, and self-presentation,
    75, 124
  and gender socialization theory, 102–3
  historical construction of, 31
  and racial categorization, 11–12, 50
gender inequality, student experiences,
  204–13
gender "molecules" as systems, ix–xv,
  79–82, 122
  "biology is destiny", x, 216
  collectivity-uniqueness, 26, 122
  cultural memory, 161
  culture-gender spiral, 214–17
  DNA mutations, 171
  gender negotiations, 124, 134–36
  inherited values of masculinity/femi-
    ninity, 149, 216–17
  longevity-mutability, 26, 38, 81,
    216–17
  malleability of, 86, 88–89
gender negotiations, 123–27
  contemporary negotiations, 78–79
  gender roles as expression of identity,
    125–26
  between individuals and collectives,
    126–27
  interviews, summary of, 168–69
  and self-reflexivity, 134–36